IMAGES
of America

NEW ORLEANS CITY PARK

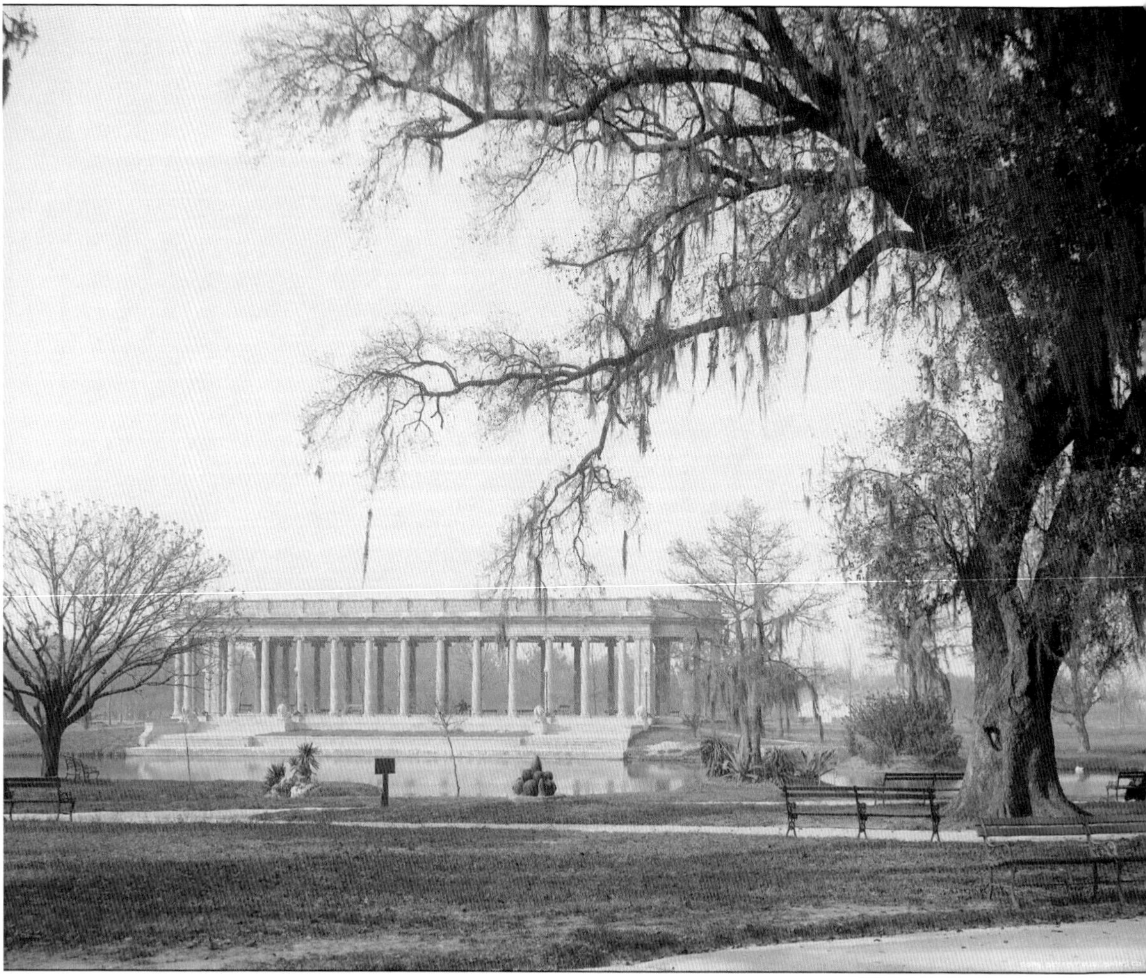

On the Cover: The most iconic structure in the park, the Peristyle, built in 1907 in the Neoclassical style that was popular at the time, was designed as a dancing pavilion by Andry and Bendernagel at a cost of $15,330.20. Along Bayou Metairie's edge, four lions guard the steps. Here, a man relaxes on a bench inside the Peristyle, a lady does the same across the bayou, and children play in the distance. Cannonballs and missiles, presumably from the Civil War, are stacked in the foreground. Looking beyond the woman, there is no bandstand or Casino Building—they would be built later. Still a popular venue for dancing at weddings and parties, the Peristyle was the centerpiece of the park, hosting galas, women suffrage and World War I peace rallies, and gatherings of all sorts through its long history. (Courtesy of the Library of Congress.)

IMAGES
of America

NEW ORLEANS CITY PARK

Catherine Campanella

ARCADIA
PUBLISHING

ISBN 978-0-7385-8758-5

Published by Arcadia Publishing
Charleston, South Carolina

Printed in the United States of America

Library of Congress Control Number: 2011920415

For all general information, please contact Arcadia Publishing:
Telephone 843-853-2070
Fax 843-853-0044
E-mail sales@arcadiapublishing.com
For customer service and orders:
Toll-Free 1-888-313-2665

Visit us on the Internet at www.arcadiapublishing.com

To Meredith and Andrew, my beloved children

Contents

ACKNOWLEDGMENTS

Many thanks go to the following people: Jill Rabalais who first helped make this book possible; Mike and Chuck Azzarello, Dolly Breaux, Vincent and Meredith Campanella, Mike Carroll, Nancy Sholl Demarest, Larry Englert, Mary Fury, Henry Harmison, Tom Munger, Barbara Pablich, Elizabeth Ohmer Pellegrin, Juanita Poche, Mary C. Schmidt, Catherine Sholl, and Maria Viages for sharing their knowledge and memories; John Hopper, City Park chief development officer, and Rodney Thoulion, Friends of City Park executive director, for guidance; Amy Perryman, my editor at Arcadia Publishing, who, from its inception, completely supported this effort; New Orleans Public Library archivist Irene Wainwright for enabling me to include historic images from my hometown library in this and my prior books; and D.C. "Infrogmation" May for sharing his beautiful photographs—Froggy has documented New Orleans's recent history better than anyone I know. My sincere thanks go to all.

The images in this book appear courtesy of the New Orleans Public Library (NOPL), Louisiana Digital Library (LDL), the Library of Congress (LOC), the Historic New Orleans Collection (HNOC), National Archives (NA), Pictometry International (PI), and D.C. May (DCM).

A portion of the author's proceeds from *New Orleans City Park* is dedicated to Friends of City Park.

INTRODUCTION

On land that was an oak forest where Native Americans traded along the banks of Bayou St. John, the Allard Plantation was carved. It evolved to become one of the largest and oldest public parks in the nation. Filling 1,300 acres, it is 457 acres larger than New York's Central Park. Its age allows for the display of the many architectural styles that came into vogue during its history, including Neoclassical, Art Nouveau, Art Deco, Arts and Crafts, Mission, and Modern.

Dueling was outlawed in 1890, and today, a plaque in the park near what is called the Dueling Oak marks the spot where many duels took place 120 years prior. Under the same tree, according to local legend, lies the body of the plantation owner in an unmarked grave. Amid 500-year-old oaks, a mule carousel once delighted local children. It was replaced in 1906 with mechanical "Flying Horses," which were listed in the National Register of Historic Places in 1989. A prominent widow bequeathed her jewels so that a fountain and wading pool could be built, complete with sculptures of a mother and children of various ages. "She loved the beautiful and gave that all might enjoy," reads the inscription on the concrete-and-bronze pool, which is still enjoyed by children today. During the 1950s, Storyland was filled with nursery rhyme figures, created by a young man who would become the most noted Mardi Gras float builder in the city; it was funded by an older man who owned and operated the most popular amusement park in the South.

Throughout its history, City Park has not changed as much as it has evolved. Until the 1930s, many improvements and additions were made at the behest of the city's wealthy philanthropists. After the Great Depression, the Works Progress Administration (WPA) constructed roads, bridges, buildings, fountains, gardens, sculptures, sculptural reliefs, a stadium, and 10 linear miles of lagoons dug with hand shovels. Federal funding of over $12 million allowed for the work and the employment of more than 20,000 people during the New Deal era. Since then, the City Park Improvement Association (as it had done in the early years), along with the support of the nonprofit Friends of City Park, has undertaken many restoration projects and additions.

New Orleans City Park is the home of the largest collection of mature live oaks in the nation and is the ninth largest city-owned recreational park in the United States. Its New Orleans Museum of Art (NOMA) is widely considered one of the finest museums in the South. The park contains the largest recreation area for the entire metropolitan area and is the largest non-hotel caterer in the city. In its forest is the highest man-made earthen elevation in New Orleans. Running two miles along Bayou St. John, it is a mile wide and three miles long with 11 miles of lagoons and lakes (the Big Lake in the shape of Lake Pontchartrain) stocked with a wide variety of fish. The park has had as many as 11 million visitors per year. Before Hurricane Katrina, approximately 14,000 mature trees thrived with some 50 species, including bald cypress, southern magnolia, pine, and oaks—with over 3,000 southern live oaks.

The oldest structures in the park are three stone bridges that were built in the early 1900s, including the much-photographed Langles Bridge over Bayou Metairie. As this book went to press, the park's architectural treasures over 100 years old include the Dunbar Pavilion (1904), the carousel (Flying Horses in the New Orleans lexicon) and pavilion housing it (1906), the Peristyle (1907), Pizzati Gate at City Park Avenue (1910), and Delgade Museum–NOMA (1911). Those over 90 years old include Janchke Fountain in front of NOMA (1912), the Casino Building (1913), Monteleone Gate at Esplanade (1914), Hyams Fountain and Wading Pool (1914), and Popp Bandstand (1917). Ten bridges are designated Historic Bridges of the United States.

Located in what was the "French part of the city," it was first called "Lower City Park"; Americans used "Upper City Park," which is now Audubon. In its early years, the park was remote and rural but is now surrounded by homes and businesses in Mid-City. The first entrepreneur to realize the park's potential to draw crowds was Jean Marie Saux who, in 1860, built and operated a coffeehouse across from it. His building would become the area's oldest structure—older than any located in the park now. We will follow its history because it closely reflects the times and the history of the park; we now know it as Ralph's on the Park at 900 City Park Avenue.

Victor Anseman is known as the father of the park, City Park Improvement Association (CPIA) has long been known as the keeper of the park, and Friends of City Park (Friends), established in 1979, is now known as a group of dedicated New Orleanians who raise funds to maintain and refurbish the park. City Park 2018, a master plan adopted in March 2005 with input from CPIA, Friends, and citizens, is currently (at the time of this writing) being implemented, and many components of the 13-year plan have been completed despite the unplanned visit of Hurricane Katrina five months after the plan was adopted.

City Park is fond in the memory of New Orleanians. We played there as children. We competed there as student athletes. We were entertained there as teenagers and returned as adults to appreciate art at NOMA, to surround ourselves with sculptures throughout the park, to stroll through Celebration in the Oaks, to ride the Flying Horses, to walk through Storyland again, or to simply enjoy the lush and beautiful surroundings. City Park has changed through the years while retaining many of the beloved historic structures and features that New Orleanians have always loved and visitors readily discover.

One

The Bayou, Road, Oaks, and Native Americans 1400–1769

When Columbus "discovered" America, oaks that are still enjoyed in City Park were nearly full-grown; the Anseman Oak and the McDonogh Oak are among the oldest and largest. When the Canadian Le Moyne brothers explored Louisiana, Iberville thought the Mississippi River was not navigable, but Bienville continued to explore it and learned from the natives that a bayou and a road had long been used for trade between Biloxi, Mississippi, and New Orleans. Their route moved them from Biloxi to the Mississippi-Breton Sound, Lake Borgne, Lake Pontchartrain, and Bayou St. John and then down the road to the river. Traveling up the river was a daunting task on sailing ships, but this issue was solved by using the Indian route instead.

The natives also showed Bienville a log bridge across the bayou, islands in the swamp surrounding it, huge moss-laden cypress trees, palmetto, reeds, and grasses. Along the steadily rising bank of the bayou were the oak, persimmon, pecan, cherry, acacia, and sweet gum trees, which would grace City Park, and the bayou would become City Park's eastern border. The first known people to settle there were the Chapitoulas who lived in cypress huts, which were abandoned and then used by the Biloxi tribe, the Houmas, who also settled along the bayou. The adjoining bayou, "Bayou Choupic," was named by the Acolapissa tribe for the mudfish that inhabited it. This bayou would later be known as Bayou Metairie.

A handful of colonists under French rule (1699–1769) settled there to grow indigo, corn, and sugar cane. Bayou St. John would become a major port of New Orleans until railroads and steam engines made it possible to easily ply up the Mississippi. The bayou, however, was navigable until 1936, when the WPA added low bridges. In 1982, Bayou St. John was placed in the National Register of Historic Places and recognized by the Louisiana Legislature as a Historic and Scenic River, which requires protection and preservation.

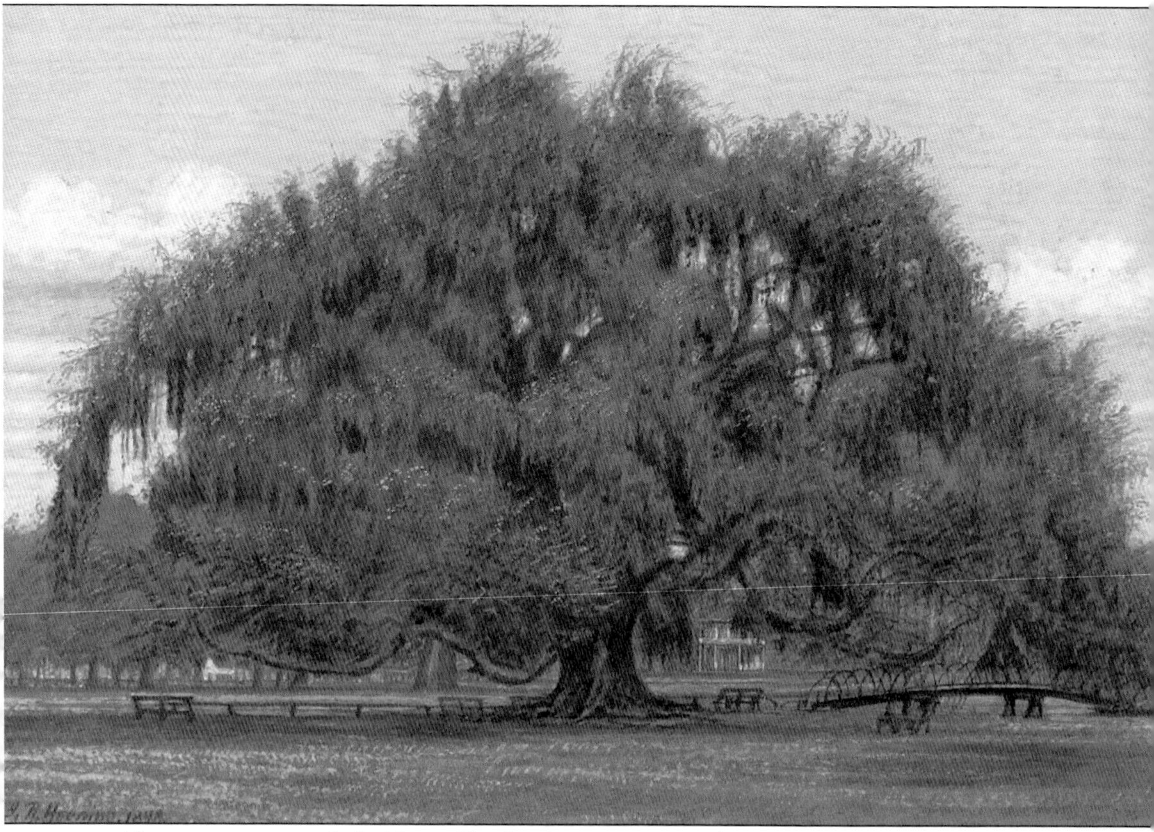

Almost a century and a half ago, Charles Gayarré wrote in his 1867 *History of Louisiana*, "On the bank of Bayou, or river St. John, on the land known in our days as Allard's plantation, and on the very site where now stands the large and airy house, which we see [shown here], there was a small village of friendly Indians. From the bank opposite the village, beginning where at a much later period was to be erected the bridge which spans the Bayou, a winding path made by the Indians, and subsequently enlarged into Bayou Road by the European settlers, ran through a thick forest, and connected the Indian village with the French settlement of New Orleans." Pictured is Julius Robert Hoening's 1898 painting titled *Plantation and Oak Tree* (*Allard Plantation*). The house fronted Bayou St. John near Bayou Metairie. The 1910 photograph on the following page offers a similar vantage point. (Ogden Museum of Southern Art.)

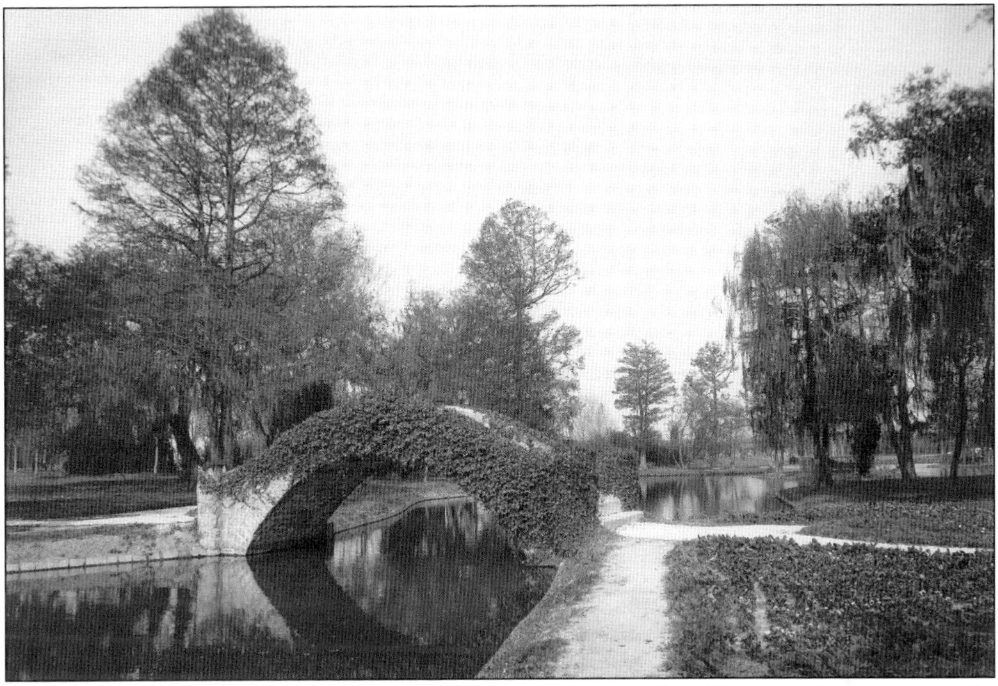

Note that the bridge shown on the previous page has been replaced by a sturdier structure; the Langles Bridge was built in 1902 and is still in use today. Many of the oaks that shaded Native Americans and graced the Allard Plantation can be seen here and still grow today. (LOC.)

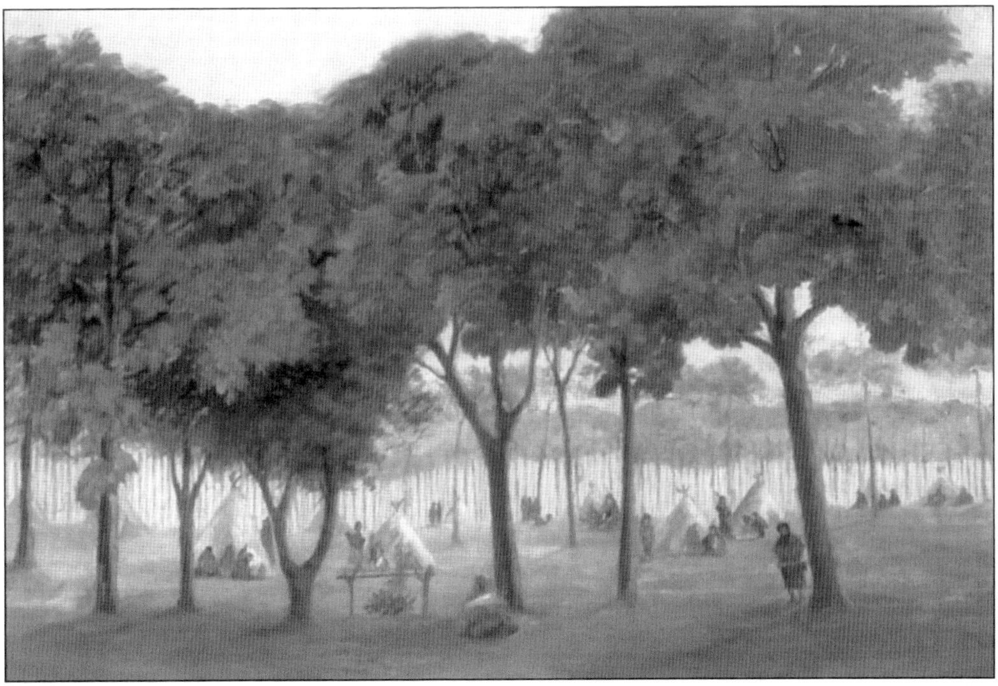

The "small village of friendly Indians" described by Gayarré shared food, medicine, and knowledge of the terrain with the European explorers who first appeared in 1699. The natives created "the winding path" as their route for trade and portage centuries before white men arrived. (LDL.)

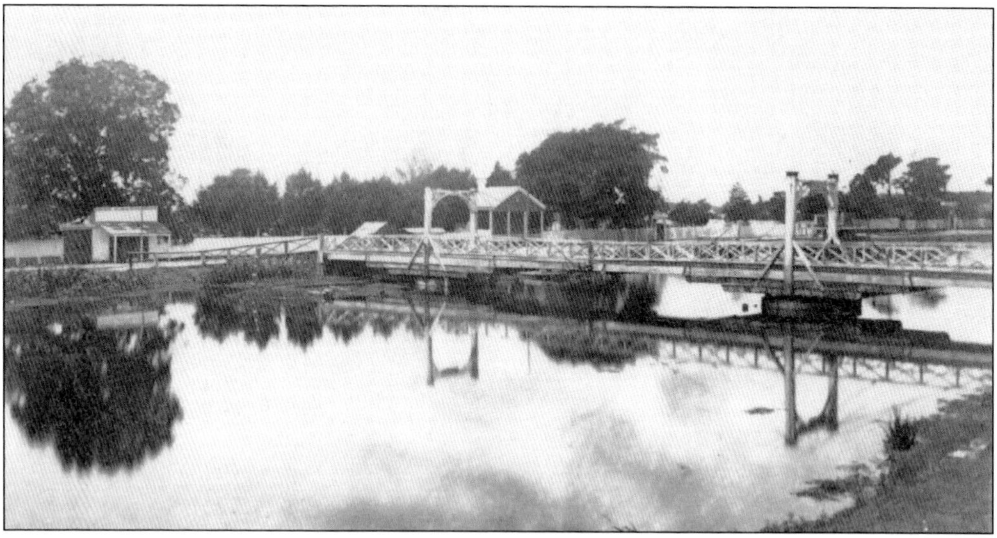

The bridge cited by Gayarré, pictured around 1864, was located at what is now the park entrance at Esplanade and Lelong Avenue. Below is a 1728 map depicting "Grand Bayou de S. Jean" (Bayou St. John), the oaks, and the "winding path [Chemin] made by the Indians . . . [which] ran through a thick forest, and connected the Indian village with the French settlement of New Orleans." (Both, LDL.)

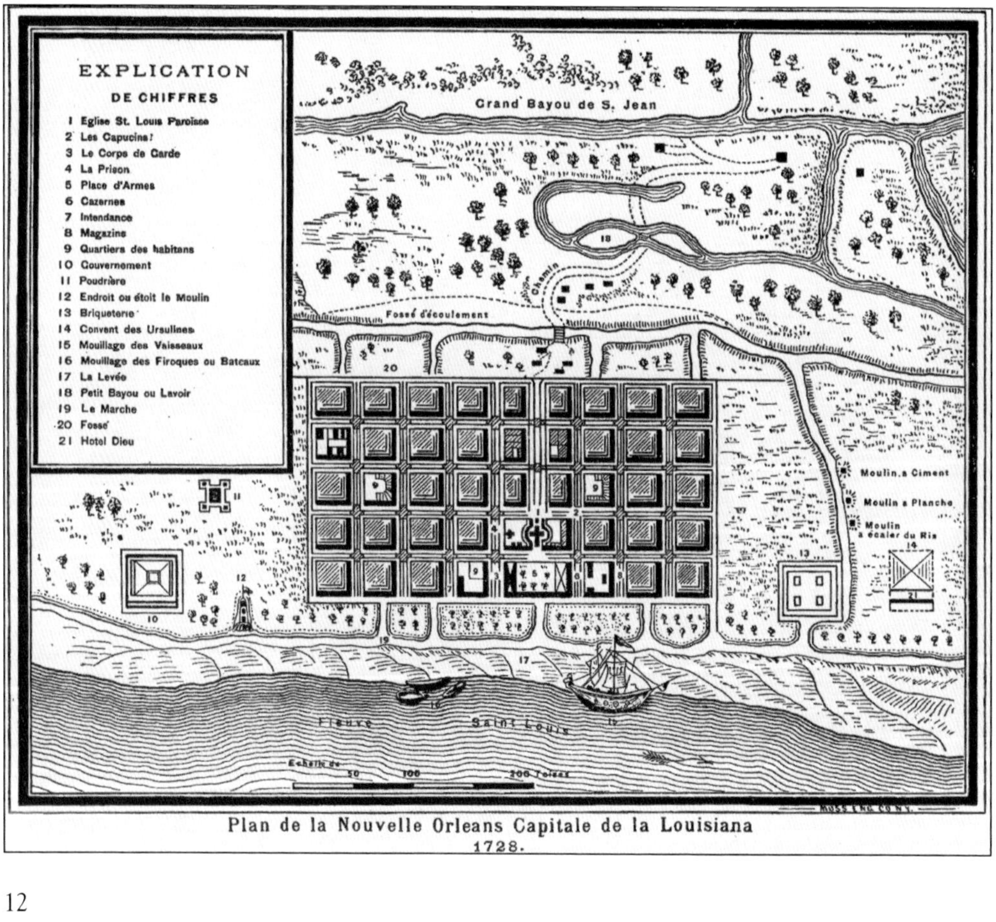

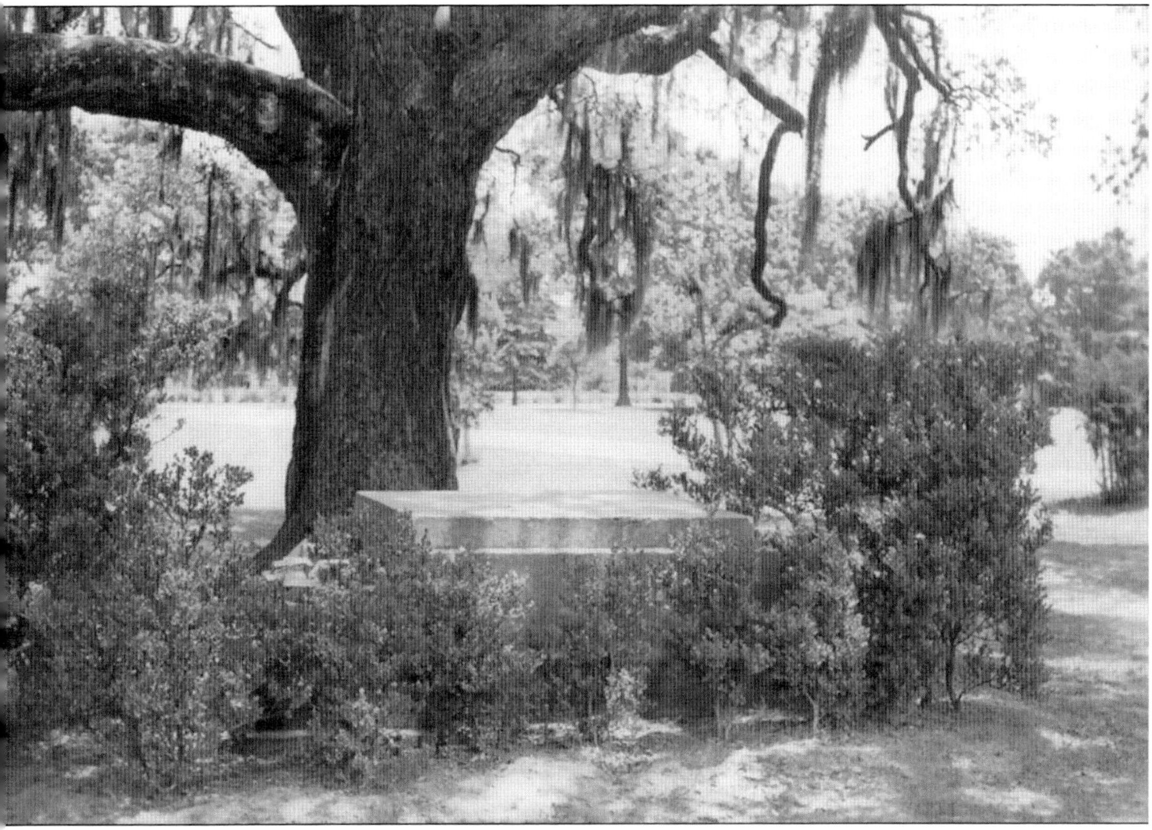

Gayarré also included the story of Chevalier d'Aubant, a Frenchman who was an officer in the Duke of Brunswick's court. After arriving with colonial troops in 1718 and with the consent of the Indians, he built a retreat on the bayou. In 1721, a woman arrived in New Orleans and asked to be taken to d'Aubant. They were wed the following day and "they planted those two oaks, which are, to this day, to be seen standing side by side on the bank of the St. John . . . a little to the right of the bridge, as you cross it, in front of Allard's plantation." Legend has it that the woman, Princess Charlotte, daughter of the Duke of Brunswick, had faked her death to escape her arranged marriage to the ruthless Alexis, son of Russia's Peter the Great. Pictured is the one remaining tree, the Dueling Oak, in a 1930s view. The tomb beside it is said to be that of Jean Louis Allard. (LDL.)

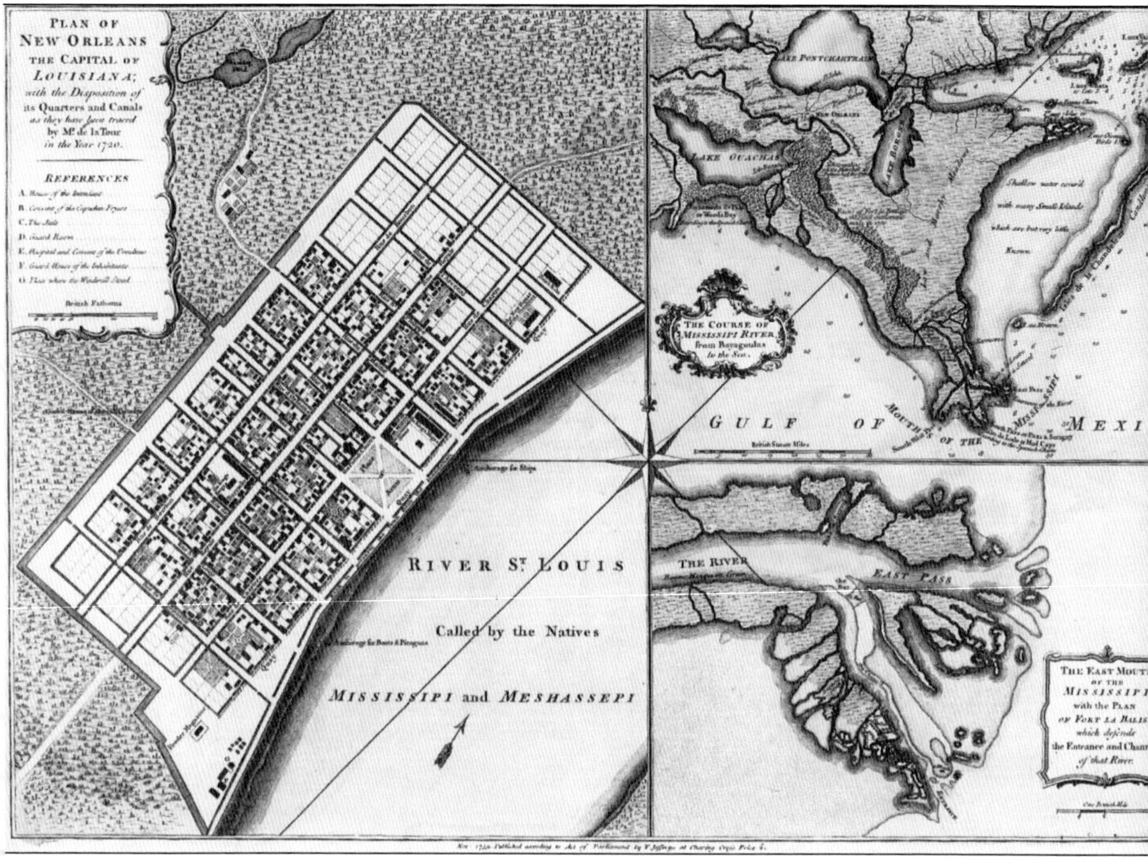

The following is from John Smith Kendall's 1922 *History of New Orleans*: "The oldest street is probably Bayou Road. When the whites first intruded into Louisiana they found it not altogether an untrodden wilderness. At the head of Bayou St. John, near the bridge, which now spans that street at the foot of Esplanade Street, stood an Indian village. The moccasined feet of the inhabitants of this tiny settlement had beaten out a pathway by the shortest possible route through the swamps to the Mississippi . . . The white settlers found it a convenient route; they appear to have used it frequently even before the site of New Orleans was definitely decided upon, and so it has happened that later when new fauxbourgs were laid out it was a thoroughfare too well established to be changed, and it still runs its ancient course, across lots and through squares." The 1747 map shows the road to the bayou and the beginnings of the city of New Orleans. (NA.)

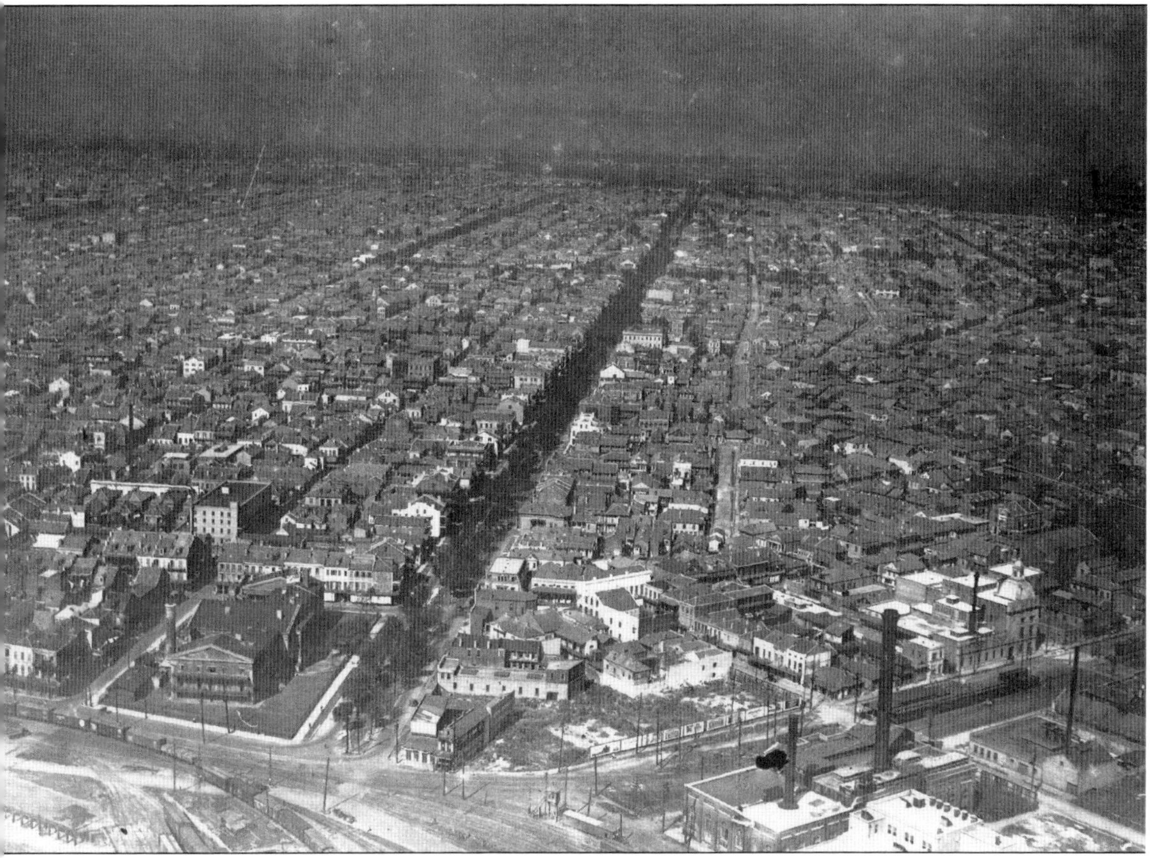

The location of the Indian village, which Kendall described "at the head of Bayou St. John, near the bridge . . . at the foot of Esplanade Street," is in the distance with City Park just beyond it in this 1941 aerial photograph. The street "still runs its ancient course, across lots and through squares." The old Bayou Road roughly parallels Esplanade Avenue, a block on either side, until it reaches Grand Route St. John. This view makes it obvious that "the moccasined feet of the inhabitants of this tiny settlement had beaten out a pathway by the shortest possible route through the swamps to the Mississippi." In the photograph, Esplanade Avenue runs from the river at North Peters Street to City Park (as it does today). The corner building of the old United States Mint can be seen to the left of Esplanade Avenue in the lower portion of the photograph. (LDL.)

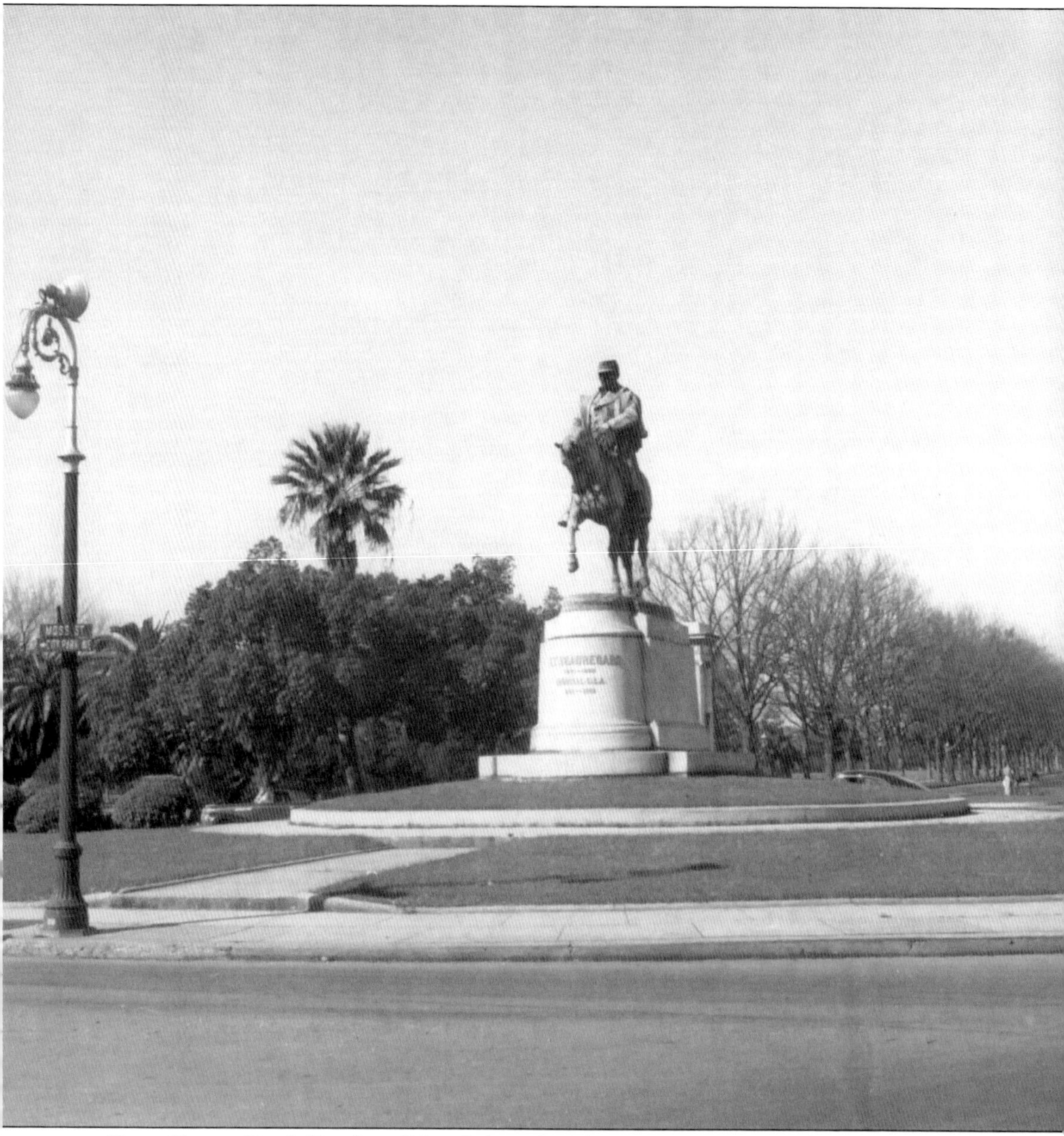

Grace King in *Creole Families of New Orleans* (1921) wrote, "A monument has been raised to him [Beauregard] at the entrance of the City Park, where ends the old road which was used by the Indians as a portage, and which Bienville traversed on his way to found the city—the road that was trod by all of Bienville's followers, the sons of France and Canada, the makers of the city. Old forest oaks are still standing that were alive then." In this 1945 photograph, Confederate general Pierre Gustave Toutant Beauregard welcomes visitors to the park at the "end of the old road," which first officially, according to municipal records, ran complete from the foot of the bank of the river to the bayou as Esplanade Avenue in 1850. (LDL.)

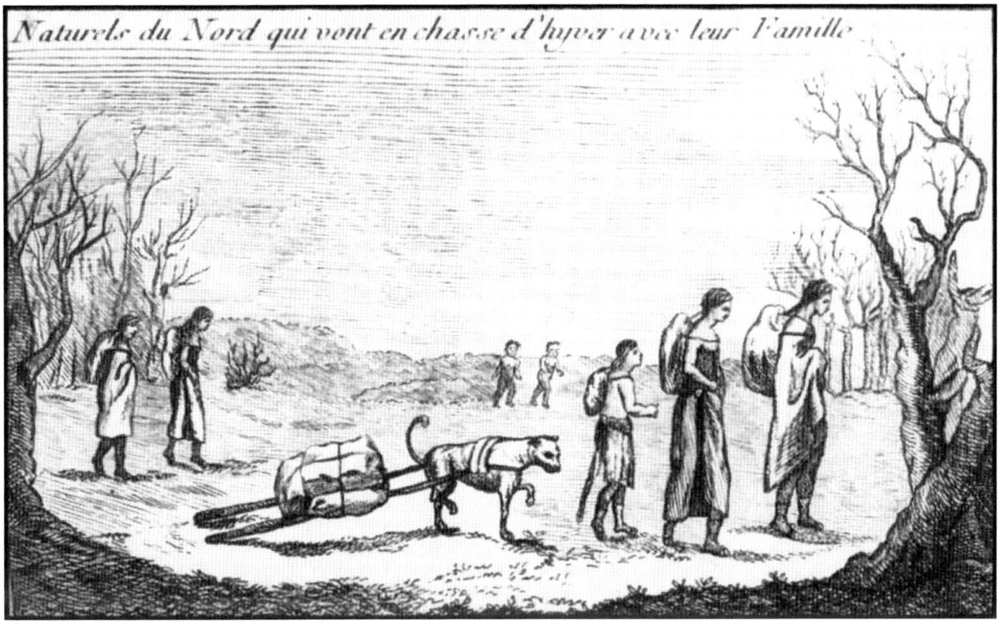

In 1699, Bienville heeded the advice of the natives as he traveled from Lake Pontchartrain down Bayou St. John through their oak-lined trail, which led to what he would claim for France and name New Orleans. It was 100 miles from the mouth of the river, located where the distance between the river and the lake was shortest. A Native American family is shown in this 1775 woodcut. (NA.)

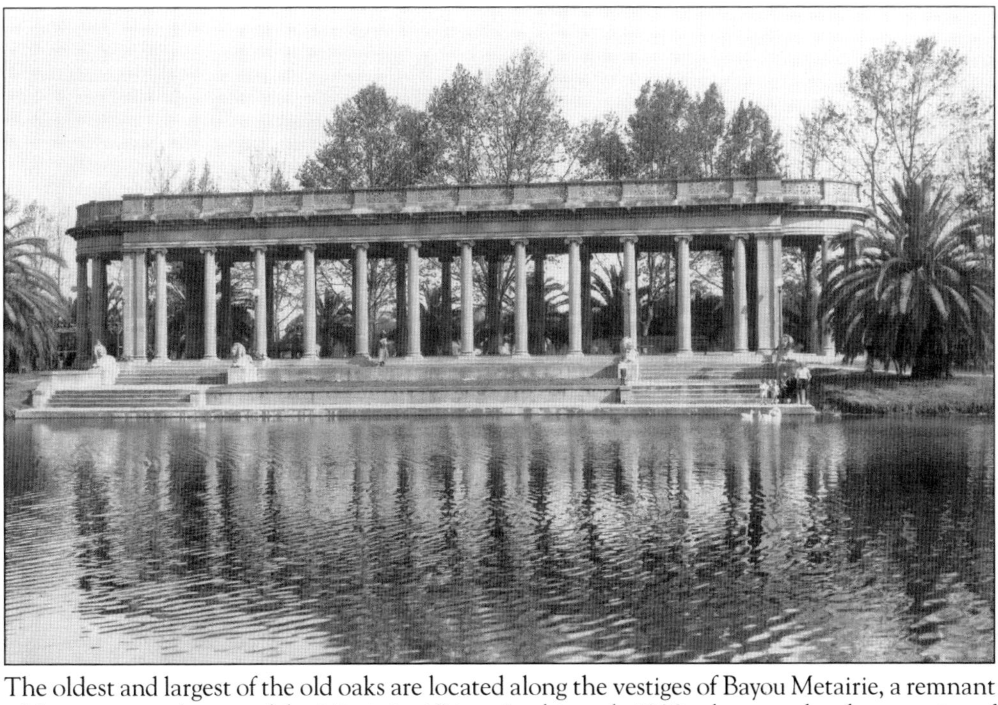

The oldest and largest of the old oaks are located along the vestiges of Bayou Metairie, a remnant of the ancient tributary of the Mississippi River. In this early-1900s photograph, what remains of Bayou Metairie runs, as it does today, along the edge of the Peristyle. (LDL.)

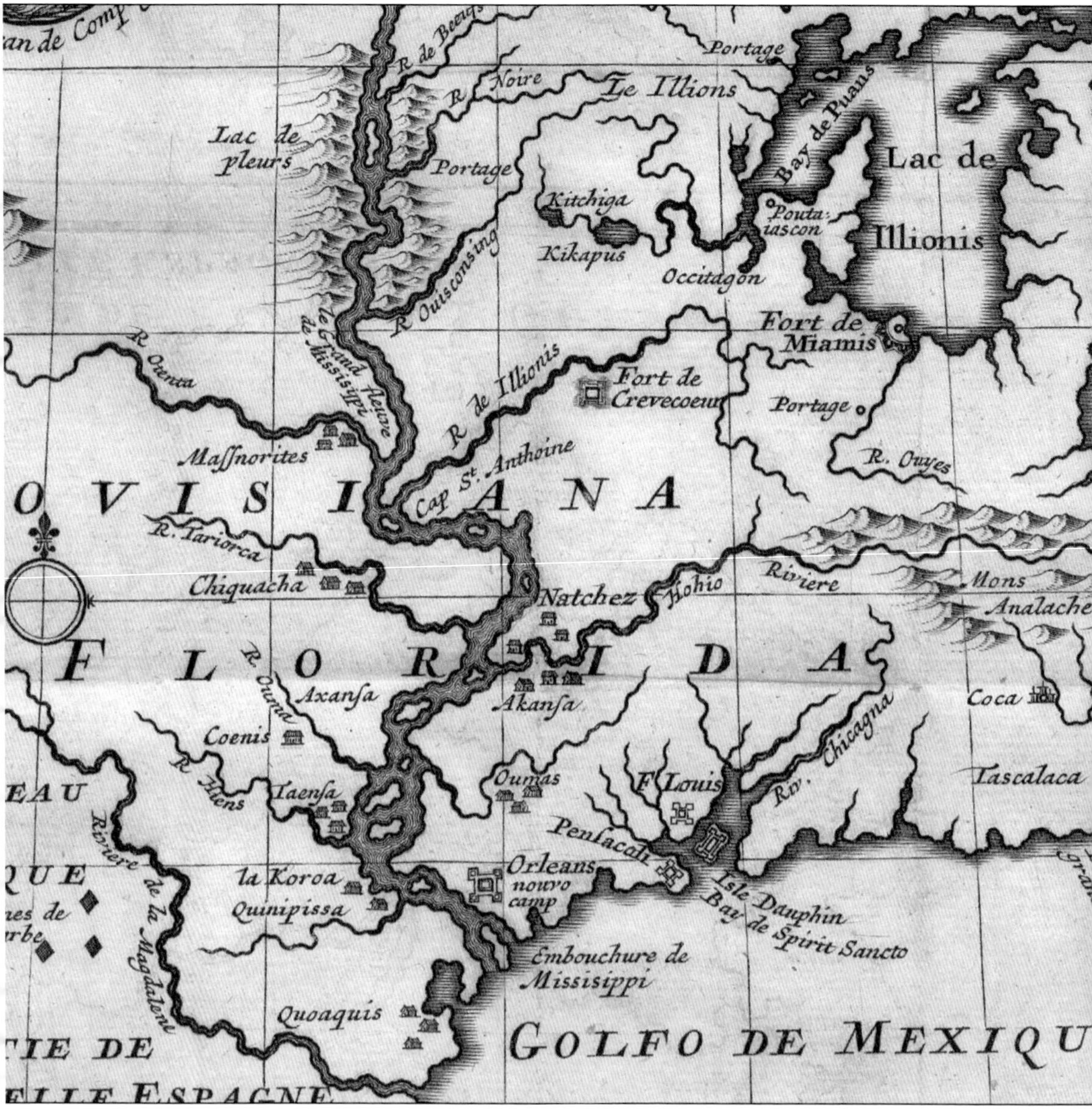

Joseph H. De Grange in *Historical Data of Spanish Fort* (*Louisiana Quarterly*) tells, "In 1699, Iberville, then located at Biloxi, was informed of a bayou that was an Indian route to the river and his guide piloted him in a pirogue to an Indian portage . . . The Choctaws, the Biloxis, Bogue Chittos and Chinchubas, made long, hazardous trips across Lake Pontchartrain in birchbark canoes. From this portage, now Esplanade street, was a pathway worn from the travel of Indians from Bayou St. John, who, journeying overland, carried their canoes over Bayou Road to Rampart street, thence through Hospital street to the highlands on the Mississippi River. Bayou St. John was the route of traffic between Mobile, Biloxi and the Mississippi River. The various tribes of Indians,—the Tchoupitoulas, Choctaw and Natchez Indians,—were wont to make an annual visit to New Orleans on New Year's Day to exchange compliments with the governor and city authorities and to receive presents stipulated by treaty." This 1720 map designates Native American territories as they existed at that time. (NA.)

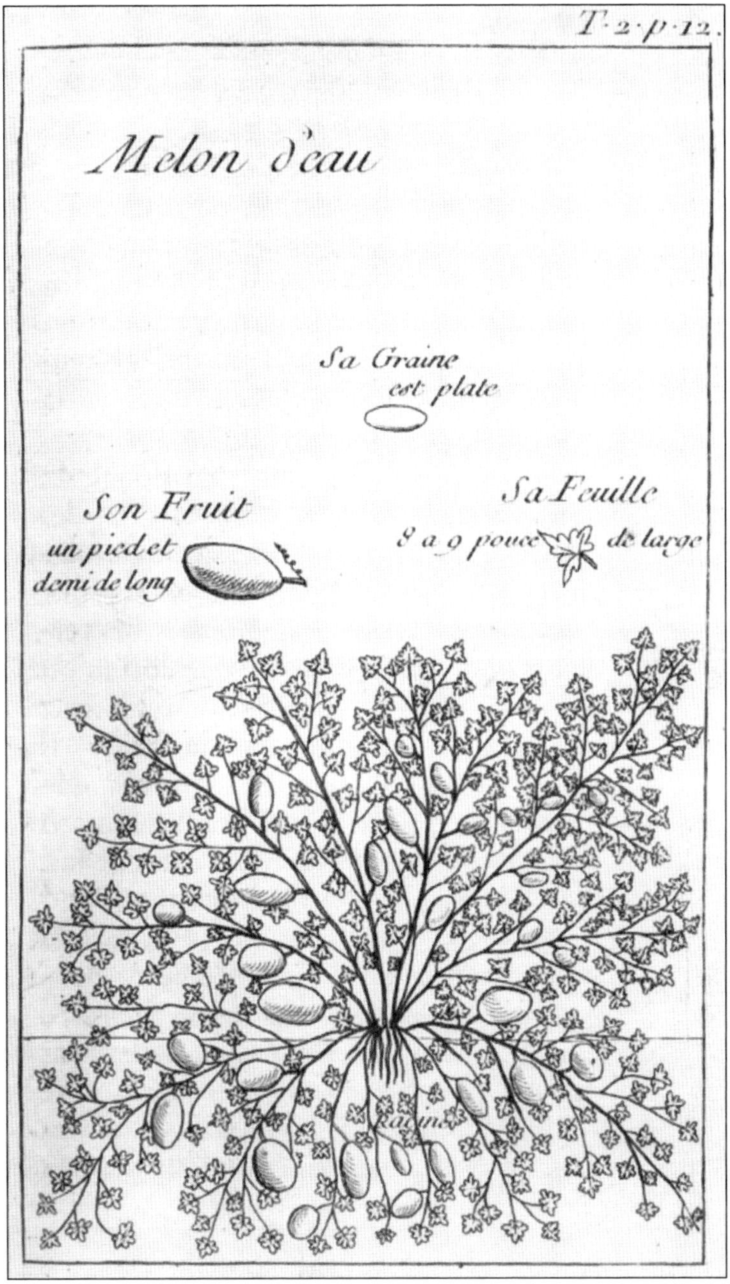

In the year that New Orleans was founded, Dutchman Le Page du Pratz arrived at Bayou St. John in March 1718. He lodged in an abandoned Acolapissa hut and wrote that New Orleans "existed only in name." He also stated that while Bienville lived in a palmetto-roofed hut, "I built my plantation about twenty-five toises (150 feet) from Bayou St. John." He described alligators and crocodiles, Muscadine grapes, and "rice in such plenty . . . that the inhabitants reap the greatest advantage from it, and reckon it the manna of the land." After purchasing a native Chitimacha female, "so as to have a woman to cook for us," he planted the first known garden cultivated by a European in the area. He said, "The quality of that land is very good." This illustration of watermelons is from his 1758 *Histoire de la Louisiane*. (NA.)

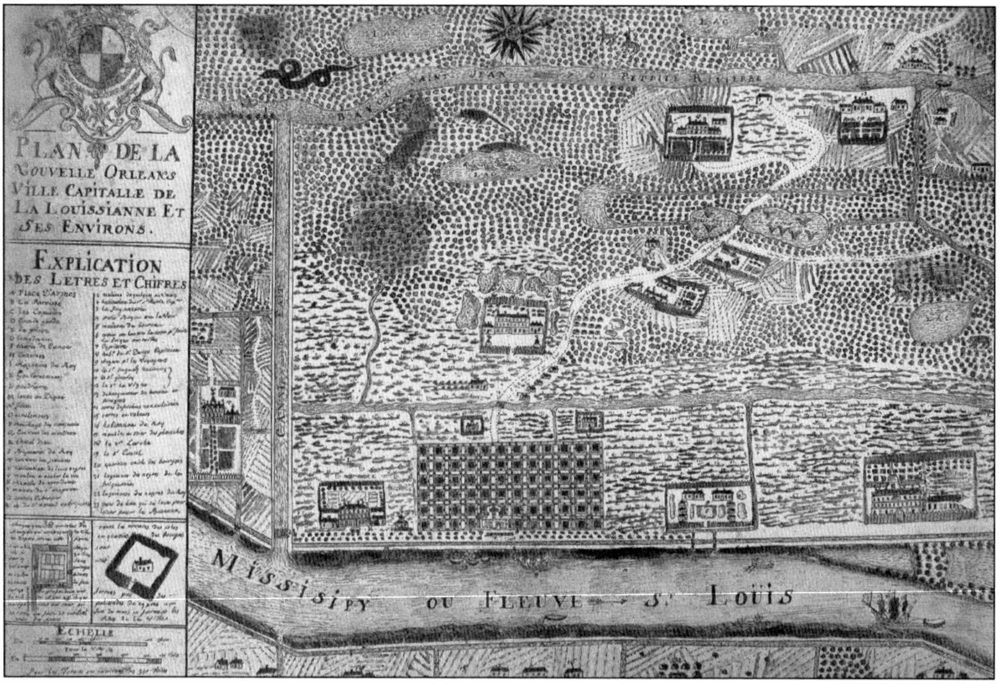

Du Pratz later "proceeded to the Bayouc Choupic [Bayou Metairie] so denominated from a fish of that name abounds not only with sea fish but with fresh water fish, some of which, particularly carp, would appear to be of a monstrous size in France. We entered this Creek Choupic: at the entrance of which is a fort at present [included in this illustration]. We went up this creek for the space of a league, and landed at a place where formerly stood the village of the natives, who are called Cola-Pissas . . . that is, the nation of men that hear and see. From this place to New Orleans, and the river Mississippi, on which that capital is built, the distance is only a league." Below is a 1930s view of the Dueling Oak, which stood when du Pratz settled there, and the Dreyfous Bridge. (Both, LDL.)

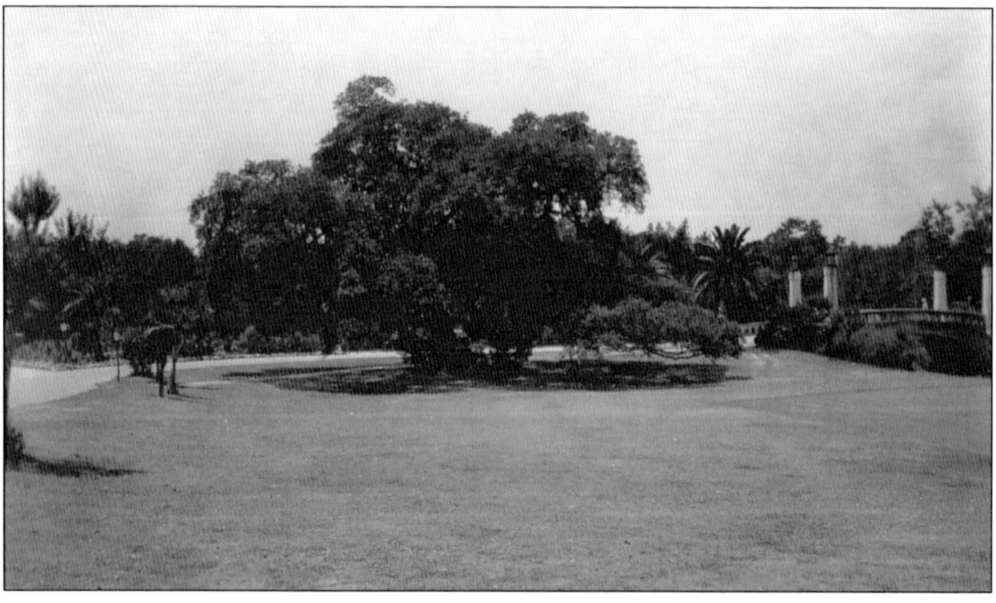

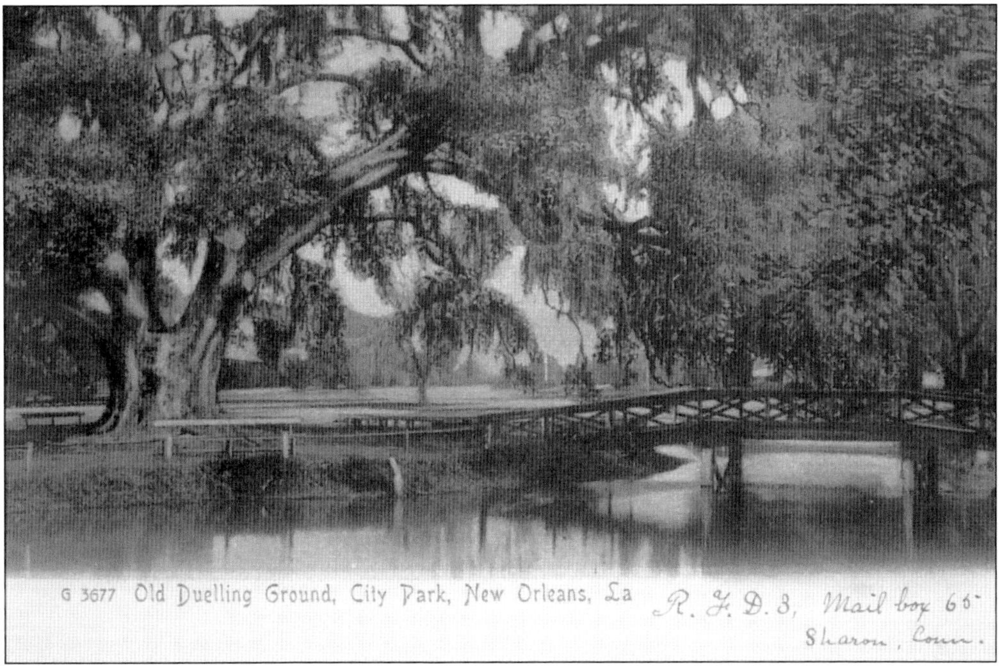

The ancient Dueling Oak is pictured in this 1906 postcard featuring the dueling ground. Note the wooden bridge, the original Grandjean Bridge. (LOC.)

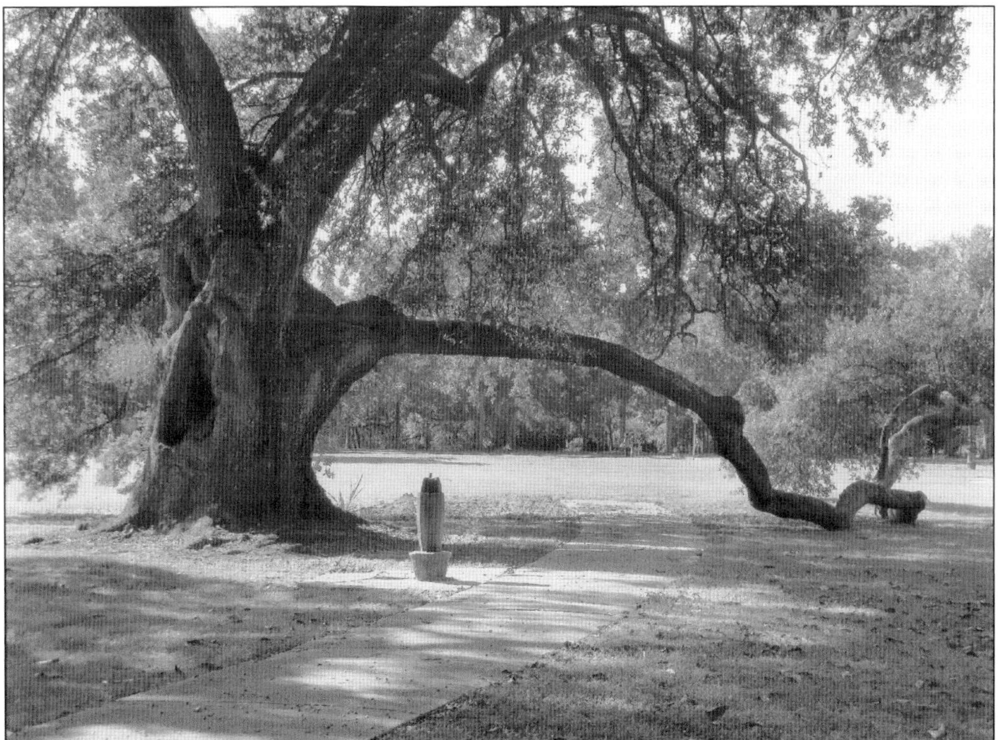
The legend of the park's Suicide Oak is that within 12 years, a total of 16 men took their own lives under its branches. (DCM.)

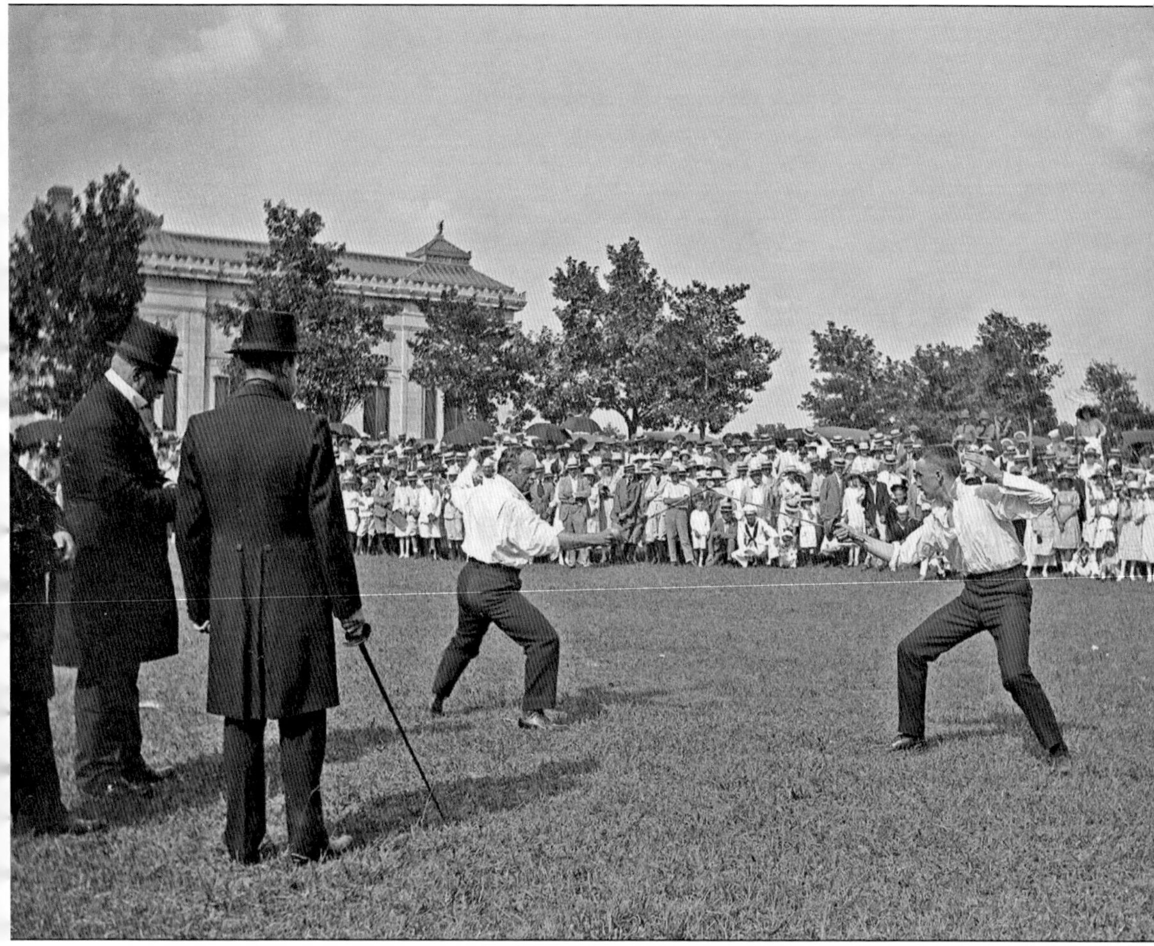

The property was famous as a dueling ground long before it was a park—more *affaires d'honneur* were fought in New Orleans than in any other American city. They resulted from serious affronts, petty insults, or deliberate confrontations for the sole purpose of displaying fencing skills. Weapons of choice included swords, sabers, pistols, rifles, and even bare hands. During the 1800s, a series of duels were fought between fencing masters. The most famous of these men, Spaniard Pepe Llula, was known as a duelist who met any man with any weapon. The *Times-Democrat* on March 13, 1892, reported, "Between 1834 and 1844 scarcely a day passed without duels being fought at the Oaks." Dueling had been outlawed two years before, and lawbreakers could have faced the death penalty if a death resulted from dueling, but it was seldom enforced. The location of exactly were to meet "under the oaks" was well-known and confined to an area appropriately 150 feet in diameter near what is now NOMA. Pictured is a 1919 reenactment on that spot. (LDL.)

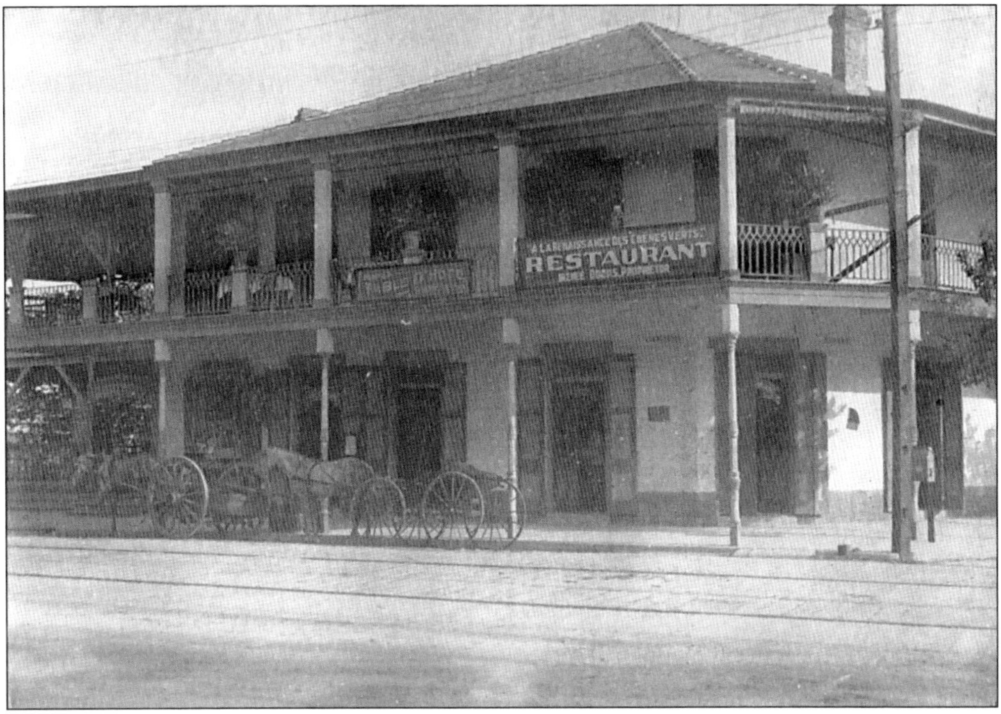

The following is from Grace King's 1926 history: "What a trooping of ghosts under the old trees, if all the votaries of honour who had fought or assisted others to fight there could revisit the place in spirit! What a throng would mine host of the restaurant opposite have to welcome, if all who quaffed a glass, in a happy reprieve from death or wounds, at that bar could return again!" Pictured is the restaurant and bar described by King, built by its proprietor Jean Marie Saux in 1860. The building pictured below still stands on City Park Avenue across from the main gate at Alexander Avenue. (Above, NA; below, DCM.)

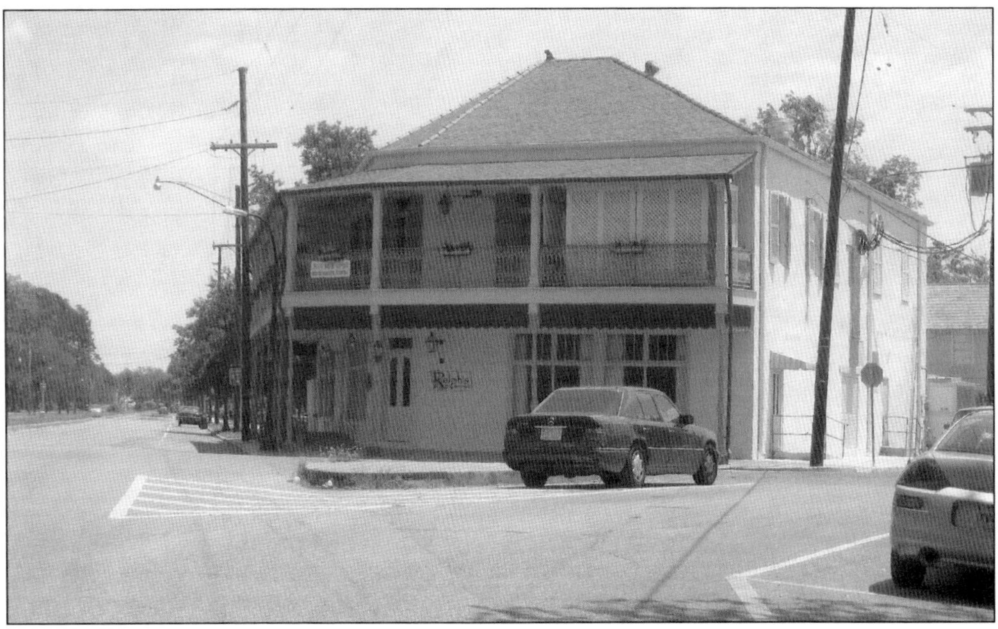

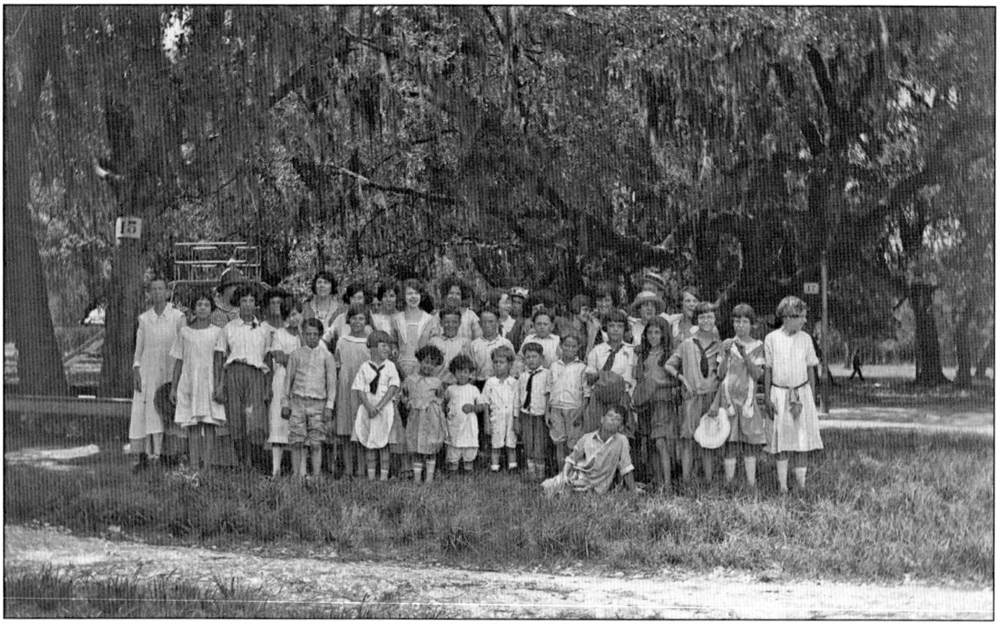

Felix Dreyfous, founding member of CPIA, walked the park every week for 55 years to check for needed trimming of trees due to wind damage or disease. He began his work in 1891 and continued faithfully until his death in 1946. Many ancient oaks would not be alive today if not for his dedication and diligence. Over 1,000 oaks were unearthed by the winds of Katrina, and 1,000 more died with roots inundated by floodwater, but the ancient oak grove, which Dreyfous had so carefully attended many years ago, sustained minimum damage. People under the oaks are pictured in 1924 (above) and 1913 (below). (Both, LDL.)

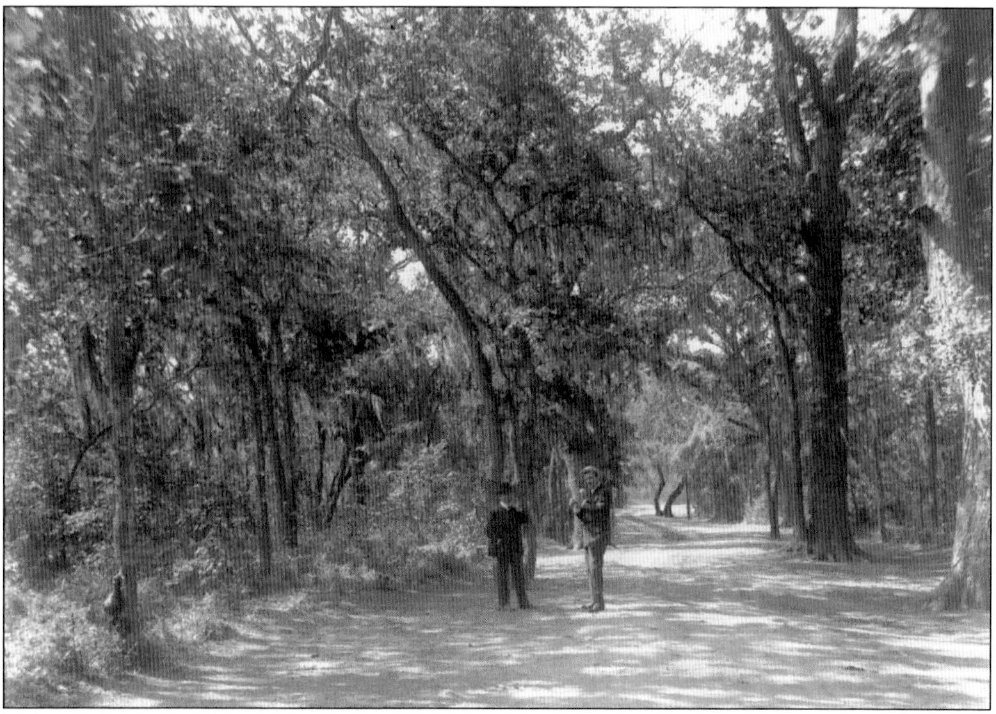

Two

Plantation to Peristyle 1770–1907

An 1829 mortgage description of Jean Louis Allard's property indicates that it included a two-story master house on 18 arpents fronting Bayou St. John, bounded by Metairie Road (renamed City Park Avenue in 1902) for 53 arpents on the ridge, which runs three feet above sea level. Allard grew corn and sugar cane but used the land primarily as a dairy farm with 40 cows. Preferring to use his time in intellectual pursuits, he had little interest in business and slowly lost portions of the property until all was sold or auctioned for taxes, which is how John McDonogh acquired the property. McDonogh was the one who willed the property to the city. Allard died in 1847, which was the same year his collection of poetry *Les Epaves* was published.

The city sold much of the Allard-McDonogh property, including the bayou frontage, but would buy much of it back later. In 1867, a park keeper was hired to cut the grass on a salary of $80, while illegally selling the grass clippings for hay, chopping trees to sell wood, and taking in $15,000 per year from charging fees for the grazing of 50 goats, 25 mules, 100 horses, and hundreds of cows. During the 1870s, the keeper, E.A. Pegroux, appointed Jean Marie Saux to oversee the park and tend the cattle. Saux also sold wood from trees cut in the park, while running his coffeehouse across from it.

An 1870 legislative act authorized the city to levy a real estate tax to establish "a New Orleans Park," and a board of commissioners was appointed. In 1871, prisoners were used to make some improvements. In 1877, the board was abolished and the city council took over the park's management. The land was roughly fenced in 1880 "to keep cows from neighboring pastureland from becoming a further nuisance."

In 1881, new commissioners were appointed, including Jean Marie Saux. In 1882, the portion of park west of Orleans Canal was detached for use as a smallpox hospital and cemetery. *Picayune's Guide to New Orleans 1903* stated, "The park contains 216.60 acres, only a portion of which, however, has been improved."

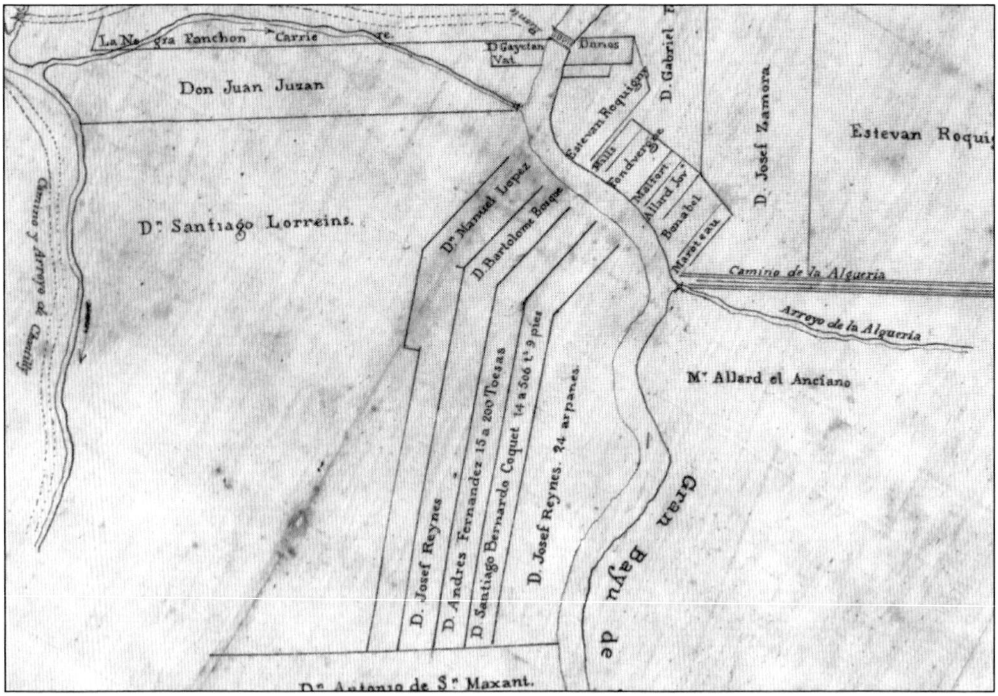

Five years after New Orleans was founded, the land, which would be City Park, was deeded to Francisco Hery in a 1723 French colonial concession. Some 50 years later, during Spanish rule, his widow, Madeleine Brazillier Hery, sold the property to Don Santiago Loreins, who would leave it to his son-in-law and daughter, Mr. and Mrs. Jean Louis Allard. The 1819 Spanish map above shows Allard's land (left of center), Bayou St. John (Gran Bayu de sn Juan), Bayou Metairie (Arroyo de la Alqueria), and Metairie Road (Camino de la Alqueria). Below is a modern map showing approximately the same area. (Both, LDL.)

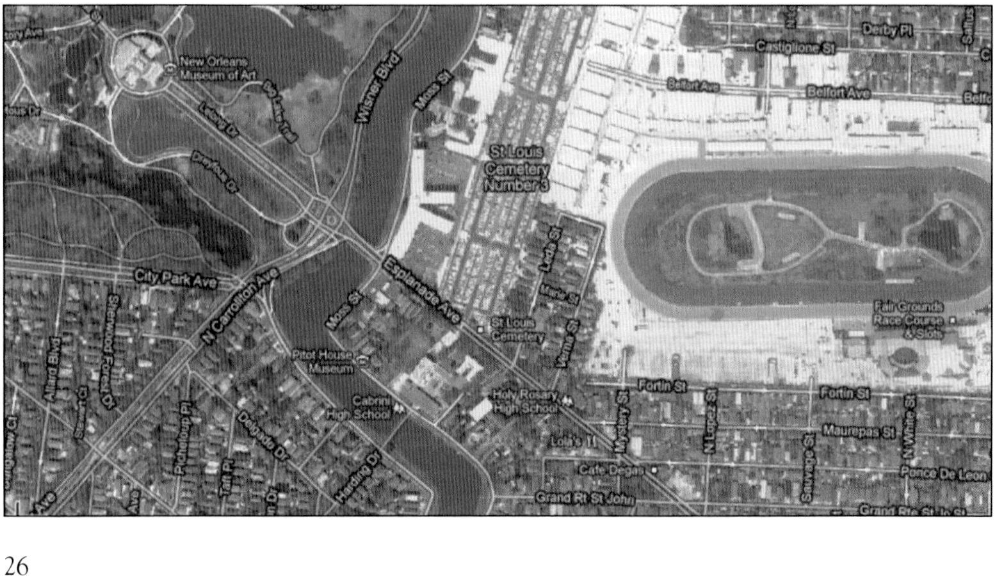

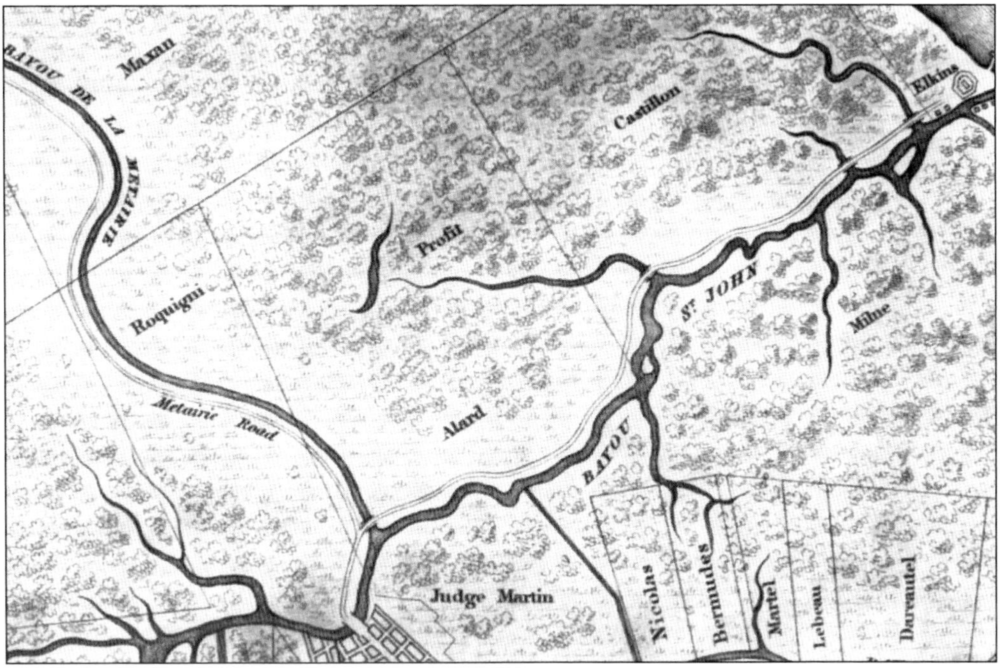

This 1828 map shows Allard's property (center) as well as Bayou St. John flowing to Lake Pontchartrain, which was where a port with a lighthouse and Harvey Elkin's popular Spanish Fort Resort were thriving; Metairie Road; Bayou Metairie; and Alexander Milne's property, which would soon boom as the Pontchartrain Railroad's Smokey Mary began its run in 1831, located east of the Bayou St. John to the lake. (NA.)

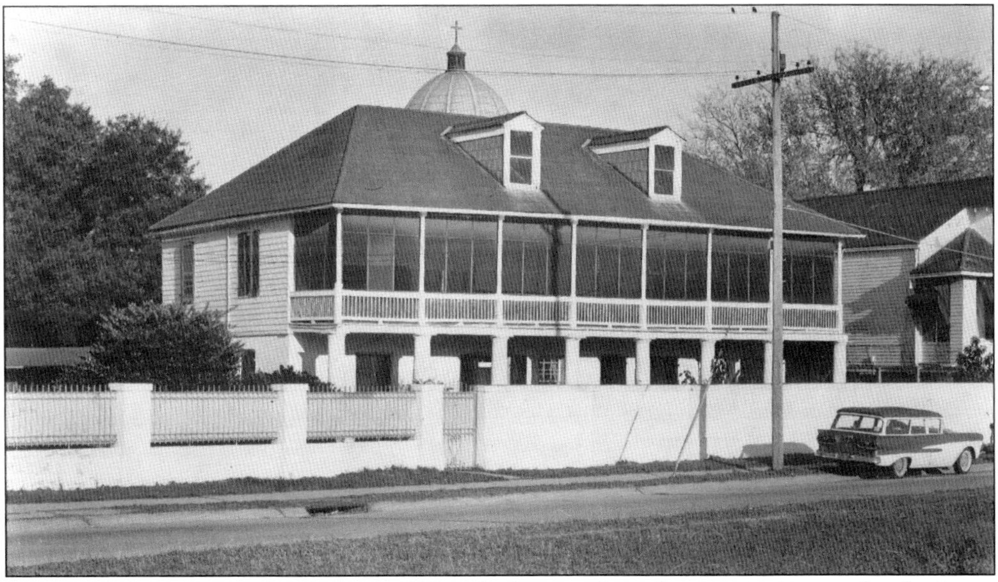

From Allard's plantation house, he could see the homes of nearby planters. Pictured is the James Pitot House, which was the home of the second mayor of New Orleans from 1810 until 1819, at 1440 Moss Street, located southeast of the park. In 1904, it became the convent of Holy Rosary Church's Missionary Sisters of the Sacred Heart. The church dome can be seen above the roof in this 1964 photograph. (LOC.)

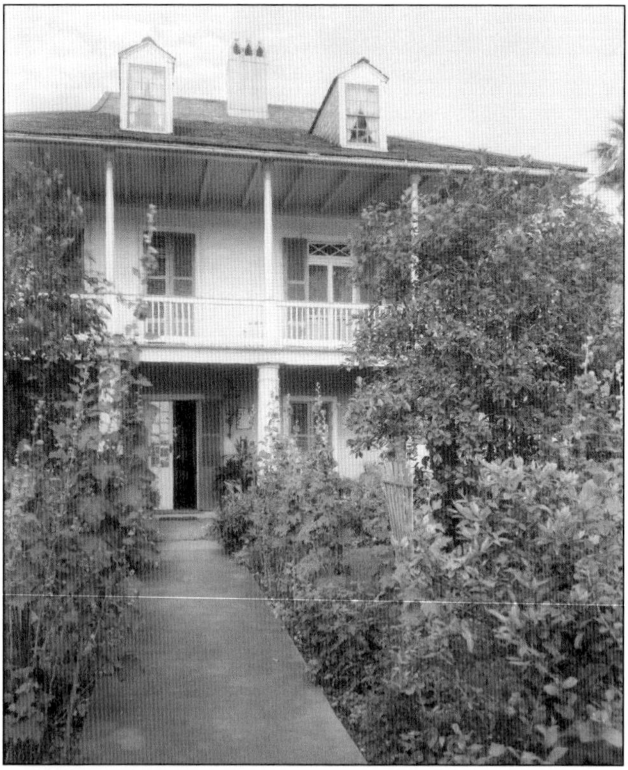

The Spanish Custom House, built in 1784 by Allard's father-in-law, Santiago Loreins, at 1300 Moss Street, is shown in this 1937 photograph. Bordering Allard's land to the south was Ferdinand d'Hemecourt's property along Metairie Road, which ran from Bayou St. John to what would become St. Patrick Cemetery. (LOC.)

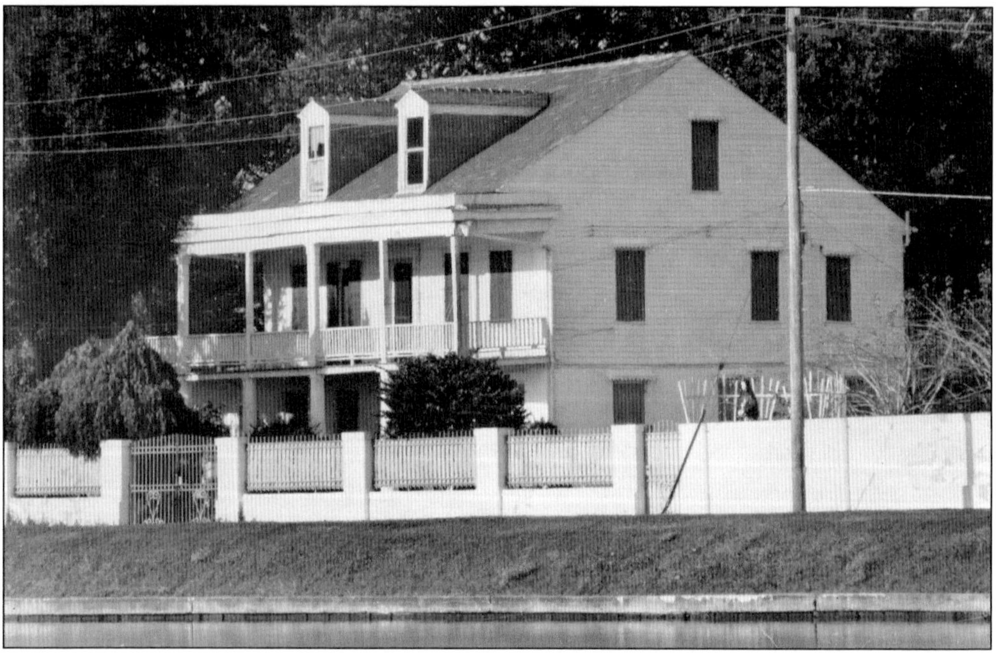

The land on which the Fernandez-Tissot House at 1400 Moss Street sat was sold by Loreins in 1800 to Andres Fernandez. The Archdiocese of New Orleans acquired a portion of the property for St. Louis Cemetery No. 3. Felix Labatut built the house in 1850. The Fernandez-Tissot House is shown here in 1937. Cabrini School used a smaller house on the property as a classroom. (LOC.)

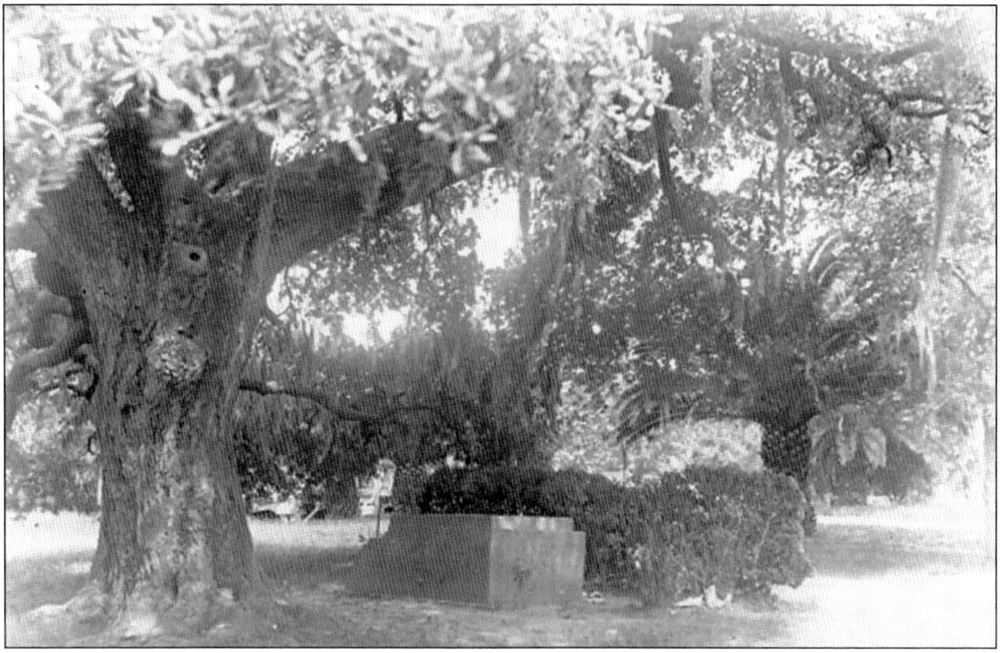

After McDonogh purchased the property in 1845, he allowed Allard to live the remainder of his life there. It is often said that Allard was buried in a quiet spot under a favorite tree, the Dueling Oak, shown here in the 1880s; however, St. Louis Cathedral records indicate that he was buried on May 18, 1847, in St. Louis Cemetery No. 2. (LOC.)

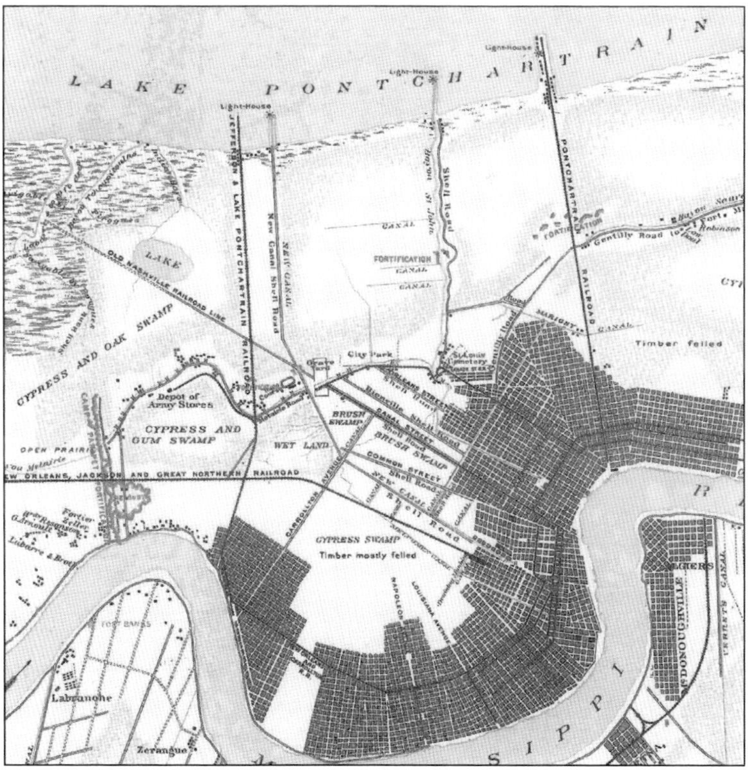

McDonogh died in 1850, and much of his bequest was used to build schools, but a portion of his property was set aside for the park. The 4th District Court's 1854 designation of approximately 100 acres of the property as a public park makes it one of the oldest in the nation. This 1863 map shows City Park in the center, relatively isolated from the city. (NA.)

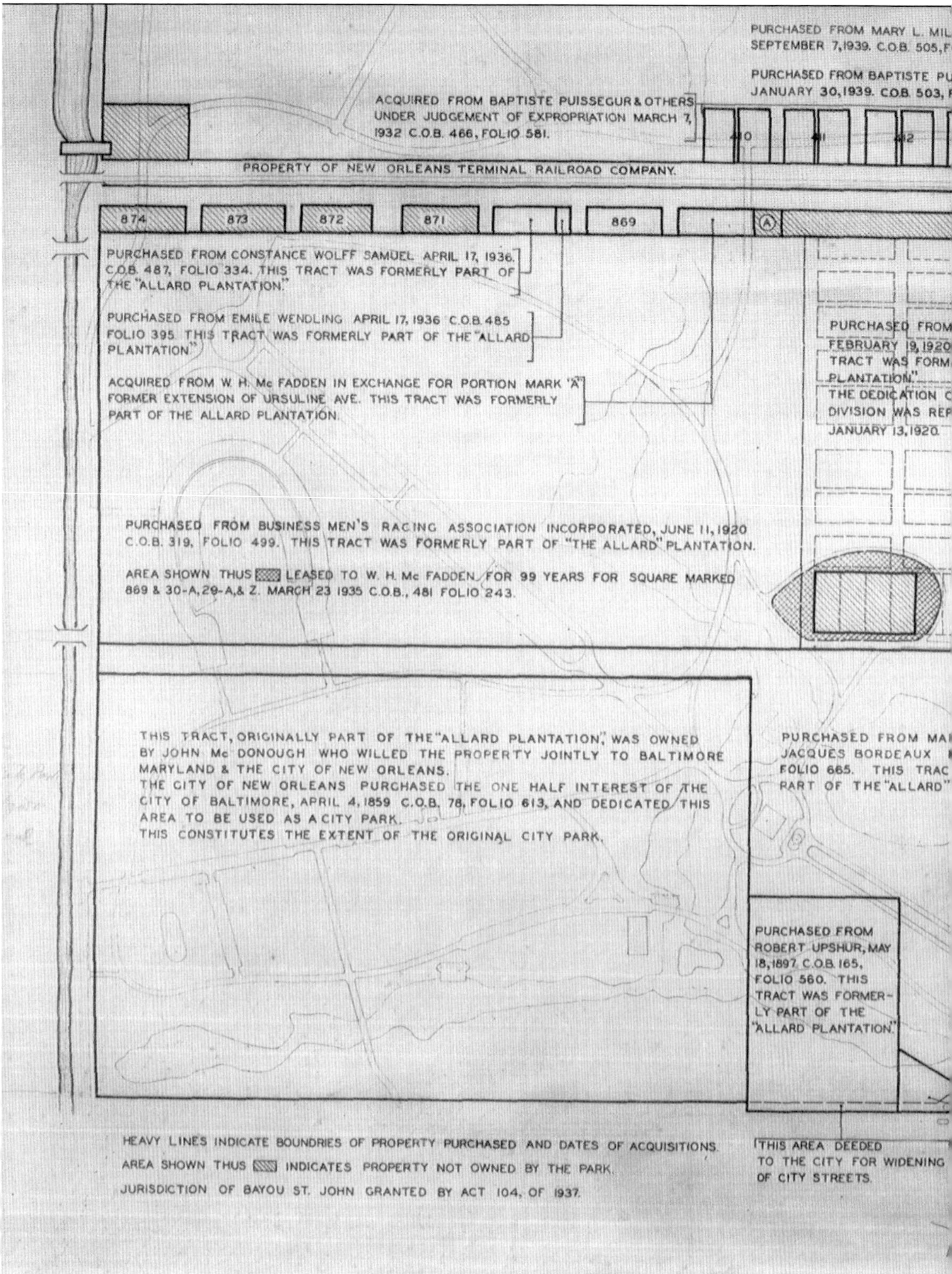
PURCHASED FROM MARY L. MIL
SEPTEMBER 7, 1939. C.O.B. 505, F
PURCHASED FROM BAPTISTE PU
JANUARY 30, 1939. C.O.B. 503, F
ACQUIRED FROM BAPTISTE PUISSEGUR & OTHERS UNDER JUDGEMENT OF EXPROPRIATION MARCH 7, 1932 C.O.B. 466, FOLIO 581.
PROPERTY OF NEW ORLEANS TERMINAL RAILROAD COMPANY.
874
873
872
871
869
PURCHASED FROM CONSTANCE WOLFF SAMUEL APRIL 17, 1936. C.O.B. 487, FOLIO 334. THIS TRACT WAS FORMERLY PART OF THE "ALLARD PLANTATION."
PURCHASED FROM EMILE WENDLING APRIL 17, 1936 C.O.B. 485 FOLIO 395. THIS TRACT WAS FORMERLY PART OF THE "ALLARD PLANTATION."
ACQUIRED FROM W. H. Mc FADDEN IN EXCHANGE FOR PORTION MARK "A" FORMER EXTENSION OF URSULINE AVE. THIS TRACT WAS FORMERLY PART OF THE ALLARD PLANTATION.
PURCHASED FROM
FEBRUARY 19, 1920
TRACT WAS FORM
PLANTATION."
THE DEDICATION C
DIVISION WAS REP
JANUARY 13, 1920.
PURCHASED FROM BUSINESS MEN'S RACING ASSOCIATION INCORPORATED, JUNE 11, 1920 C.O.B. 319, FOLIO 499. THIS TRACT WAS FORMERLY PART OF "THE ALLARD" PLANTATION.
AREA SHOWN THUS LEASED TO W. H. Mc FADDEN, FOR 99 YEARS FOR SQUARE MARKED 869 & 30-A, 29-A, & Z. MARCH 23 1935 C.O.B., 481 FOLIO 243.
THIS TRACT, ORIGINALLY PART OF THE "ALLARD PLANTATION," WAS OWNED BY JOHN Mc DONOUGH WHO WILLED THE PROPERTY JOINTLY TO BALTIMORE MARYLAND & THE CITY OF NEW ORLEANS.
THE CITY OF NEW ORLEANS PURCHASED THE ONE HALF INTEREST OF THE CITY OF BALTIMORE, APRIL 4, 1859 C.O.B. 78, FOLIO 613, AND DEDICATED THIS AREA TO BE USED AS A CITY PARK.
THIS CONSTITUTES THE EXTENT OF THE ORIGINAL CITY PARK.
PURCHASED FROM MA
JACQUES BORDEAUX
FOLIO 665. THIS TRAC
PART OF THE "ALLARD"
PURCHASED FROM ROBERT UPSHUR, MAY 18, 1897 C.O.B. 165, FOLIO 560. THIS TRACT WAS FORMERLY PART OF THE "ALLARD PLANTATION."
HEAVY LINES INDICATE BOUNDRIES OF PROPERTY PURCHASED AND DATES OF ACQUISITIONS.
AREA SHOWN THUS INDICATES PROPERTY NOT OWNED BY THE PARK.
JURISDICTION OF BAYOU ST. JOHN GRANTED BY ACT 104, OF 1937.
THIS AREA DEEDED TO THE CITY FOR WIDENING OF CITY STREETS.

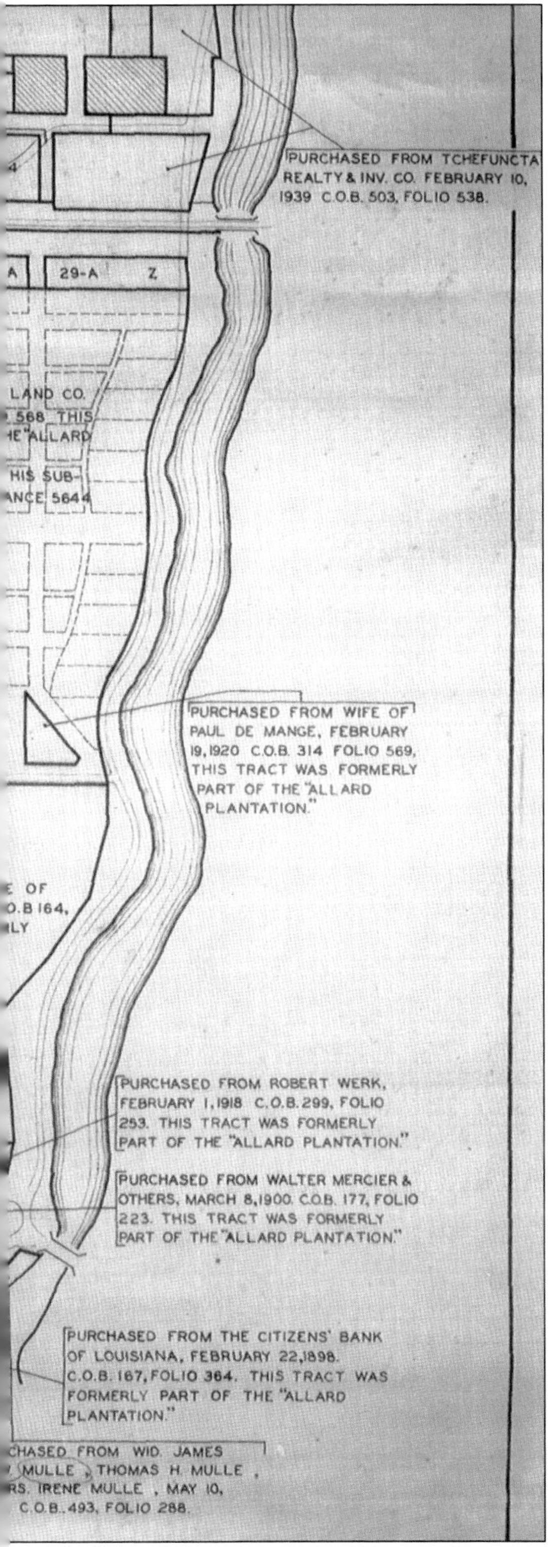

An 1855 ordinance mandated that the chief of police appoint one officer to patrol the park to prevent destruction of trees. Ordinances in 1858 called for the selection of a caretaker, the building of a keeper's lodge, and the authorization to contract for fencing along Metairie Road. The park officially opened in 1859. This diagram shows land acquisitions from 1859 through 1939. Note that the original park extended only along Metairie Road to the Orleans Canal (McDonogh's land also extended west of Orleans Avenue but was never used for the park) to just south of what is now the stadium and west of NOMA. The park expanded eastward until 1918 and did not grow northward until the 1920s, when city streets were taken. The largest acquisition, 900 acres, which was extended and improved by the WPA during the 1930s and 1940s, is not included here. (NOPL.)

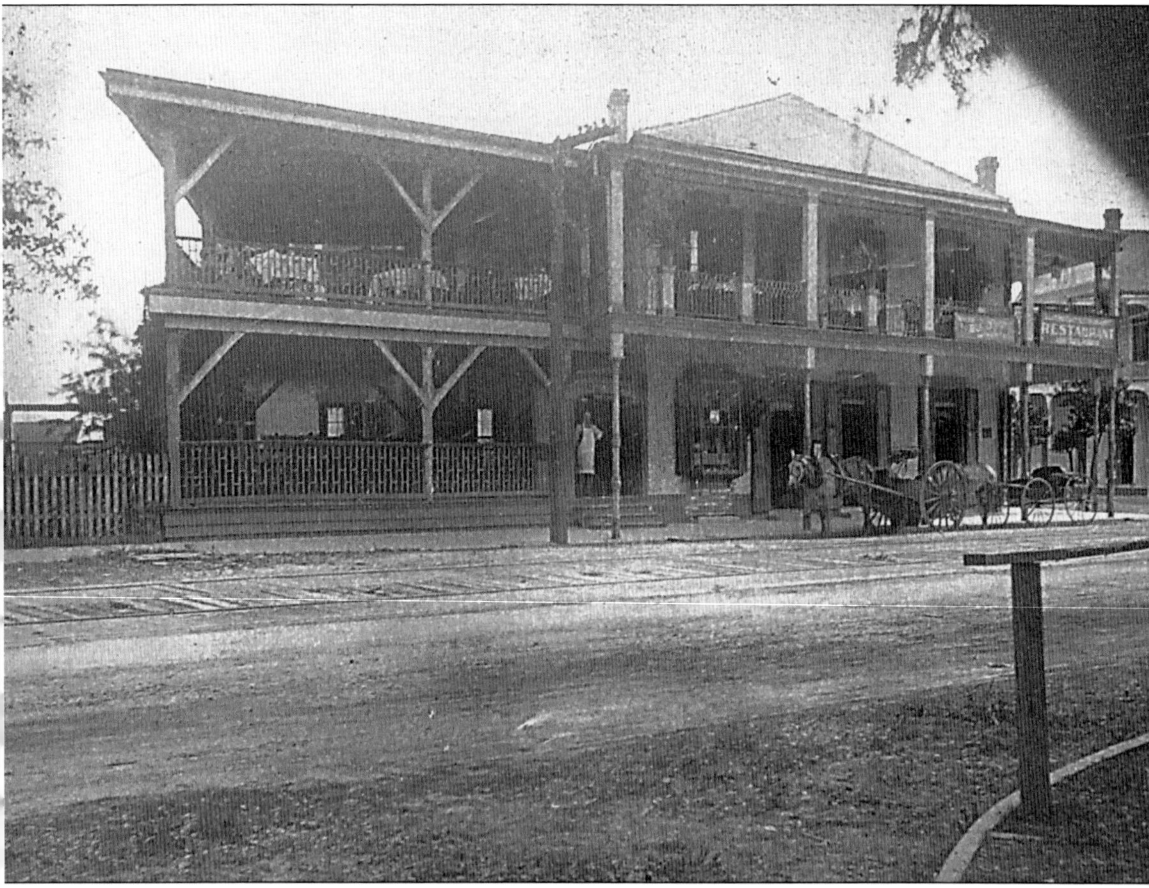

Here, one can see again Jean Marie Saux's building at the end of Alexander Street where he sold refreshments to park visitors since no potable drinking water, restroom facilities, or concessions were available in the park. In 1861, the *Daily Picayune* glowingly reported, "A large home of refreshments, stocked with the best liquors, and to which is adapted an ice cream saloon for the ladies. The proprietor will have nothing neglected to deserve the patronage of the citizens." This would become the entire area's oldest structure by at least 30 years. (LDL.)

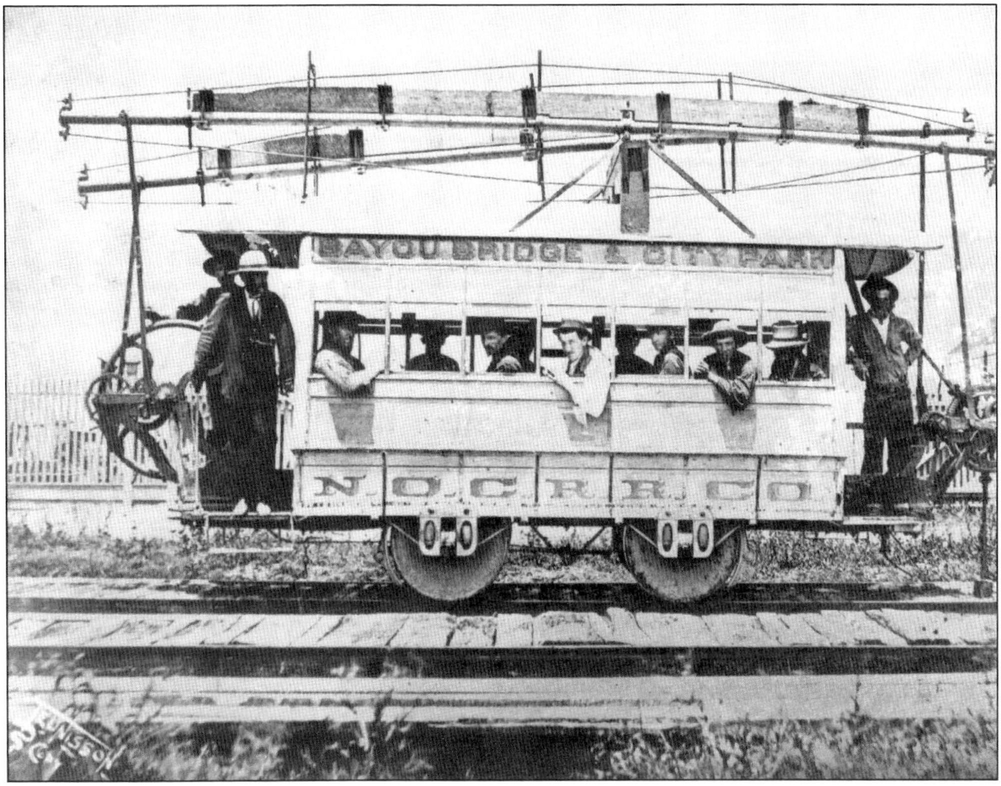

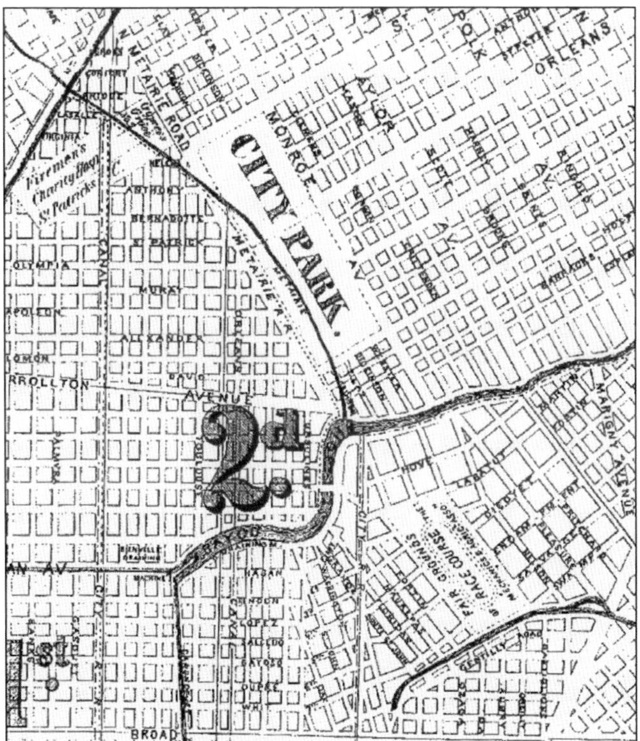

A trip to the park required a ride from the city by horse and carriage on unimproved roads. Transit companies saw an opportunity to capitalize on the growing popularity of City Park by adding new lines. These afforded easy access, and consequently, interest in the park rose, which led to the call for park improvements. On the riverside of Bayou St. John, the New Orleans City Railroad Company (NOCRR) operated the Esplanade and Bayou Bridge streetcar line (above) beginning June 1, 1861. On the lakeside of the bayou, the New Orleans City Railroad Company, whose route can be viewed on the map, ran the Bayou Bridge and City Park streetcar line beginning in the fall of the same year; it became part of the Esplanade line around 1900. (Both, LDL.)

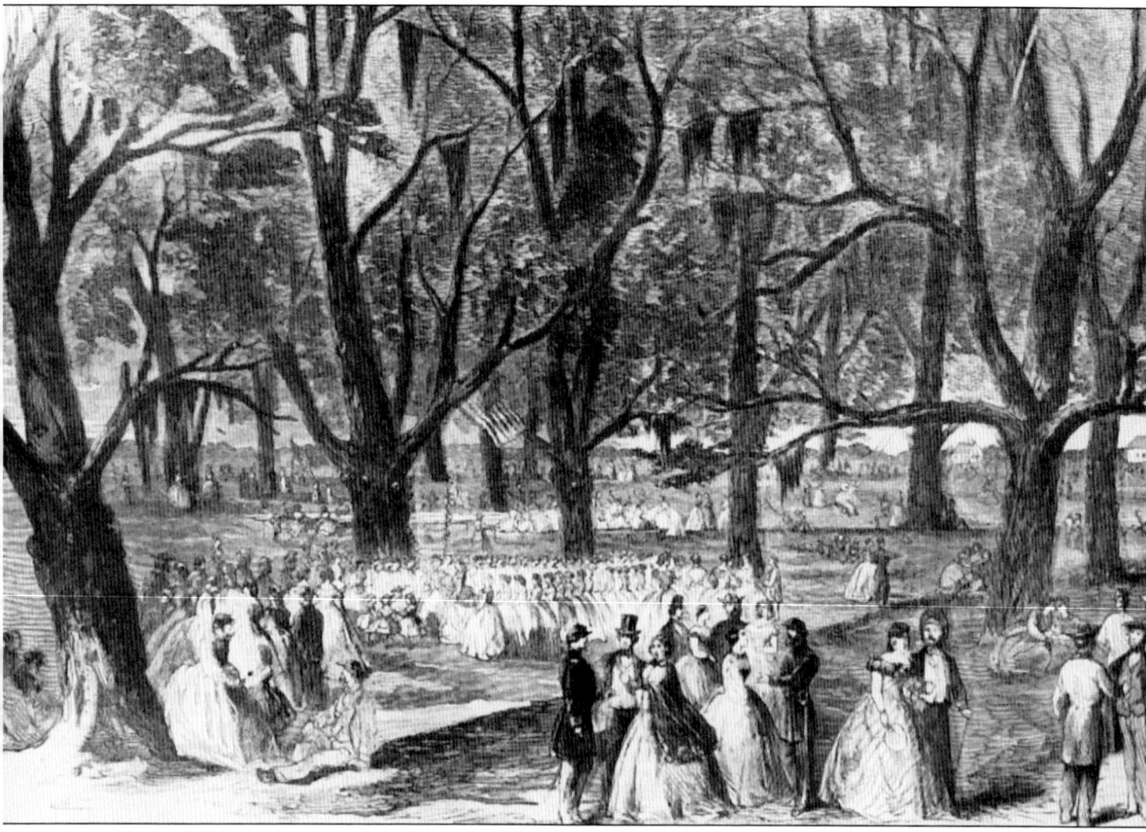

Harper's Weekly reported on June 6, 1863, "Captain Walters, Commander of the gunboat *Kineo*, had kindly sent there a large quantity of canvas to lay on the grass for dancing, with abundance of ropes for swings, and detailed two or three of his sailors to come and arrange matters for his young friends . . . It was really interesting to watch some little dark-haired Southern beauty innocently romping with her blue-eyed playmate—the daughter of some officer from Maine or Massachusetts—and then to be reminded that the father of the former was a 'registered enemy.' " The accompanying sketch is shown here. During the 1860s, the *Daily Picayune* noted numerous picnics, many including groups of "colored people." The following is from an 1864 article: "No doubt more than two-thirds at the large concourse were formerly slaves and treated as if they were unfit for freedom . . . they have so used their freedom as to convince any candid minded that they are capable of appreciating their freedom." (NA.)

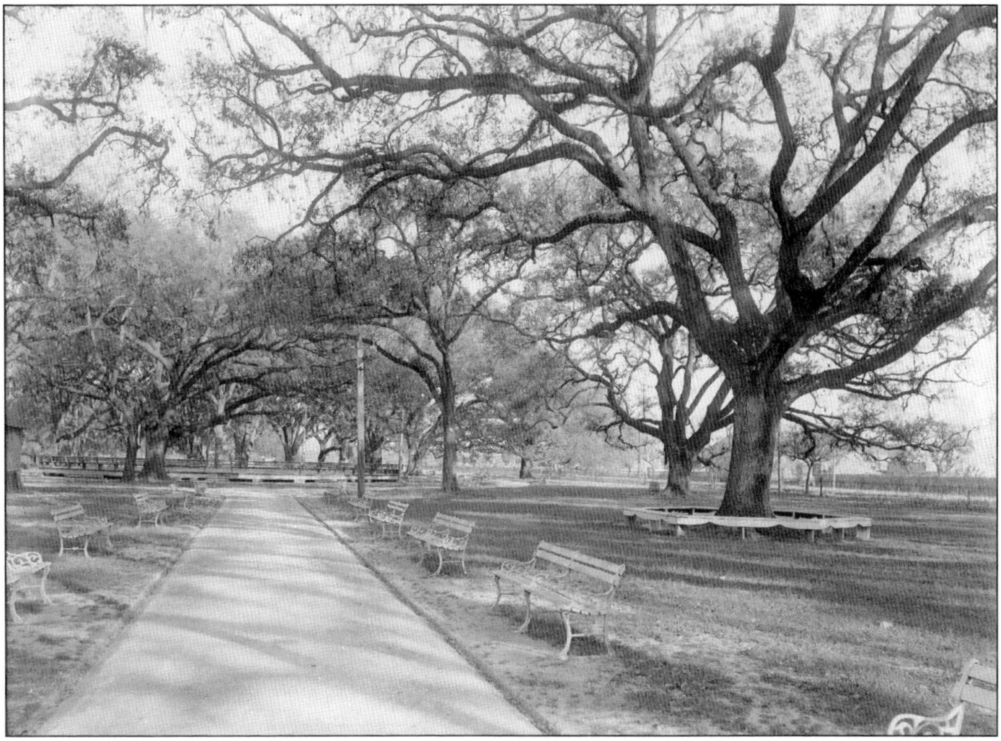

An 1879 ordinance removed what is now Holt Cemetery, pictured right, from the park's jurisdiction. In 1891, CPIA was incorporated, and the property was officially named "City Park." Victor Anseman was appointed keeper with a $40 salary. He called for a fence on the front side with an iron gate, prohibition of shooting and trapping (with a $10 fine), cattle pasturing in the rear as an income source, iron benches, an octagon-shaped dance pavilion, and that a plan be designed. Anseman planted orange and Chinese umbrella trees. By the end of 1891, CPIA had received fees and donations amounting to $3,000 from 2,000 members. About 50 more benches were budgeted, and a series of entertainment for additional revenue was planned. In May 1892, the first Fete Champetre (country feast) was held as a fundraiser. The celebration's lengthy program included the Washington Artillery Band, military drills, fencing exhibits, and children's games—all for a 25¢ admission (children free). The event reportedly attracted 5,000 people, who also enjoyed food and drink concessions, for a profit of $1,532.97. (Above, LDL; right, LOC.)

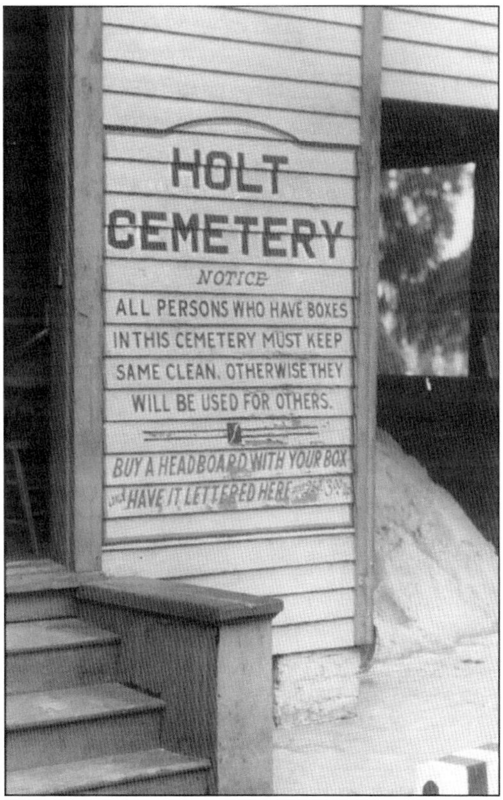

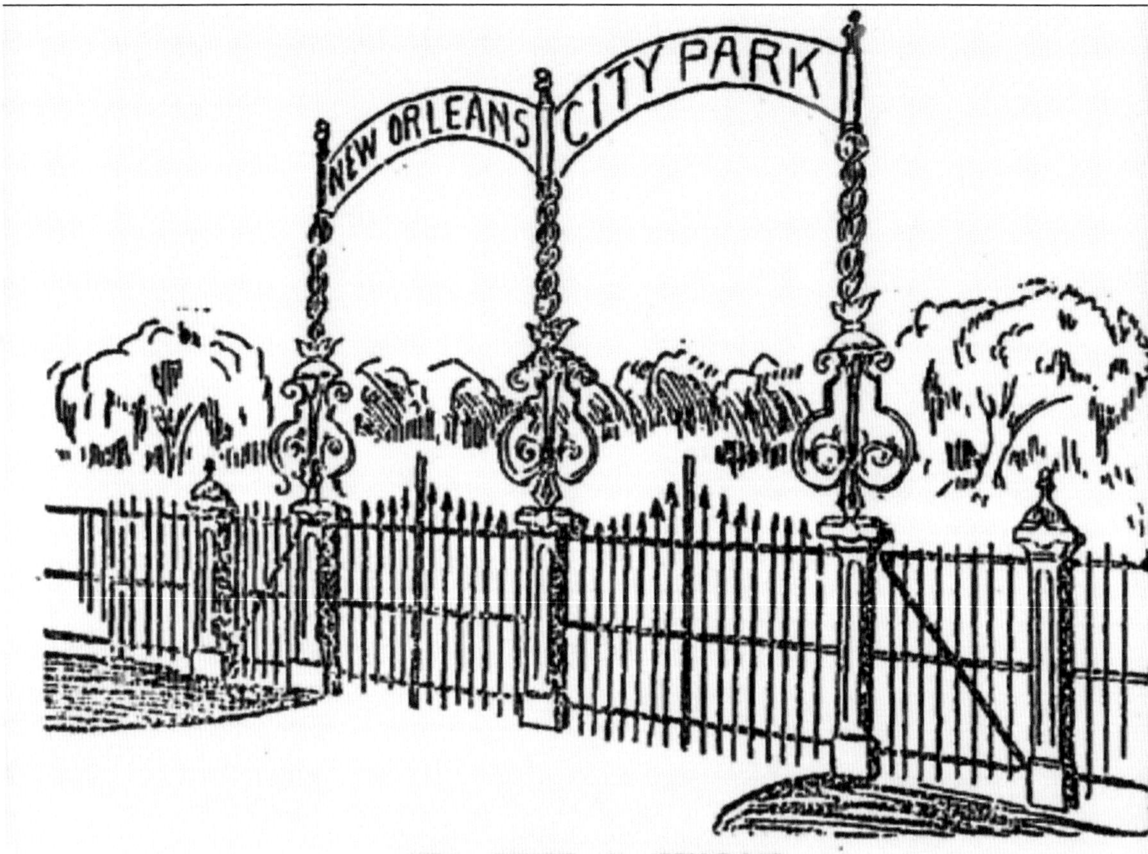

THE NEW GATEWAY.

On March 13, 1892, the *Daily Picayune* described park improvements since Anseman's appointment, including this drawing of the new "3,000-foot fence and iron gate on Alexander Avenue painted red." The article stated that CPIA had collected $1,000 from the city and $8,000 in donations and membership fees and that it had cut weeds, placed circular benches around the dueling oaks, built the Ladies' Cottage rest area (with parlors, closets, and porches) near the gate and the Men's Cottage near Bayou Metairie, and constructed a footbridge across the bayou. It described "50,000 oranges, lemon, and fruit trees for revenue" and a "palmetto alley with Spanish dagger plants and lantanas." And the *Picayune* described the Saux Building as "the stuccoed hostelry of Jean-Mario [sic] on Alexander Street with its rose garden and green pea and thyme and orange trees where in the past the order be given of pistols for two and coffee for one." (*Daily Picayune*.)

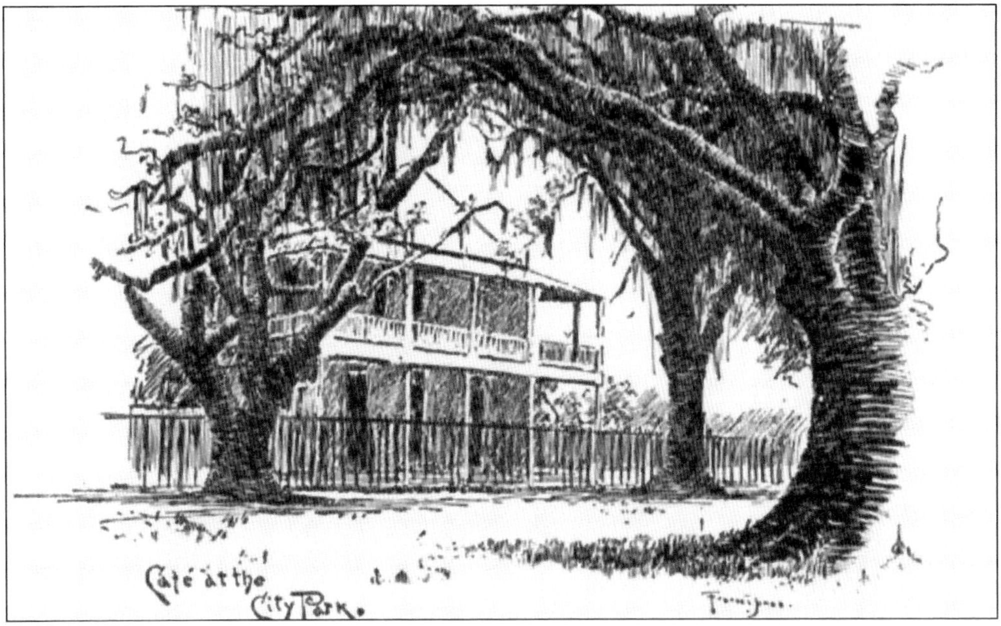

In 1893, Fernand Alciatore, the son of Antoine's Restaurant's Antoine Alciatore, purchased and renovated the building to serve fine food at A la Renaissance des Chenes Verts (green oaks). The illustration is from Grace King's history. Across the street in the park, 2,000 barrels of shells extended walkways, and along these walkways, the second Grand Fete featured a procession, Indian dances, battle reenactments, performances by the City Park Pocahontas Dramatic and Social Club, games, and fireworks. About 10,000 tickets were printed, and 3,000 people attended. (NA.)

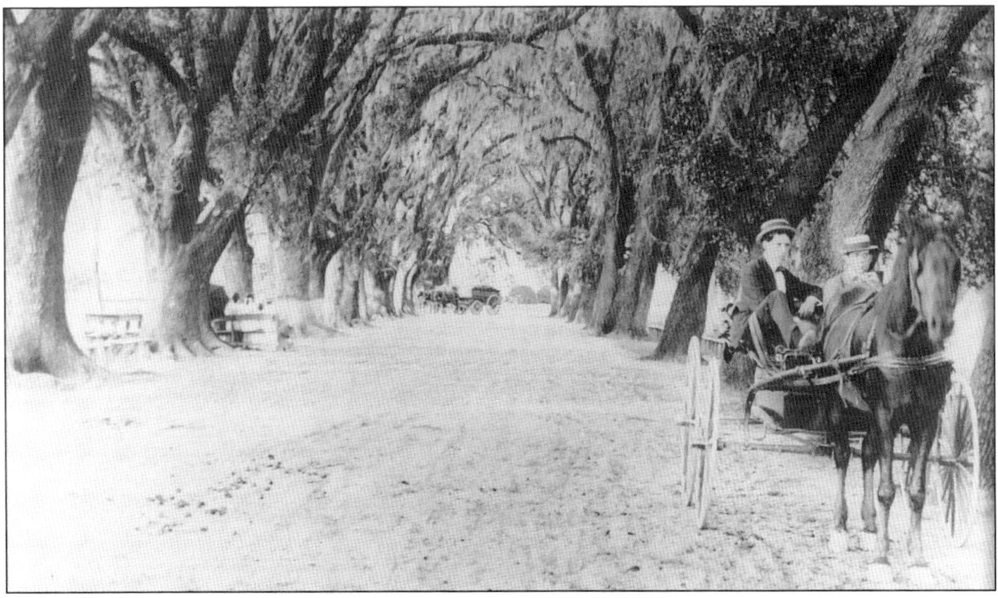

In 1895, under park board member and engineer George H. Grandjean's direction, low areas were filled and 100 million gallons of water pumped from Bayou St. John to create a half-mile lake at the cost of 16.7¢ per cubic foot. The US Commission of Fish and Fisheries offered bass, crappie, catfish, perch, and carp to augment the fish, which would swim down the bayou from Lake Pontchartrain. This photograph is dated 1895. (LOC.)

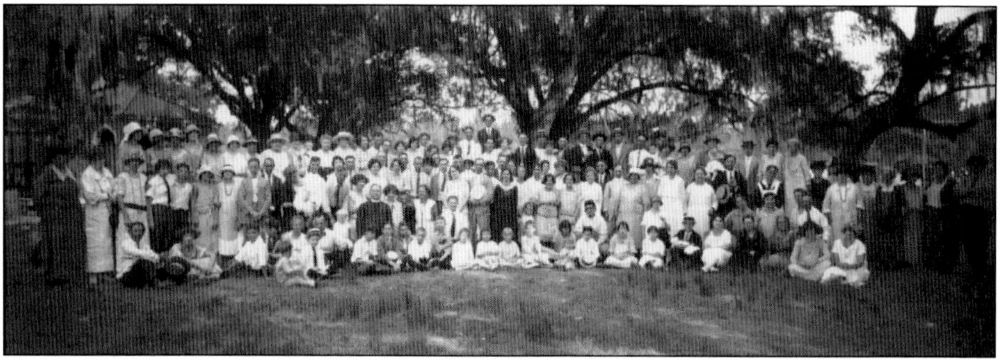

In the short-lived zoo resided doe, hogs, macaws, parrots, goldfish, and several monkeys, which were killed by predators. The zoo's wildcat was "causing problems," which led to a resolution not to accept wild animals unless approved by the board. Fifty permits were issued for group picnics, one pictured above, averaging about 200 people. Two-hundred family picnics were held as well. Tickets, at 25¢ each, were issued by the Beauregard Monument Association for a battle reenactment fundraiser. After the commission and residents secured a grant from the city council, six blocks of Alexander Street near the park entrance were paved with shells in 1895, which was when the photograph below was taken. In celebration, a dinner was held at Fernand Alciatore's restaurant under the oaks in the yard accompanied by an orchestra, opera, and fireworks. (Above, NOPL; below, LOC.)

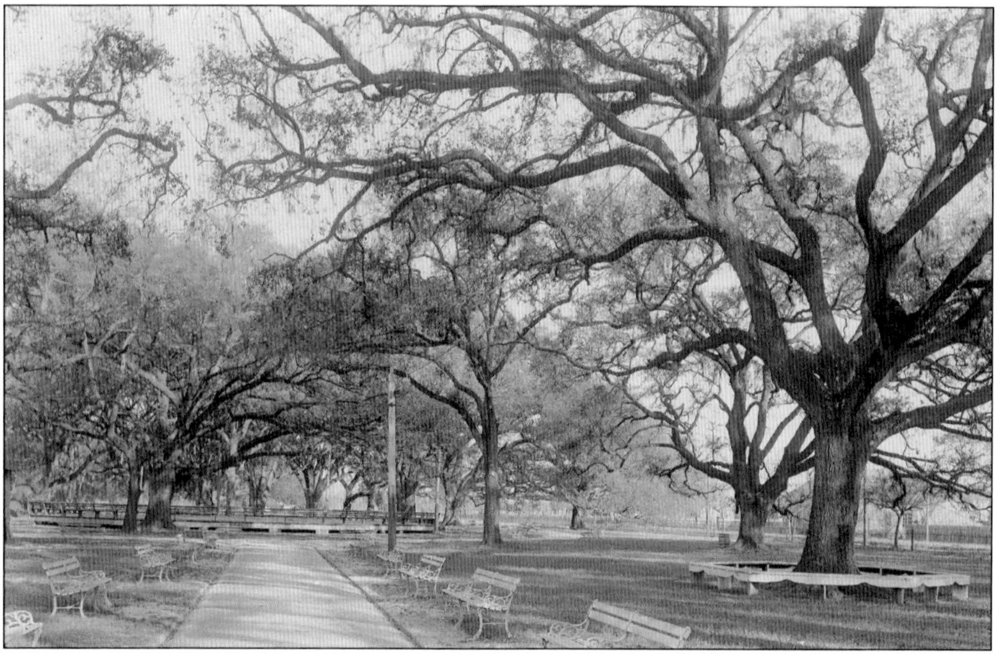

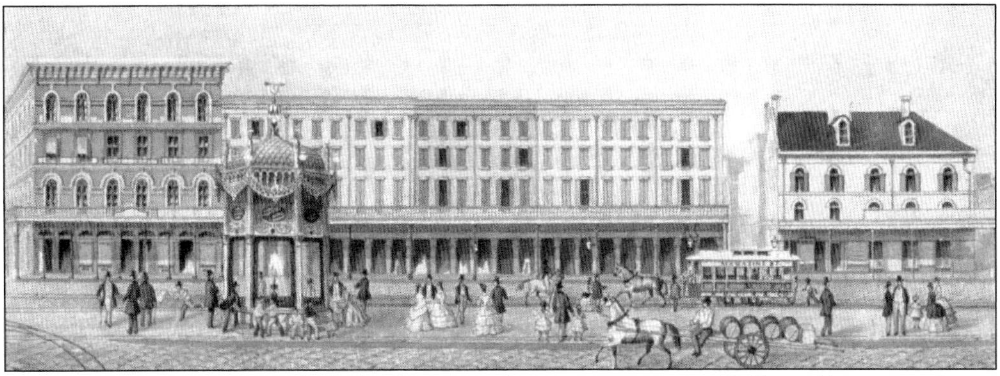

In 1870, Jackson Ogden Belknap built the gas-lit, ornate, cast-iron Belknap Fountain, shown on the left-hand side of the image. Ogden's intention was to use it primarily as an advertising stand on the neutral ground of Canal Street. Note the NOCRR streetcar, as mentioned on page 33. (HNOC.)

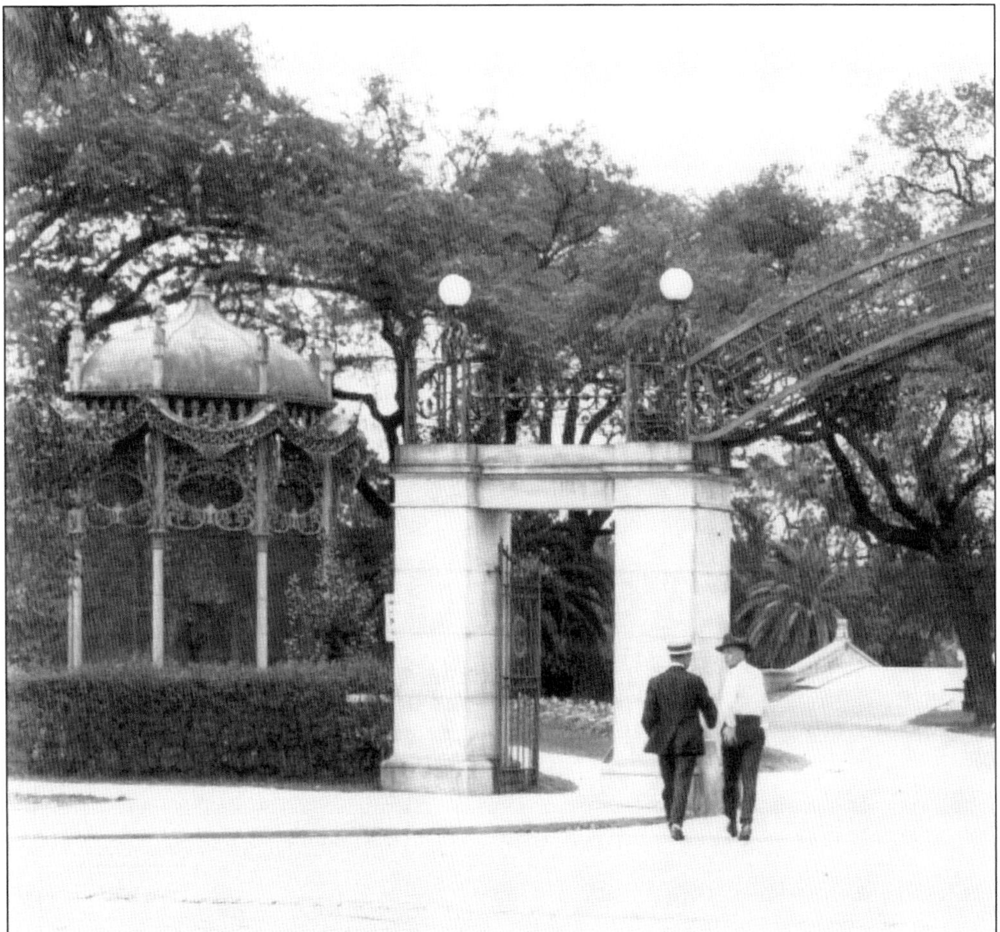

The *Daily Picayune* reported on May 11, 1895, that the "Manager of the Traction Company presented the Iron Pavilion which would be moved to the front entrance of the park and painted the appropriate colors," seen here inside the Alexander Street entrance. (LDL.)

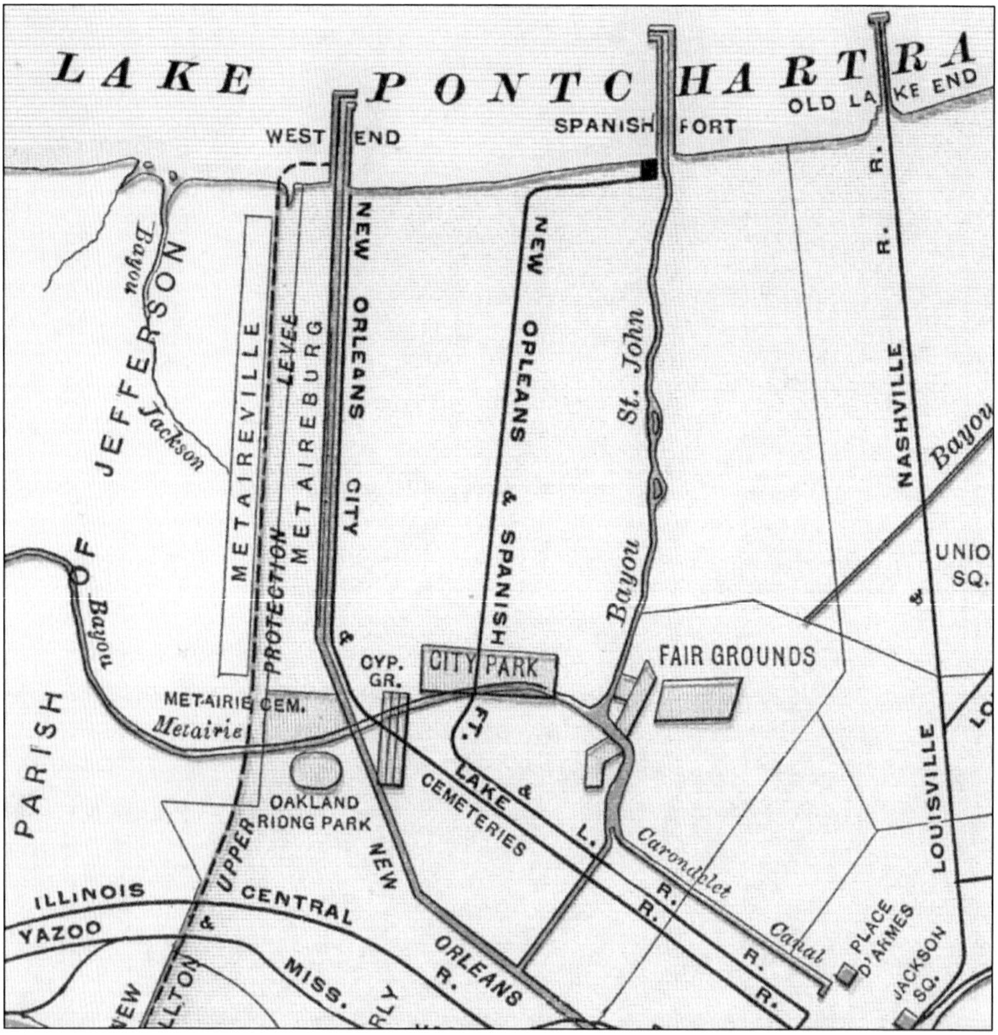

The Louisiana Legislature gave CPIA authority to operate and develop the park in 1896 and provided a reserve fund in addition to city revenues of $10,000. In addition, the Louisiana Legislature ordered the city to set aside annually not less than $15,000 beginning in 1897. At this time, weekly musical performances were provided by the New Orleans & Spanish Fort Railroad (whose route is show on the map). An electric trolley extended a single track from the Halfway House at the New Basin Canal to the park. In 1897, a mule-driven carousel first operated, and the park gained property, located 1,805 feet along Bayou St. John and 4,685 feet on Metairie Road, which increased the park size to 213.5 acres. The City Park superintendent position was created, and Victor Anseman was selected. Also in 1897, the State Military Rifle Range was inaugurated and designated to use the park. (NA.)

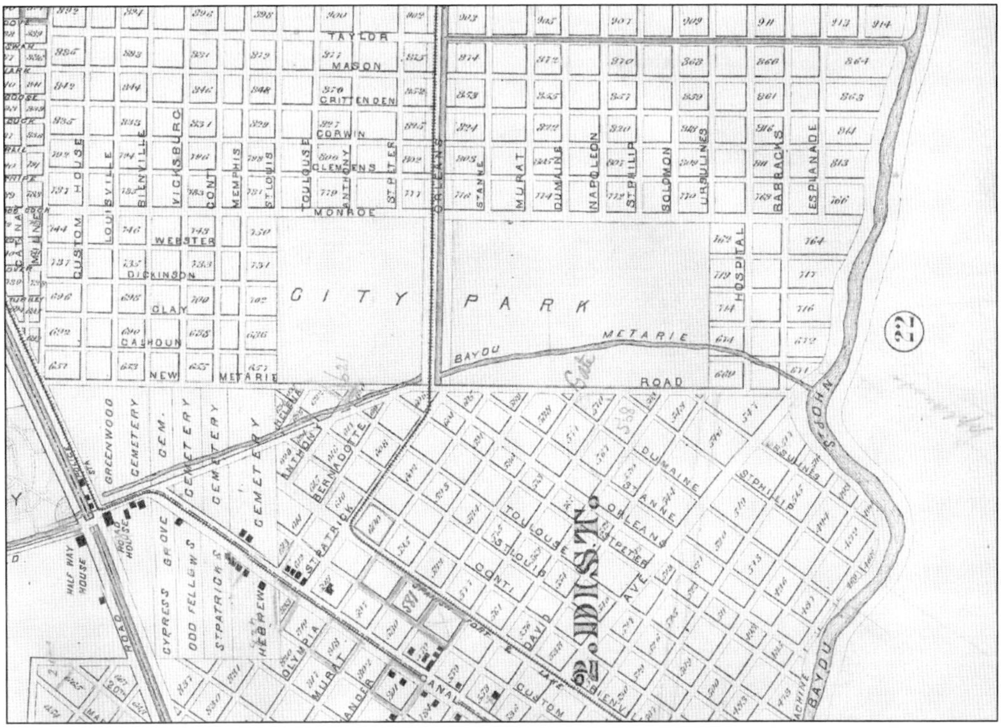

In 1898, Orleans Avenue was extended to Metairie Road, which bordered the park as did St Louis Street, Monroe Street, and Ursulines. The local firm Daney and Wadill submitted the "Plan of Existing and Proposed Improvements in the New Orleans City Park," with many ideas largely attributed to George Grandjean. Also in 1898, the first miniature train ran in the park and 6,000 attended Recreation Day in September. (NA.)

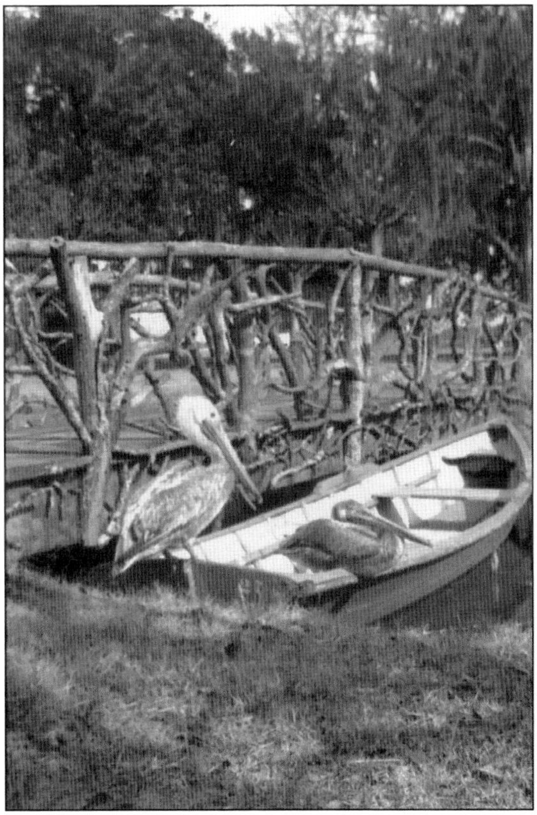

In 1899, local photographer Alexander Allison captured this sighting of Louisiana's state bird, the pelican. In that same year, the cavalry mustered here during the Spanish-American War. The following year, Henry Rightor wrote in his *Standard History of New Orleans*, "Racquette is still played in New Orleans at the old City Park . . . by the Creoles who have always been very fond of the game." Local Frenchmen had learned it from the Indians. (NOPL.)

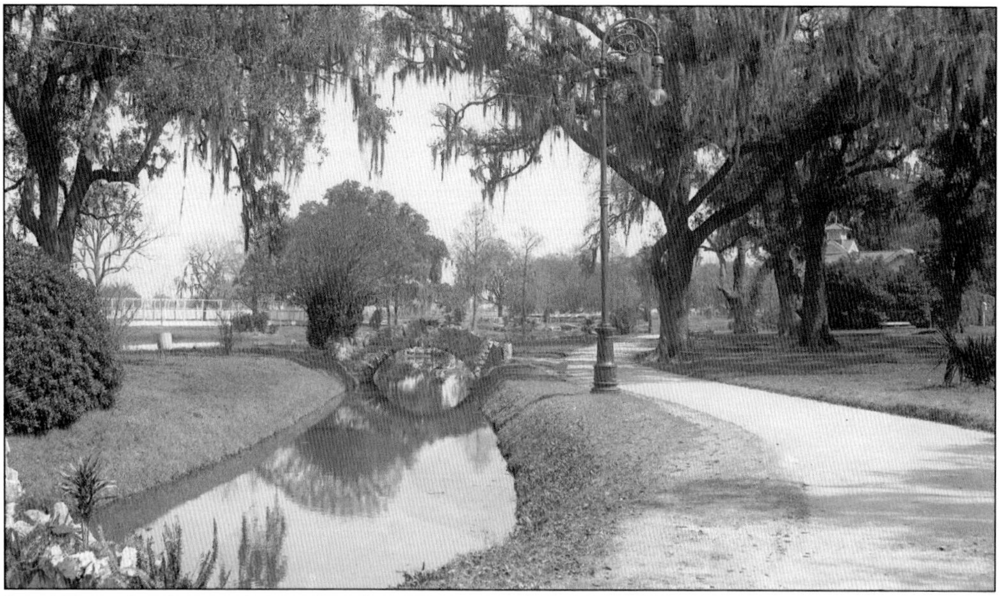

In 1902, with a $650 gift from local socialite Angele M. Langles and other donations, the lovely Langles Bridge was built over the Bayou Metairie south of what would be the Casino Building. Local architects Andry and Bendernagel, designers of the Ursuline Convent, several McDonogh schools, and buildings on Tulane's campus, were commissioned to design the Neoclassical Anseman Bridge, shown below in 1904. It lasted only until 1938, when the WPA replaced it with the stark monolithic structure used today. The Langles Bridge can also be seen in distance of this undated photograph. (Both, LOC.)

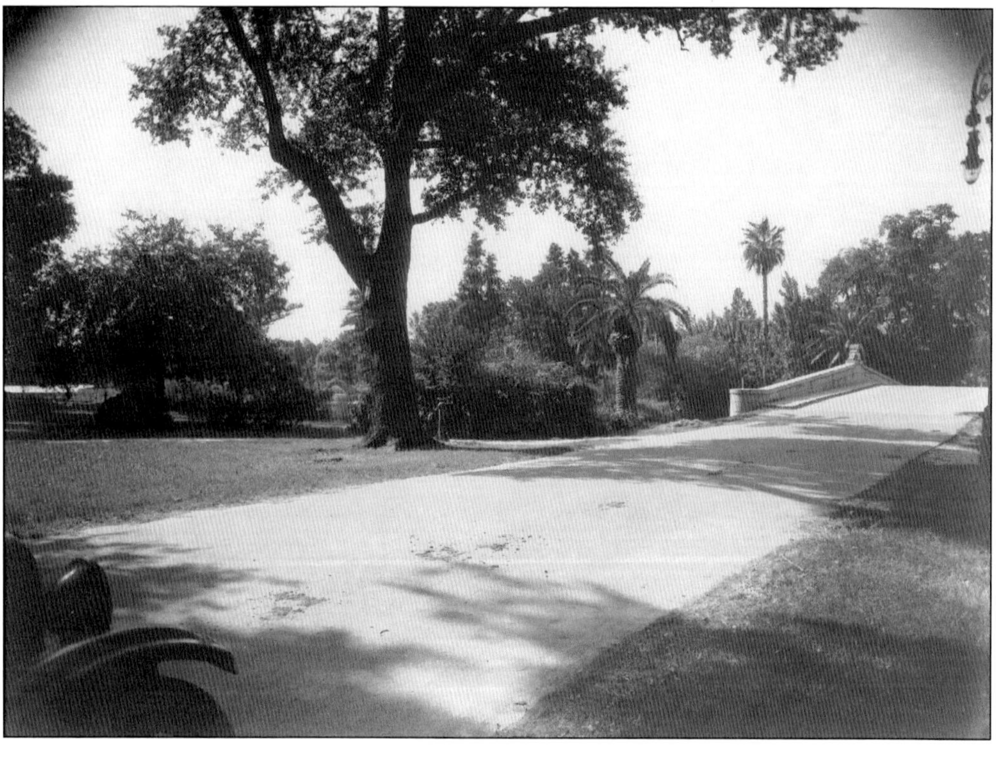

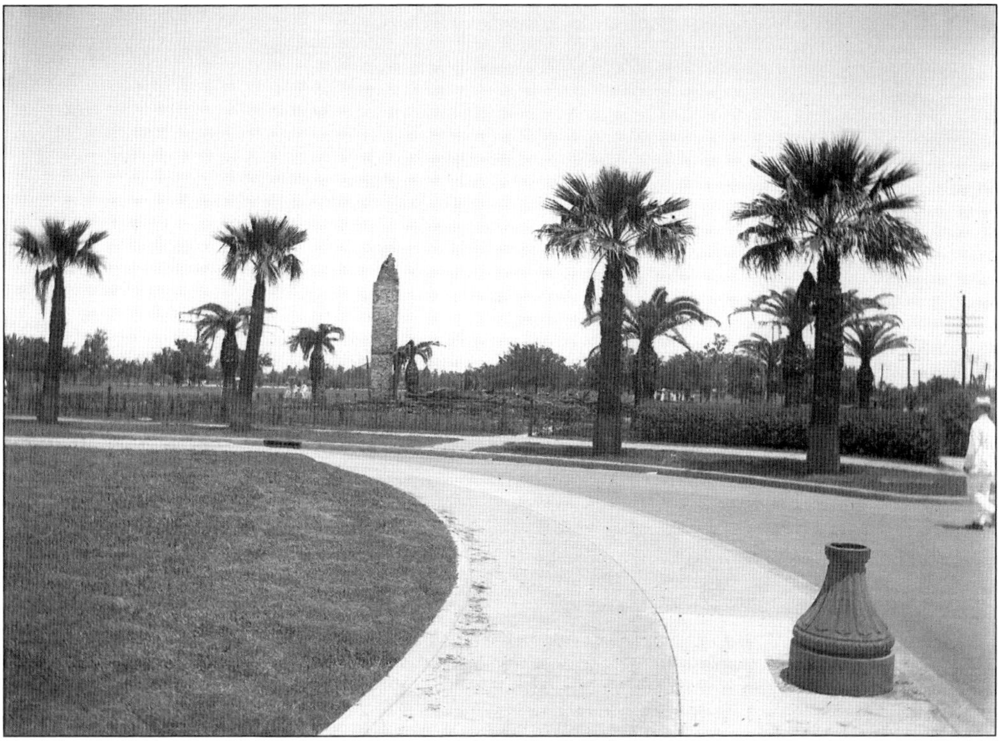

The Country Club of New Orleans, organized in 1903, was adjacent to the park near Bayou St. John, located about 100 yards from where the Beauregard statue stands. Built in 1905, the club's building was destroyed by fire on May 8, 1917, shortly before this photograph was taken. The land was later acquired by the park. (LDL.)

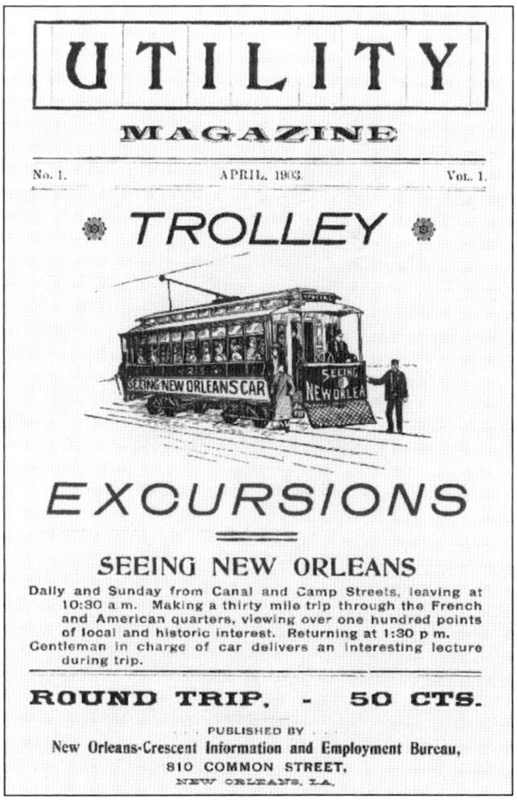

Beginning on Canal Street at Camp and Chartres Streets, the trolley headed for Esplanade Avenue to the park and then along City Park Avenue to the cemeteries, where it turned toward West End. From there, it returned to Canal Street, making its way to Audubon Park before heading back to its origin in the city proper. Viewed here is a 1903 advertisement. (NA.)

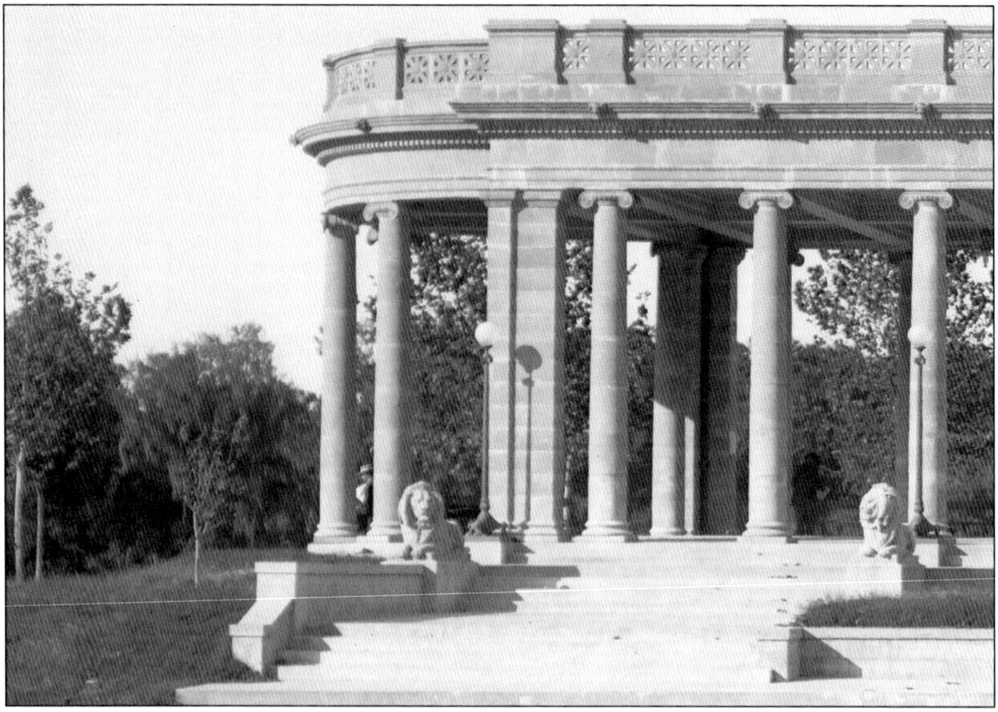

A 1904 ordinance allowed for the expropriation of property at the rear of the park, and $60,000 was appropriated. The land was exchanged with the owners of the country club. Mayor Paul Capdevielle ended his term in office, and so the New Orleans Public Library acknowledged his contributions: "City Park stands as a monument to his energy and civic spirit. The upbuilding of the park was his constant care, and he served continuously as president of the CPIA for more than two decades, holding the office at the time of his death [in 1922]." Victor Anseman, founding member of CPIA, City Park superintendent, keeper, planter, and visionary, died at age 63. He is remembered as the "Father of City Park." Pictured here are children walking along the road named for him. (Both, LDL.)

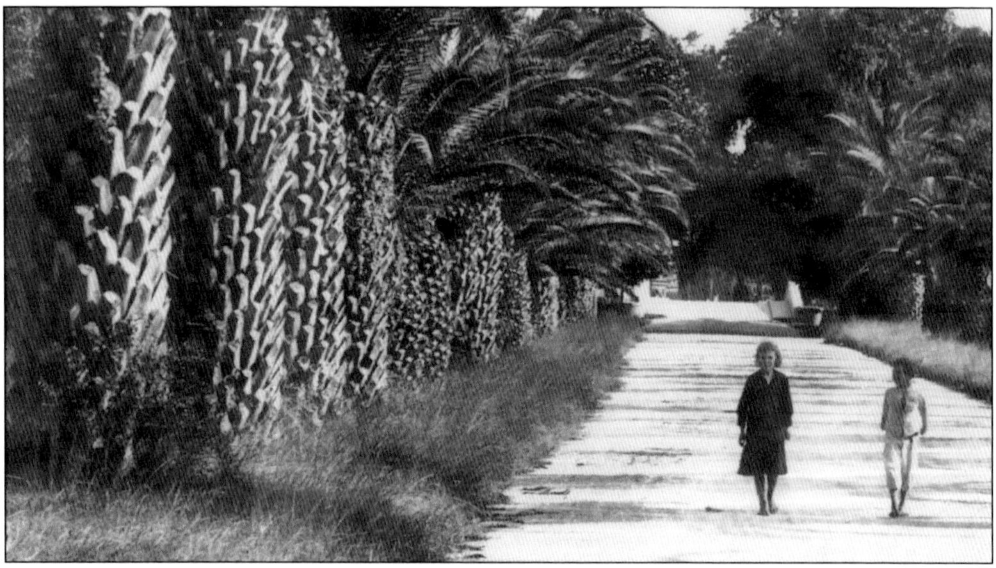

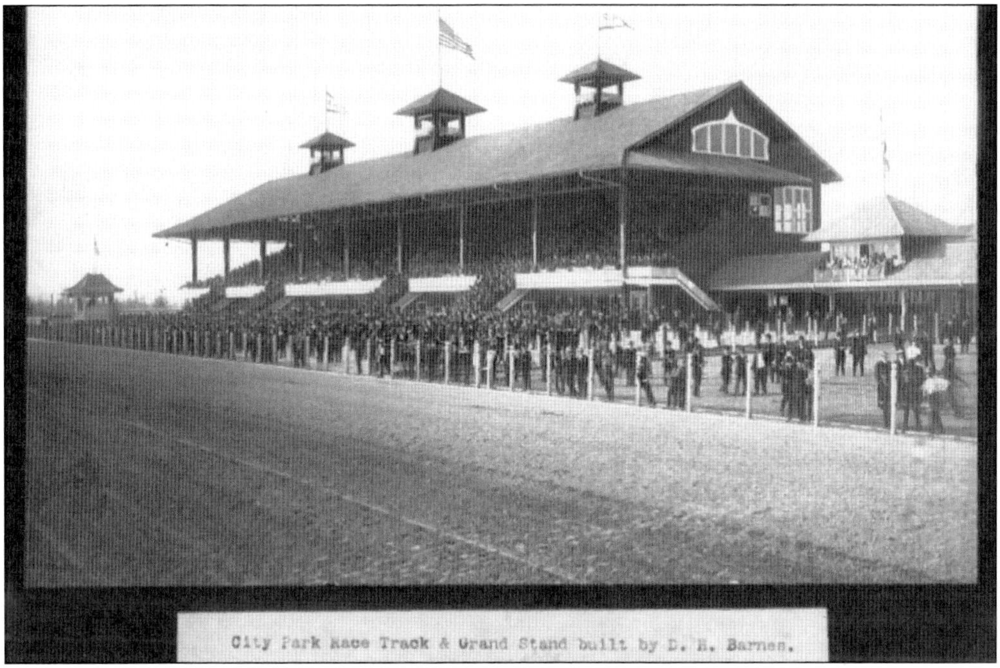

Joseph Bernacii was appointed superintendent with plans to light the lake for night rowing. In 1905, the Parkway Commission was created by city ordinance to devise a plan for a connecting link of roadway between Audubon and City Park. Armand Veazey led the band at the opening of the mile-long City Park Racetrack. The racetrack ran along what would become the Roosevelt Mall and competed for business with the nearby fairgrounds. David H. Barnes (cited in the 1905 photograph) was the president of the City Park Jockey Club. The grandstand was in the area where the stadium sits today. Closed to racing in 1908 when the Locke Law prohibited betting on horses, the track was used for aviation shows. Below is a view looking toward the park on Explanade Avenue in 1906. (Both, LDL.)

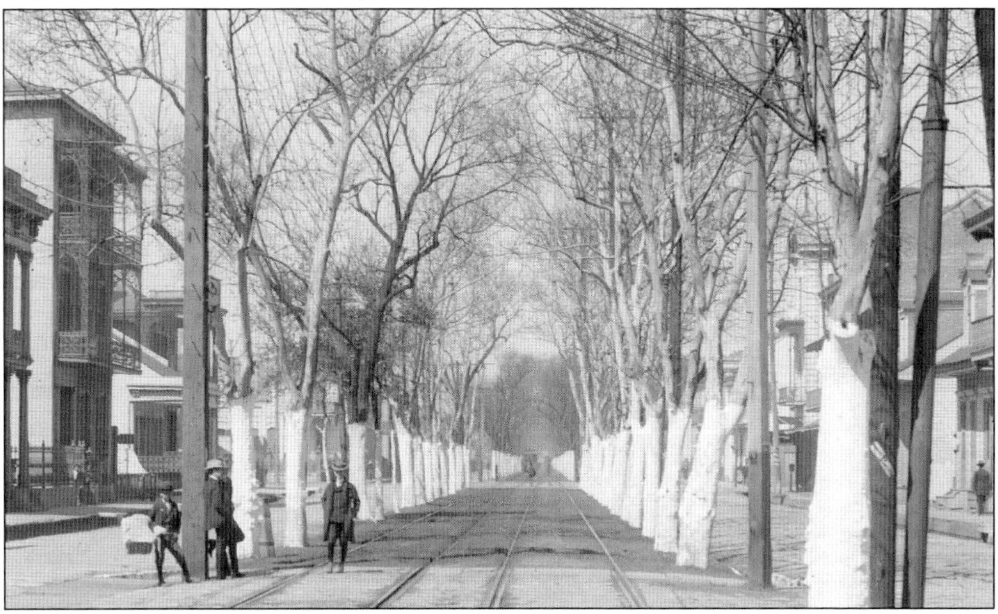

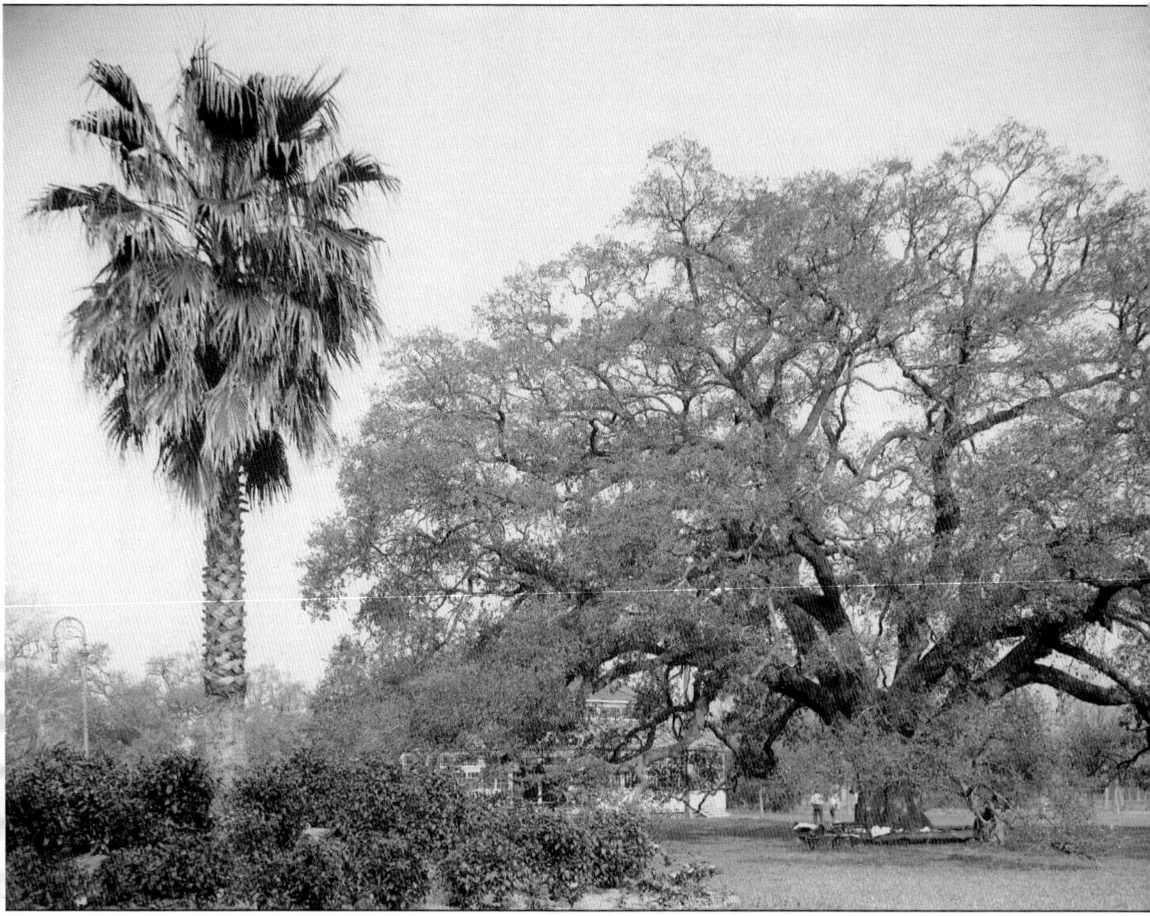

One of only 100 antique wooden carousels in the country and the last in Louisiana, the City Park Flying Horses first delighted children and adults in 1906. Carved by Looff and Carmel, the Flying Horses were listed, along with their pavilion (shown here in 1910), in the National Register of Historic Places in 1986. Some carved horses from the Spanish Fort carousel are now believed to be among the park's Flying Horses, now located in the Hines Carousel Gardens along with modern amusement rides. Also in 1906, a skating rink was designed, pony rides began, and several tracts of land were purchased at a total expense of $28,000. The firm of MacKenzie and Goldstein drew a new plan for improvement. By 1907, CPIA had 592 supporting members, and so a new deer pen was built and a new hothouse was under construction at a cost of $12,000. Orleans Street was filled and widened, allowing more visitors to attend the Sunday and Wednesday concerts from May though September. (LOC.)

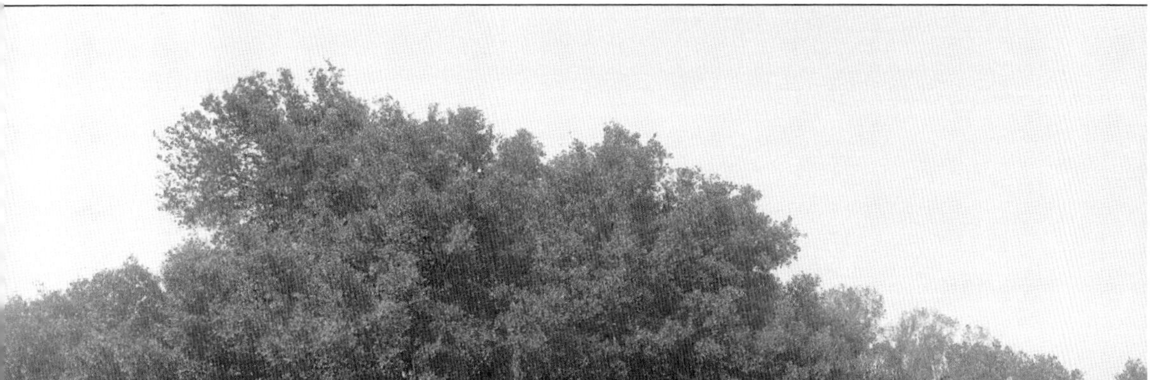

Describing City Park during the 1860s and 1870s, *Times-Picayune* reporter James M. Augustin wrote in a 1908 article, "Cattle was pastured in the park, and it was fully abandoned. At night it was the rendezvous of people of unsavory character and respectable people avoided the place, even in the daytime. Many fist fights occurred here and such was the desolation and gloom of the park that frequent suicides took place there. The favorite site for such tragedies was a big oak tree, with very low, overhanging branches. It is even now still known as 'suicide's oak'. In July 1881, an attempt was made to rescue the property." This photograph of that oak tree was taken in 1910. It survives today in a park that is lovingly being rescued, yet again, but this time after the ravages of Katrina. (LDL.)

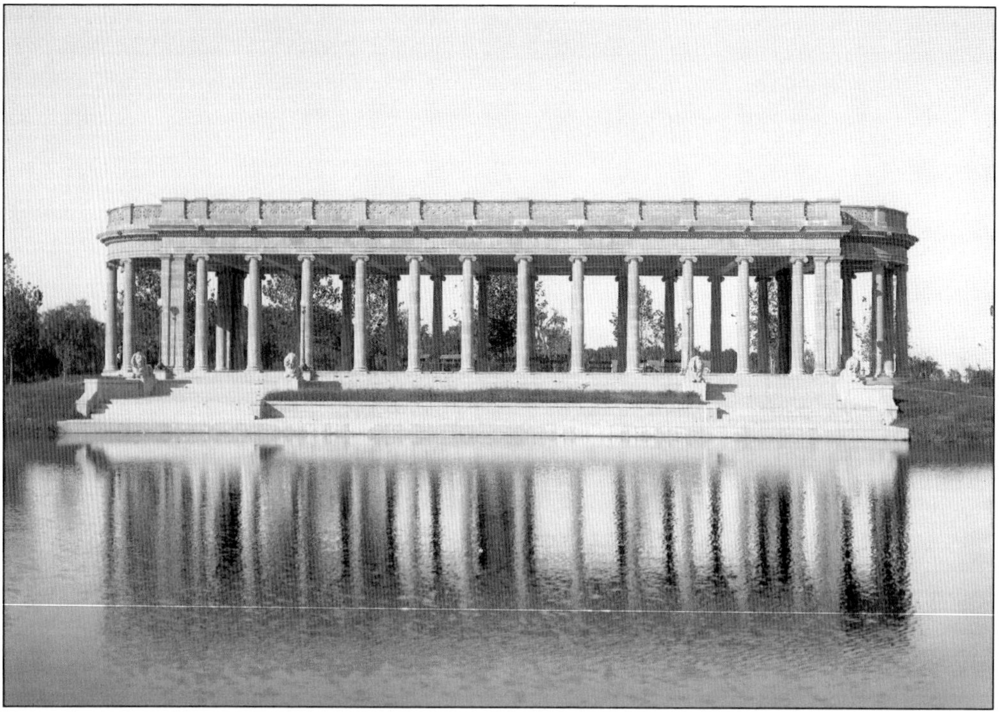

Note the beautifully ornate parapet surrounding the top of the Peristyle in 1910. Deemed to be causing roofing problems, it was removed by WPA workers in 1936, as seen below during the 1940s. In 1989, Mae and Vincent Saia, along with Friends of City Park, generously funded its renovation. The Peristyle is now an anchor of the Goldring-Woldenberg Great Lawn, which was completed in the spring of 2010. (Both, LOC.)

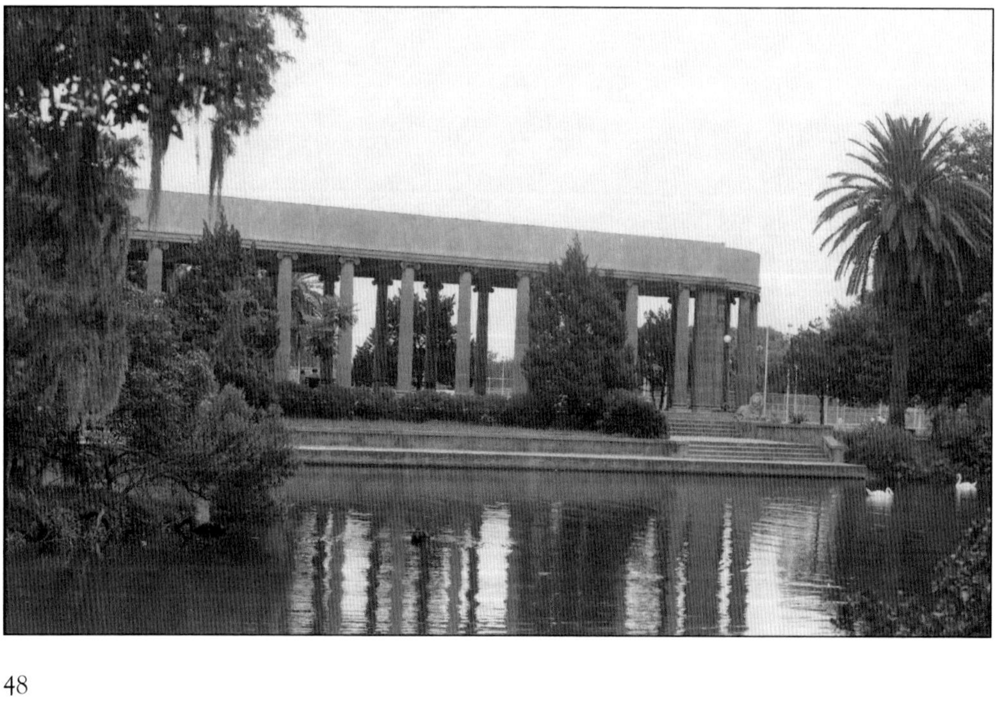

Three

EXPANSION AND MODERNIZATION 1908–1928

In 1912, the Saux Building was bought in a sheriff's sale by the New Orleans Brewing Company, the makers of Double Eagle and 4XXXX beer, and was leased by Frank LaMothe, the former proprietor of LaMothe's Restaurant and Oyster Saloon at 137 St. Charles Street, which claimed to be New Orleans's oldest restaurant. He renamed his new place LaMothe's City Park Restaurant and advertised a "fine banquet hall and accommodations for ladies" in local directories and in City Park festival programs. Men were entertained there by "ladies" from Storyville who relaxed on the balcony during free time. In 1922, the brewery sold the building to Anthony Compagno whose sons operated it as Holland House, offering dining upstairs, ice cream on the first floor, and a barroom in rear. The backroom was purportedly used by a bookie who exchanged bootlegged rye and scotch for rent. Elkin's Coffeehouse was later housed in this building.

When asked about the danger of flying, John Moisant responded, "I do not expect to die in an airplane," but he did after taking off from City Park in 1910. A decade later *American Magazine of Art*, while glowingly praising the Delgado Museum in 1921, described its visitors as "A quiet and well-behaved company, including a number of Jews, a few Creoles, and almost no negroes." A park Aesthetic Committee was formed in 1922, whose members Richard Koch (architect), Julius Dreyfous (engineer), and Marcel Garsaud created a long-range plan. In 1926, the city paid $1,750 for an additional 11 swampy acres between the park and the lake. In 1927, a 900-acre extension was acquired, and in 1928, the first tennis courts were built.

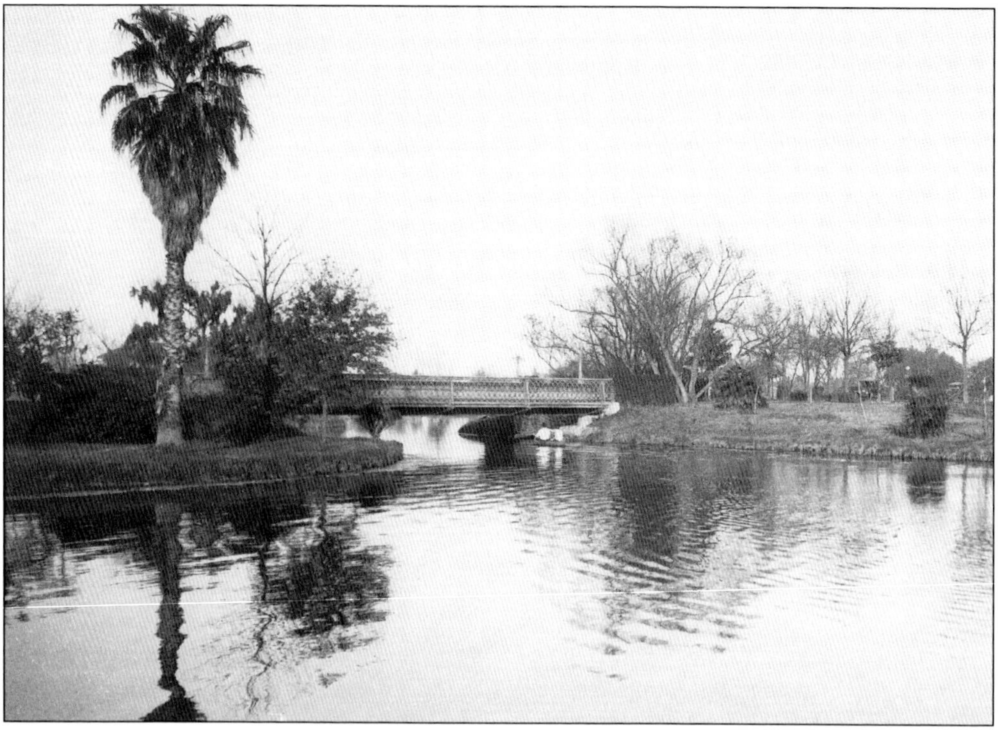

After a 1909 hurricane caused much damage to the park, a wood-and-iron girder bridge (shown above) replaced a simple wooden one over the lagoon behind what would become NOMA. It was dedicated to the memory of former City Park commissioner George H. Grandjean (1892–1900) who had supervised construction of the lagoons. In 1938, this second bridge was demolished and replaced by the bridge that is currently used (below), constructed by the WPA. (LDL.)

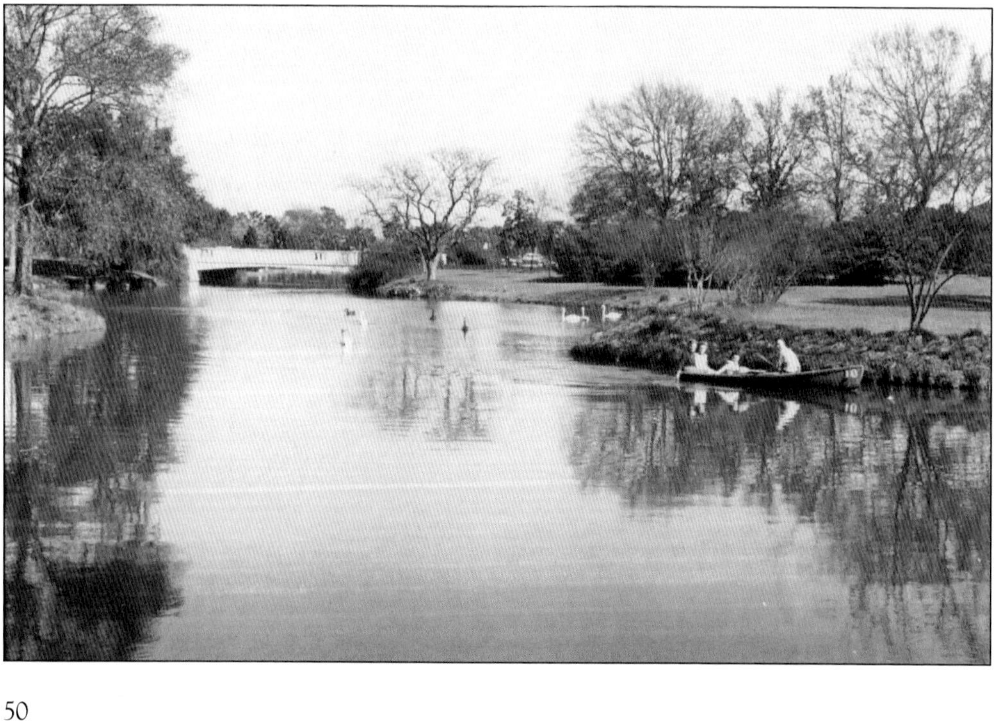

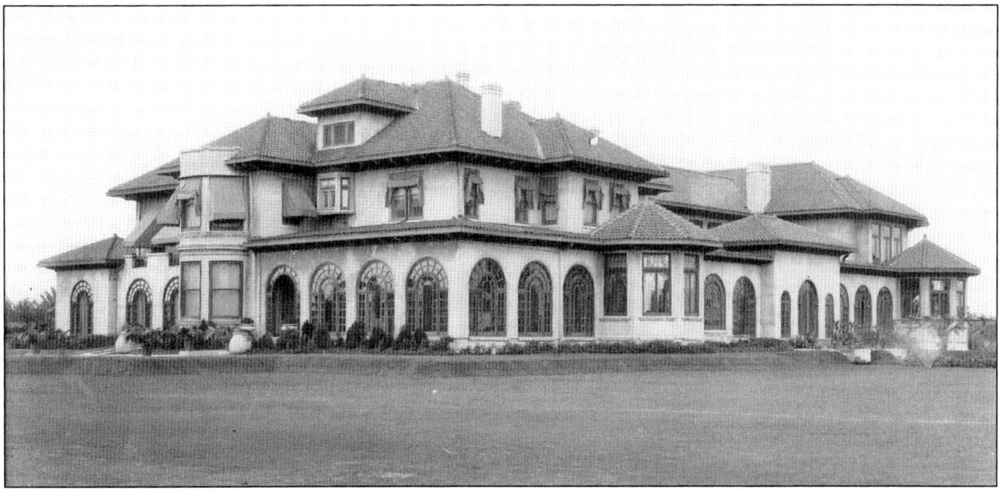

Fred Bertrand built a five-bedroom, two-bath house on four acres edging the park in 1909. Ten years later, Texas oil millionaire William Harding McFadden bought, remodeled, and greatly enlarged it to use as a second home while he and his wife visited New Orleans for the carnival season, the racing season, and Sugar Bowl games. The mansion contained 11 bedrooms, 11 baths, a ballroom, trophy room, and drawing rooms. On one side of the house was a sunken garden, on the other an Oriental garden. On the property was a lovers' lane featuring an iron arbor, bamboo canes, roses, and wisterias. A large, marble-lined, indoor swimming pool was surrounded by lush plantings. There was also a fountain that featured a bronze sculpture of a young boy holding one of his boots high while water trickled through a hole in it. (See page 52.) (Both, LDL.)

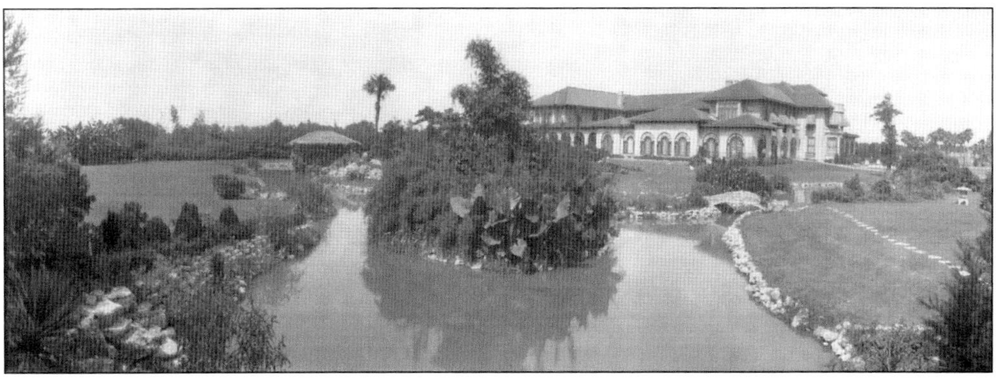

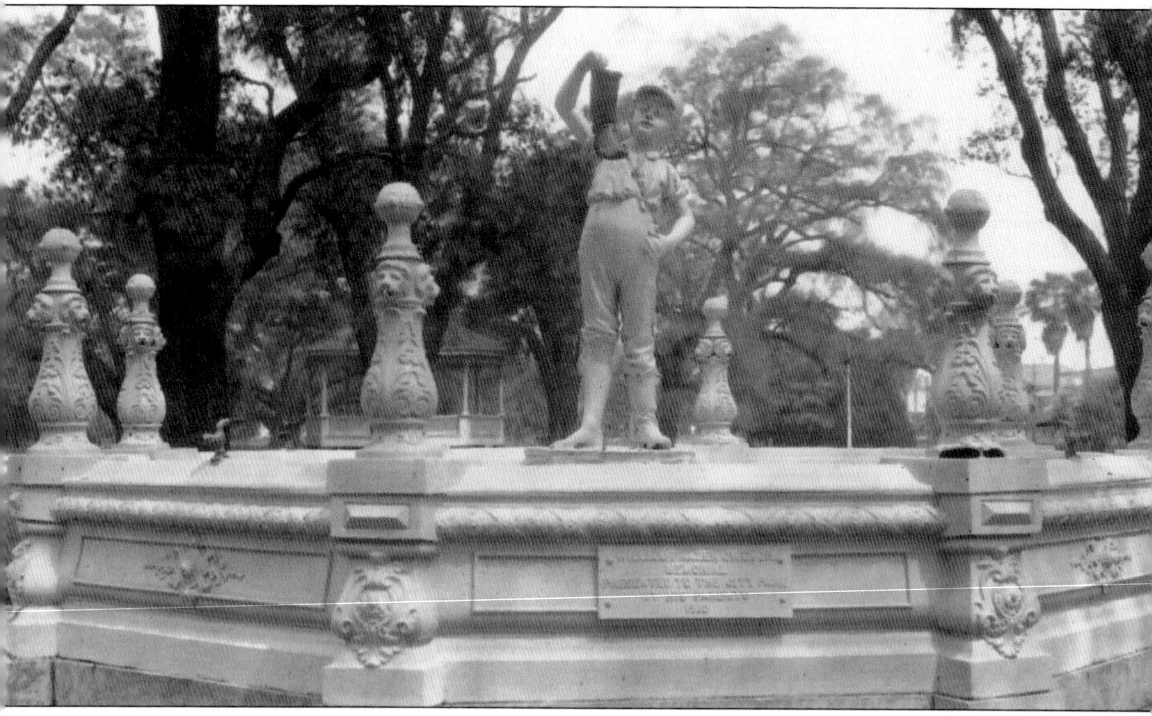

McFadden's fountain contained a replica of the same statue. Located near the Peristyle, the bronze sculpture of a young boy was titled *Unfortunate Boot*. The park's fountain was dedicated in 1910 to the memory of William Frazer Owen Jr. by his parents. In 1929, the statue was broken, and the board of commissioners ordered a 400-pound bronze replica at a cost of $270. McFadden, then a park board member who had moved near the park some 10 years after the Owen Memorial was dedicated, objected to its replacement because it has been speculated his wife wished to own the only unfortunate boot in the city. The park's statue was sold; the spindles, which had surrounded the boy, were removed; and a bronze statue of Chloe, the water nymph, which is seen today, replaced the sculpture. In 1994, the family and friends of Patrick J. Butler (1934–1992) along with Friends of City Park and the City Park Neighborhood Association restored the fountain. (LDL.)

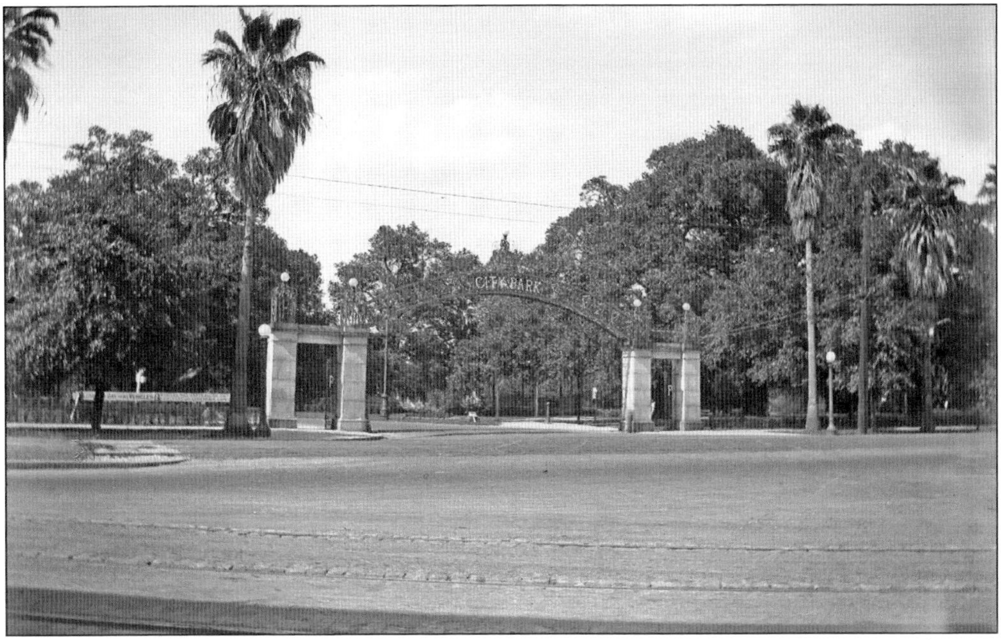

The Pizzati Gate, erected in 1910, is one of the oldest structures in the park. It is located at the former main entrance at Alexander Street and City Park Avenue. Donated by steamboat captain Salvatore Pizzati, the gate was rededicated on October 25, 2001, in memory of Edgar A. Luminais, an original member of the board of commissioners. Note in this 1924 photograph that the Belknap Fountain has been removed. (LOC.)

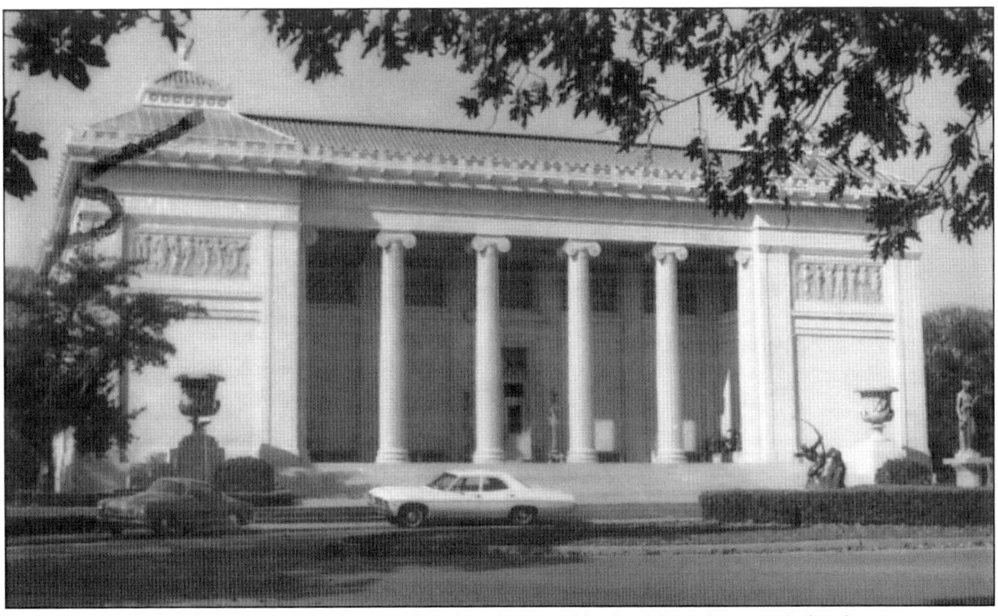

In 1910, Lebenbaum and Marks submitted a plan designed by builder Julius Koch for the art museum, which was made possible by the generous donation of $150,000 from Isaac Delgado. Gifts from wealthy New Orleanians included paintings, precious stones, Etruscan glass, Greek vases, bronzes, and ceramics. The New Orleans Artists' Association contributed several paintings. The museum opened on December 16, 1911. The permanent collection now contains over 40,000 objects. (LDL.)

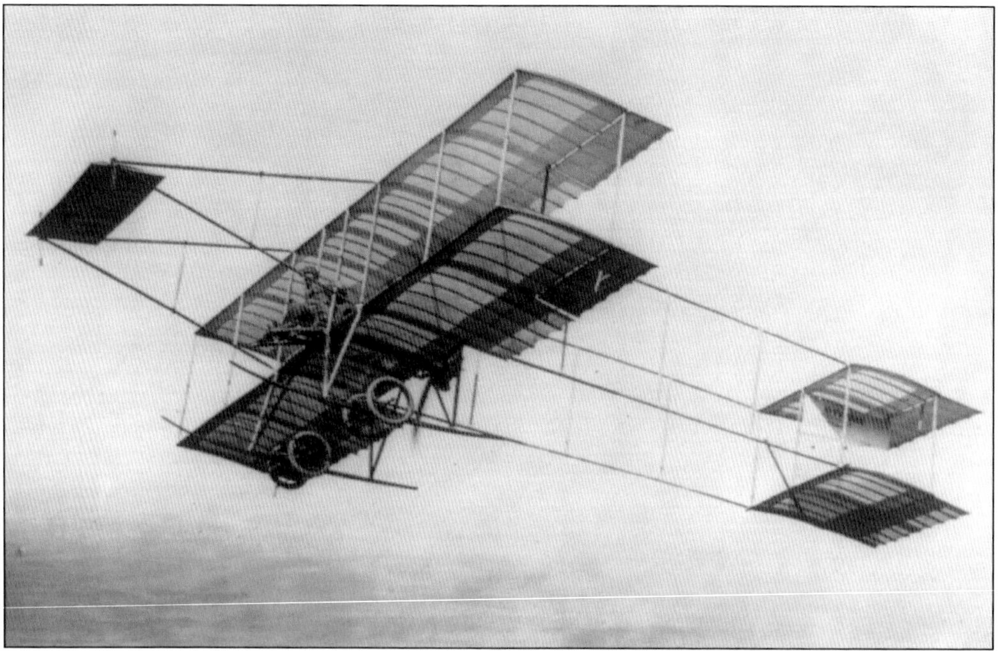

From December 24, 1910, through January 2, 1911, the first international aviation competition in the South was held at the park's racetrack. Louis Paulhan flew his biplane at 35 miles per hour and drew a crowd, reportedly, of 25,000 who paid 50¢ each for a ride in the plane, which can be seen here. On opening day, John Bevins Moisant, shown below, circled the business district four times, while Christmas Eve shoppers waved. Moisant returned to the park with the record for the longest sustained flight over a major city at 46 minutes. During the competition, Moisant lost a race with an automobile by seconds while setting the record for a one-mile flight for 57 seconds. (Both, LOC.)

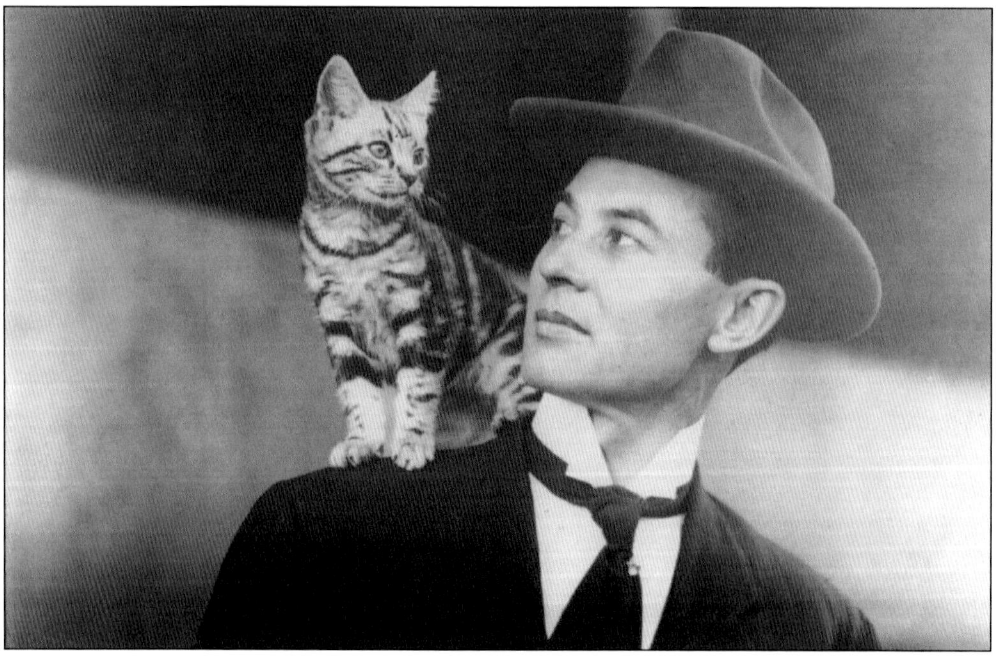

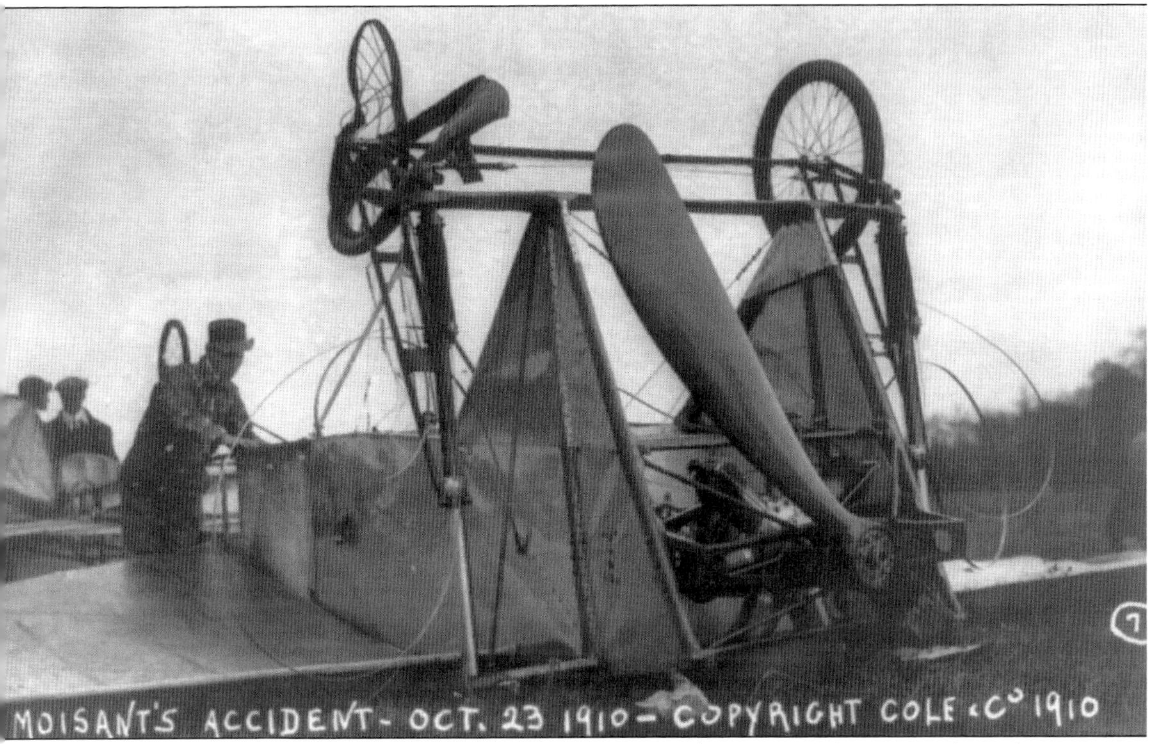

On New Year's Eve, Moisant competed with four pilots for the $4,000 Michelin Prize to beat the sustained flight record of 362.66 miles. He flew from City Park and headed for the competition's start field in Harahan. After circling three times at 200 feet, wind shear at 25 feet caused the plane to crash as he attempted to land. *Scientific American* magazine reported that he was the first aviator to be thrown from a plane in a fatal accident. In 1946, the city named its new airport Kenner Moisant Field, which is now Louis Armstrong International. At the dedication ceremonies, aviator Jimmy Doolittle was present to unveil the monument, which reads, "In commemoration of a pioneer in aviation, who lost his life in an airplane accident near this site December 31, 1910. He was the first pilot: to carry a passenger across the English Channel, inventor of the early all-metal airplane, a man of lovable character whose tragic death was a great loss to aviation." Note the date on this photograph—Moisant had also crashed in October 1910 but escaped serious injury. (LOC.)

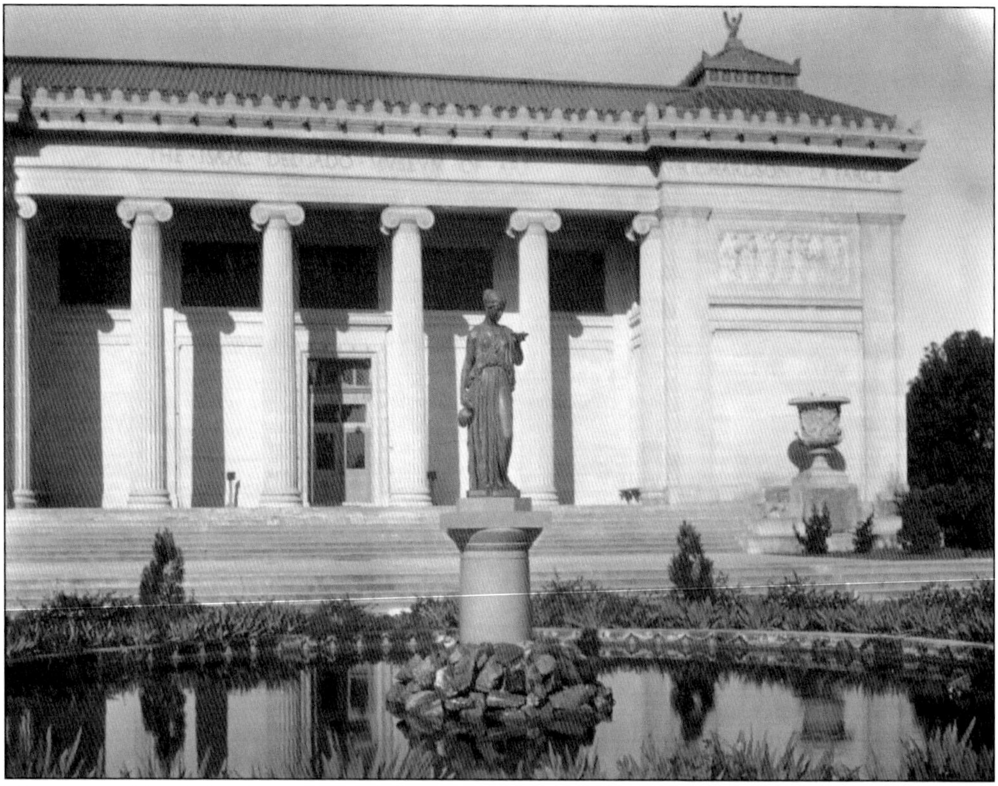

The sons of Fritz Jahncke, who made his first fortune with Lake Pontchartrain shells, donated this fountain in front of the Delagado Museum in 1912 in their father's memory. In 1928, Ernest Jahncke added the statue of Hebe, the Greek goddess of youth and a cupbearer to the gods, which can be seen in this photograph. (LDL.)

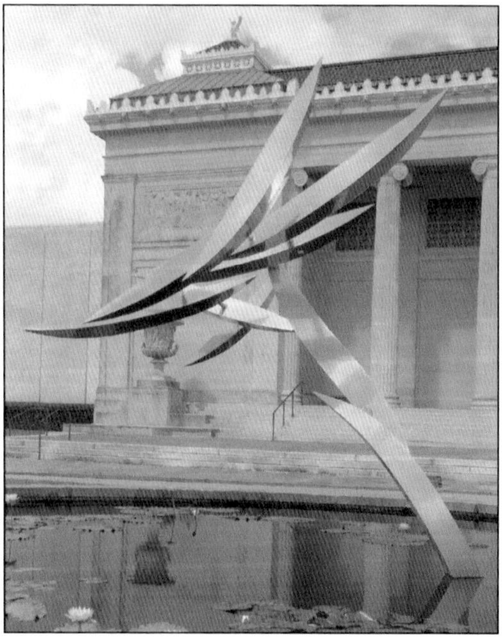

In 1988, the sculpture of Hebe was replaced with *Wave* by New York–born kinetic sculptor Lin Emery. It was a gift of the Frederick Weisman Company; Frederick Weisman was a Californian philanthropist and a supporter of the arts. Created from discarded metal serving trays, coffee pots, and miscellaneous items from the Roosevelt Hotel after it closed in the 1960s, New Orleanians dubbed it "Morrison Wave" because it was commissioned during Mayor Chep Morrison's administration and was originally placed in city hall's Duncan Plaza. (LDL.)

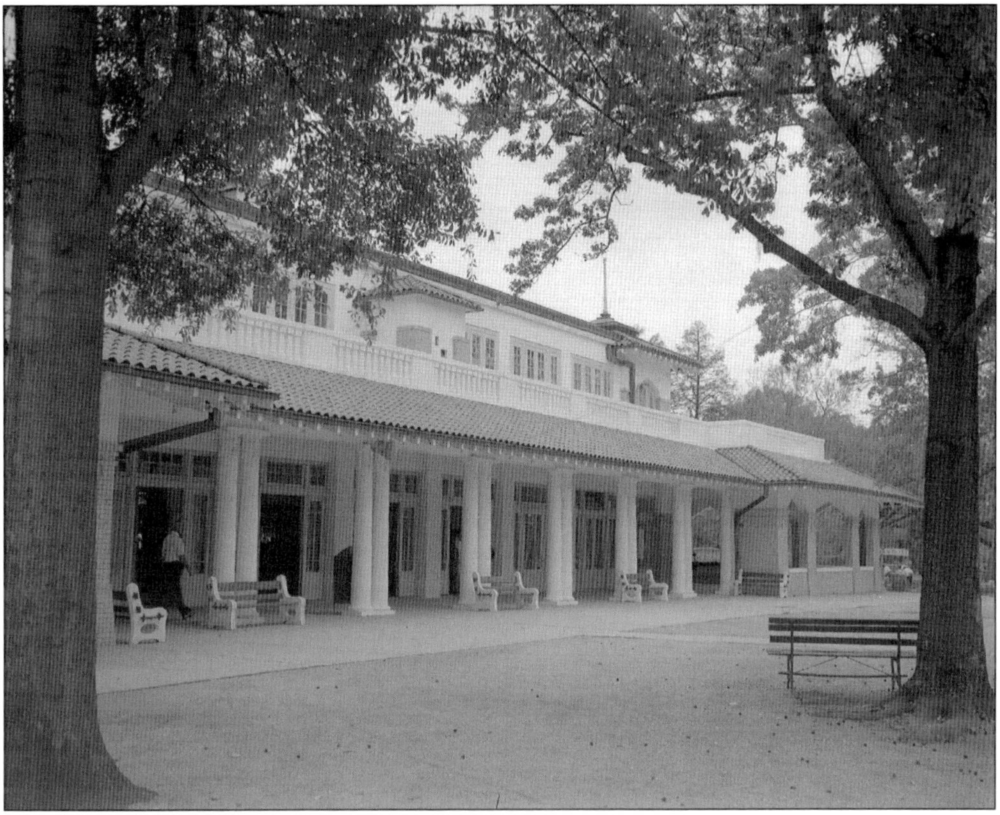

The Casino, opened on July 11, 1913, is now one of the park's few surviving Spanish Mission–style structures. Renovated in 1999 and renamed the Timken Center, its second floor is used for meetings and parties. This photograph was taken in 1939. Workmen with the WPA can barely be seen on the right-hand side of the image completing renovations of a boarding dock for the swan boat. (NOPL.)

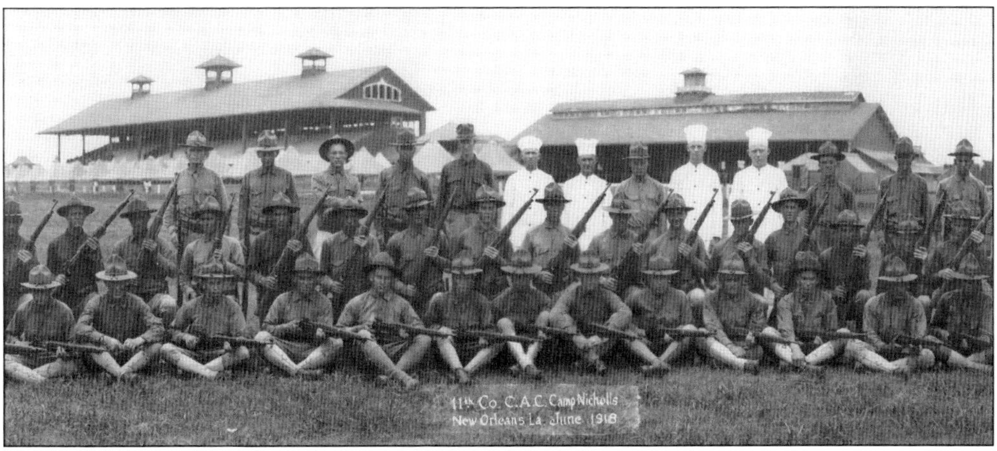

During World War I, City Park Racetrack was used as a camp where soldiers were quartered before being sent overseas. Pictured here is the 11th Company of the Coast Artillery Corps. Although the photograph is captioned "Camp Nicholls," the City Park Racetrack's grandstand is clearly visible. (LDL.)

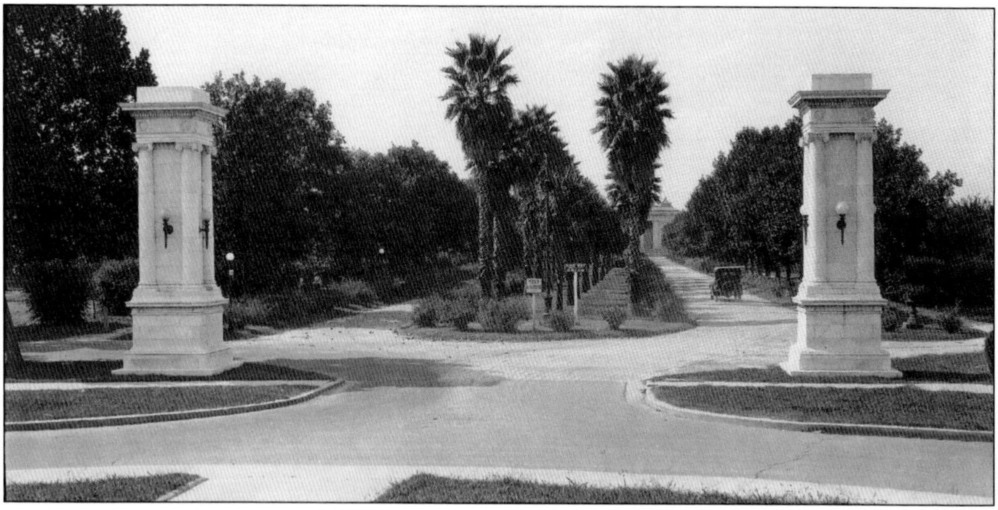

At the Esplanade Avenue entrance, the beautiful Monteleone Gate has stood at the intersection of Lelong Avenue for almost 100 years. Constructed in 1914 with two 25-foot marble pylons, eight bronze lamps, and 600-pound capstones, it was dedicated to the memory of New Orleans hotelier and City Park commissioner Anthony Monteleone following his death in 1913. (LDL.)

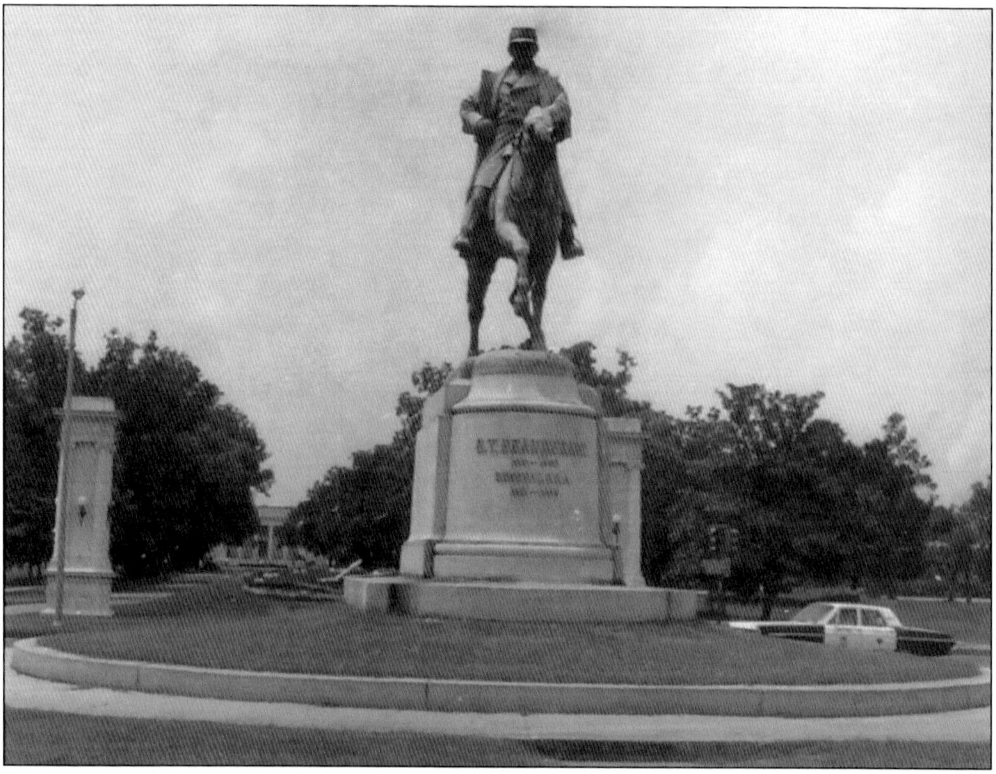

It was a year after the Monteleone Gate was erected that the monument to General Beauregard was placed in front of it in 1915. The bronze figure on a base of granite was dedicated by the Beauregard Monument Association at a cost of $22,000 on the 97th anniversary of Beauregard's birth. Alexander Doyle, who also designed the Robert E. Lee statue at Lee Circle, created the sculpture. (LDL.)

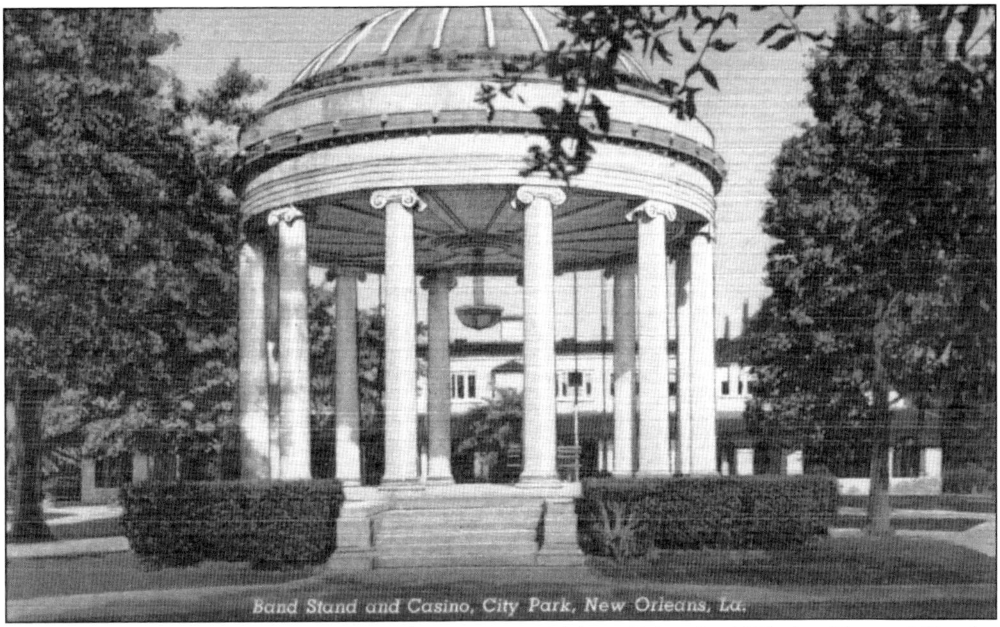

In 1916, a bandstand was dedicated to the memory of Alexis Ribet. In 1917, the Classical Greek–styled Popp Bandstand, viewed here in the 1930s, replaced it. Designed by Emile Weil at a cost of $75,000, it was dedicated on the Fourth of July. Its 12 granite, ionic columns are topped with a bronze dome. Named for its benefactor John F. Popp, who had made his fortune in the lumber business, it is a replica of Temple of Love in Versailles. The memorial to Ribet is embedded into the structure. Many New Orleanians enjoyed their first glimpses of moving pictures here on summer evenings. Generations of musicians have played here, including John Philip Sousa who performed in 1928. In 1916, City Park Avenue, pictured below, was paved and palm-lined, but the park lost land on the lake side of the avenue, which eventually became Delgado Trades School, opened in 1921. The park received $178,500 for the land. (Both, LDL.)

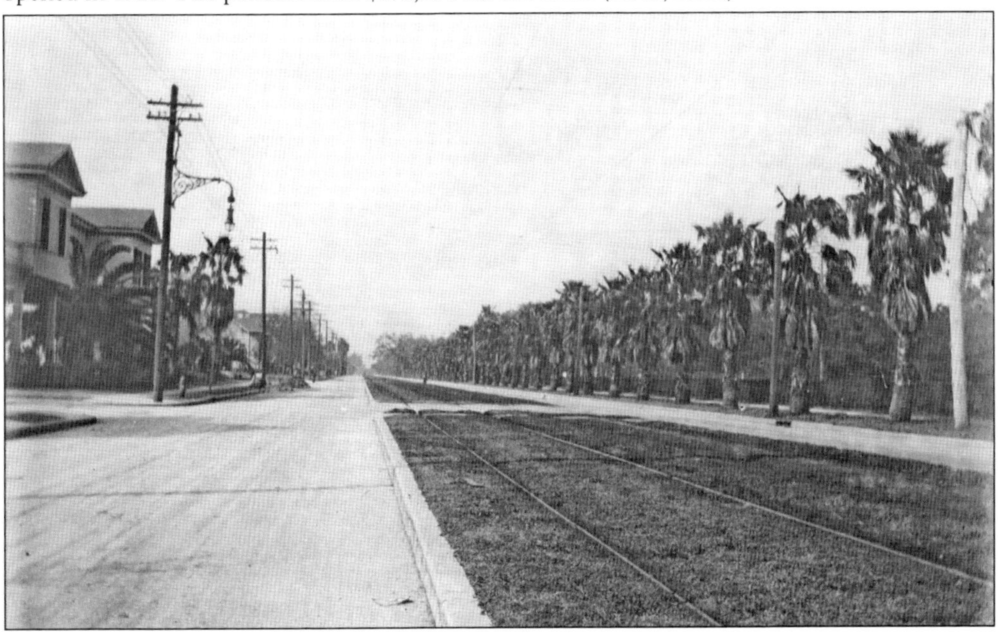

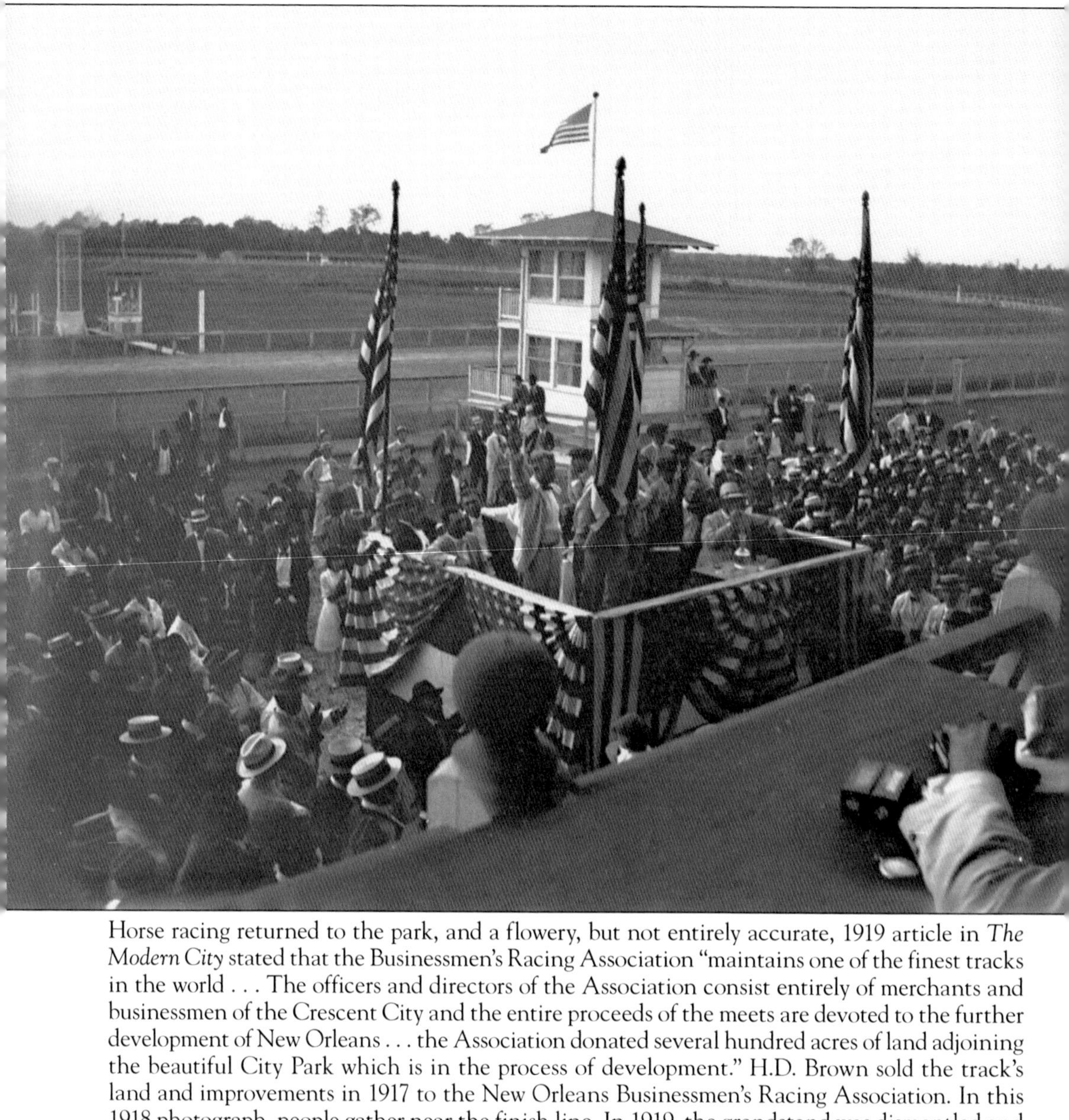

Horse racing returned to the park, and a flowery, but not entirely accurate, 1919 article in *The Modern City* stated that the Businessmen's Racing Association "maintains one of the finest tracks in the world . . . The officers and directors of the Association consist entirely of merchants and businessmen of the Crescent City and the entire proceeds of the meets are devoted to the further development of New Orleans . . . the Association donated several hundred acres of land adjoining the beautiful City Park which is in the process of development." H.D. Brown sold the track's land and improvements in 1917 to the New Orleans Businessmen's Racing Association. In this 1918 photograph, people gather near the finish line. In 1919, the grandstand was dismantled and reassembled at the fairgrounds to replace the grandstand that burned to the ground in 1918. The park acquired the land in 1920, which would become the site of Municipal Stadium. The old City Park grandstand stood at the fairgrounds until a seven-alarm fire destroyed it in 1993. (LDL.)

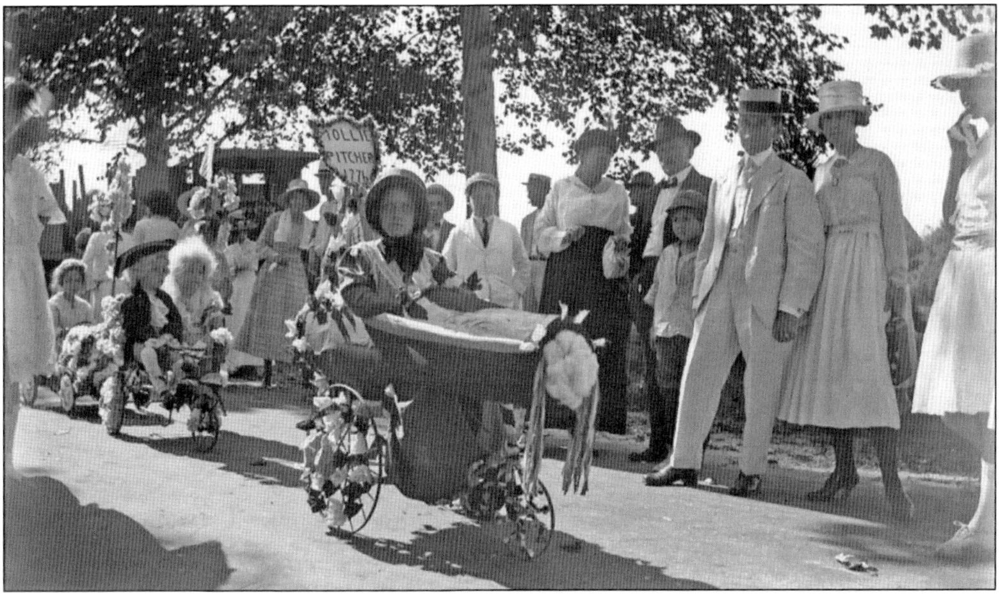

In 1918, the US Bureau of Fisheries distributed 15,000 large-mouth bass into the park's lake. In 1920, the American Medical Association held an April Fete Champetre in the park. Also in 1920, large sightseeing cars were allowed in the park; however, there was a growing concern that they caused damage to the roads. In the same year, carriages and Shetland ponies were added for children's rides. Pictured is a glimpse of the 1918 Children's Play Week, an annual event involving playgrounds throughout New Orleans. (LDL.)

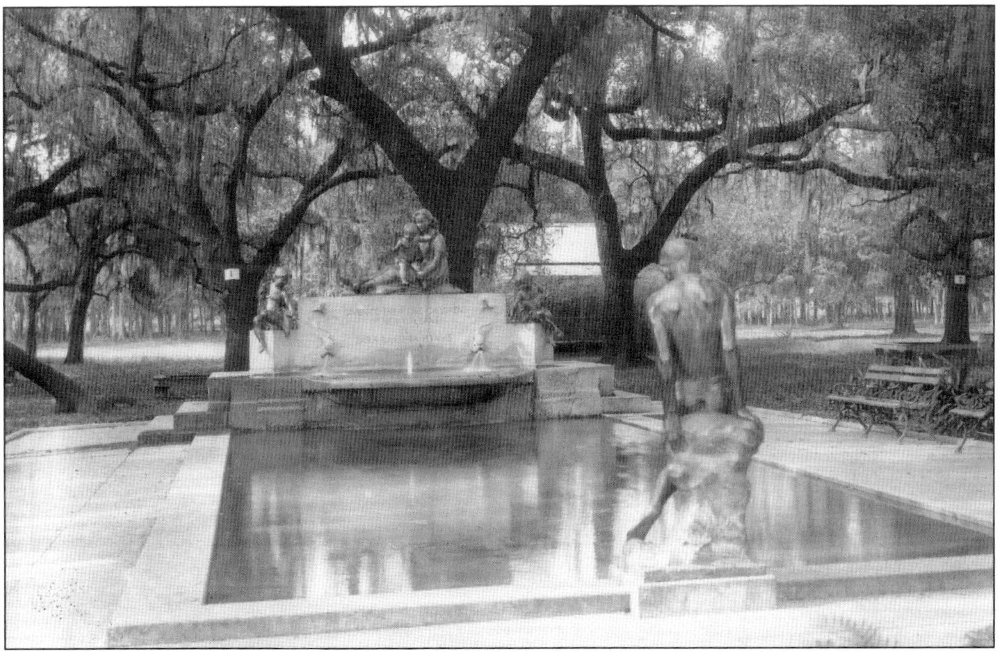

The following is the inscription on the 1914 concrete-and-bronze wading pool designed by Isodore Konti, which is still enjoyed by children today: "By bequest Mrs. Chapman H. Hyams left her jewels to Audubon and City Parks, the proceeds of which were to build a testimonial of her love for her home city . . . She loved the beautiful and gave that all might enjoy." (LDL.)

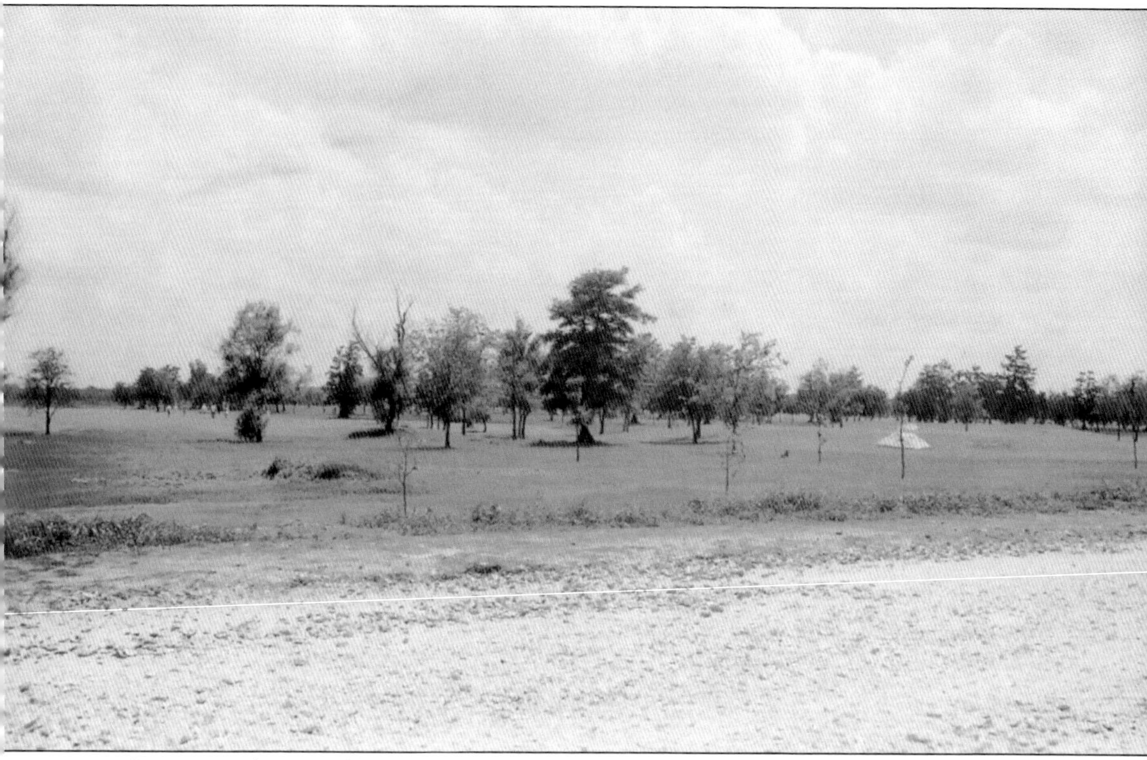

The No. 1 and No. 2 golf courses were completed in 1923, both designed by Joseph M. Bartholomew Sr. (1881–1971). After eight years of schooling, he caddied at Audubon Park and then became the greenskeeper as well as an excellent golfer. Bartholomew then moved to Metairie Golf Club, where members, led by H.T. Cottam, suggested that the club send him to New York to study golf course architecture. After returning home in 1922 to design a new 18-hole course in Metairie, he began work on the City Park courses. In 1924, Bartholomew designed the Pontchartrain Park Municipal Course, which was not completed until 1956. Segregation laws prohibited Bartholomew from playing on any but the Pontchartrain course, and so he built a seven-hole course on his property in Harahan. Bartholomew was the first African American to be inducted in the Greater New Orleans Sports Hall of Fame. In 1979, the newly renovated Pontchartrain Park Golf Course was renamed Joe M. Bartholomew Sr. Municipal Golf Course, some eight years after his death. (LDL.)

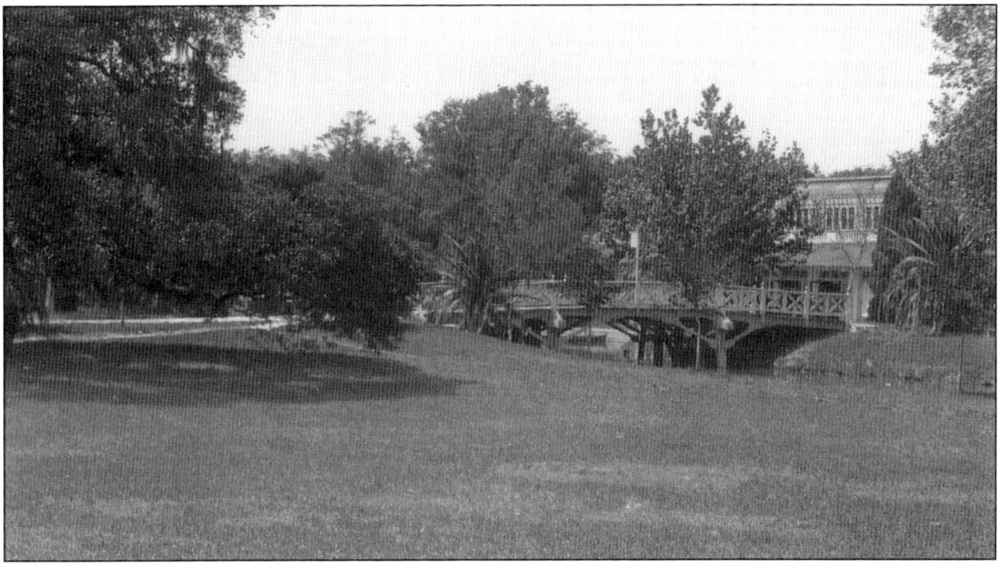

Pictured above is the first bridge built over the lagoon behind the Casino. In 1924, Felix J. Dreyfous and his wife, Julia Seeman Dreyfous, donated the beautiful bridge, seen below in a 1920s photograph by George Francois Mugnier. Their son architect F. Julius Dreyfous designed it at a cost of $36,000, and it still graces the park. As the Dreyfous Bridge was being constructed, so was the Irby Swimming Pool and Bathhouse, which was made possible by the $60,000 donation by local tobacco magnate William Ratcliff Irby. In 1921, the biennial report of the Louisiana State Museum stated that workers, while digging the park extension at Bayou St. John, found three-inch cannon balls. In 1925, Enrique Alferez was contracted to design the main fountainhead for Popp Memorial. (Both, LDL.)

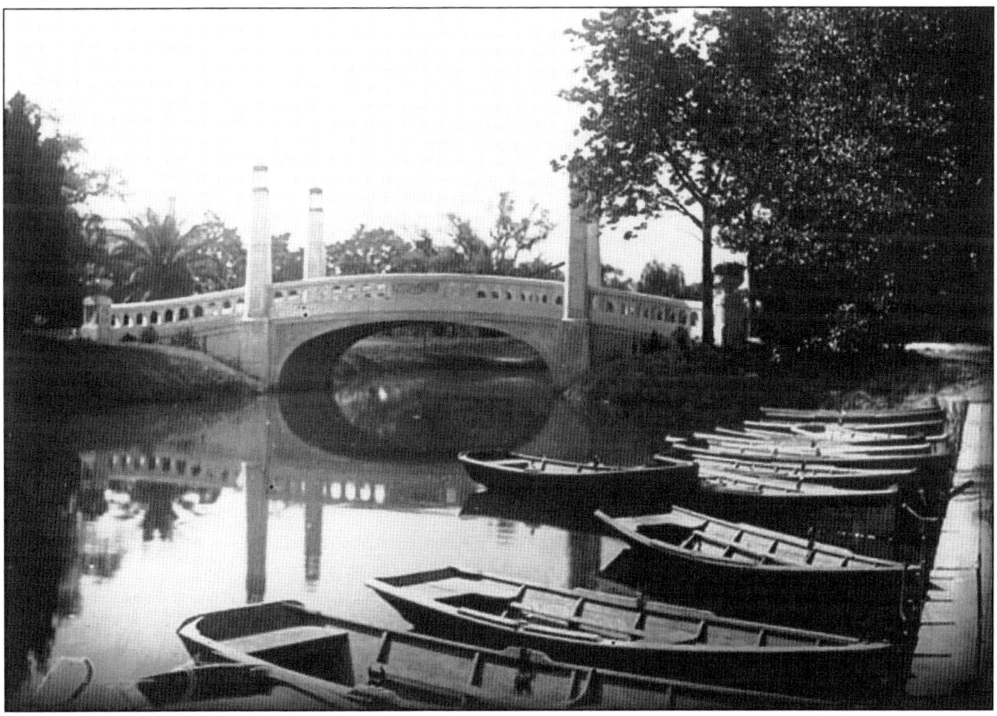

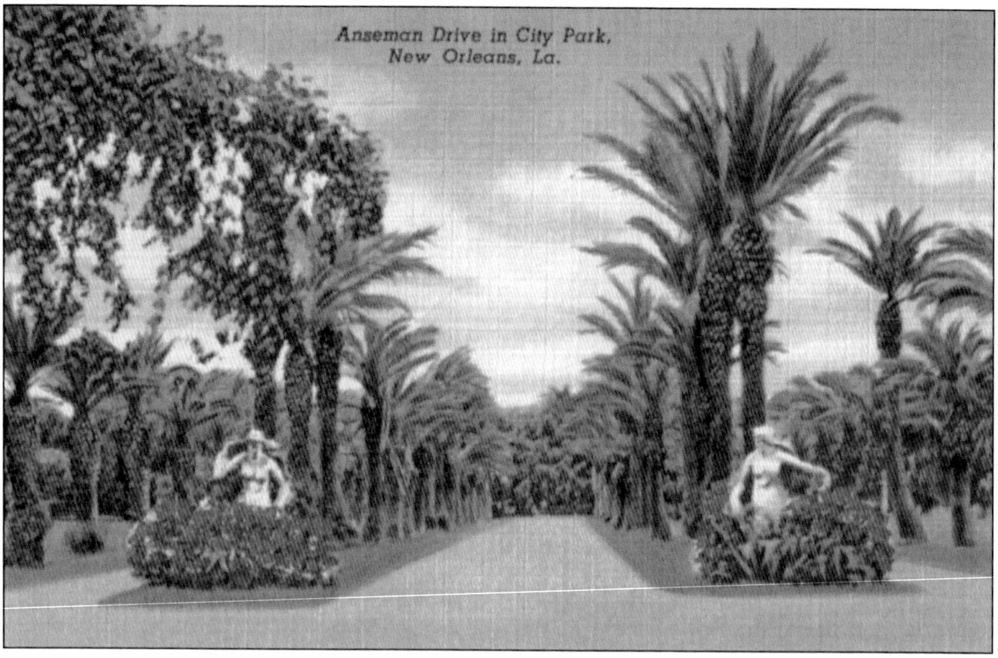

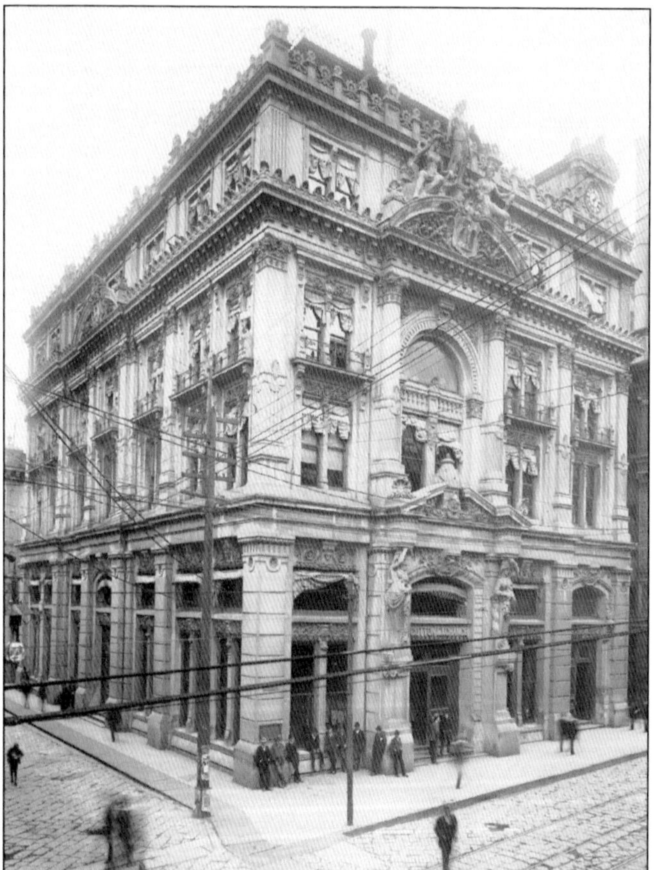

During the 1920s, these 100-year-old bare-breasted ladies would greet visitors entering the Pizzati Gate on Anseman Avenue. They had originally hovered high above the main entrance to the New Orleans Cotton Exchange Building, seen at left in 1903. The building was constructed in 1823 and was being readied for demolition in 1920. The women were acquired by the park, along with the standing, clothed figure between the two ladies and the granite caryatids at the front doors of the Cotton Exchange Building. Their tenure in the park was brief; some citizens were outraged. The ladies went on to reside at Metairie Cemetery, and the caryatids can still be seen near the cemeteries on City Park Avenue. (Both, LDL.)

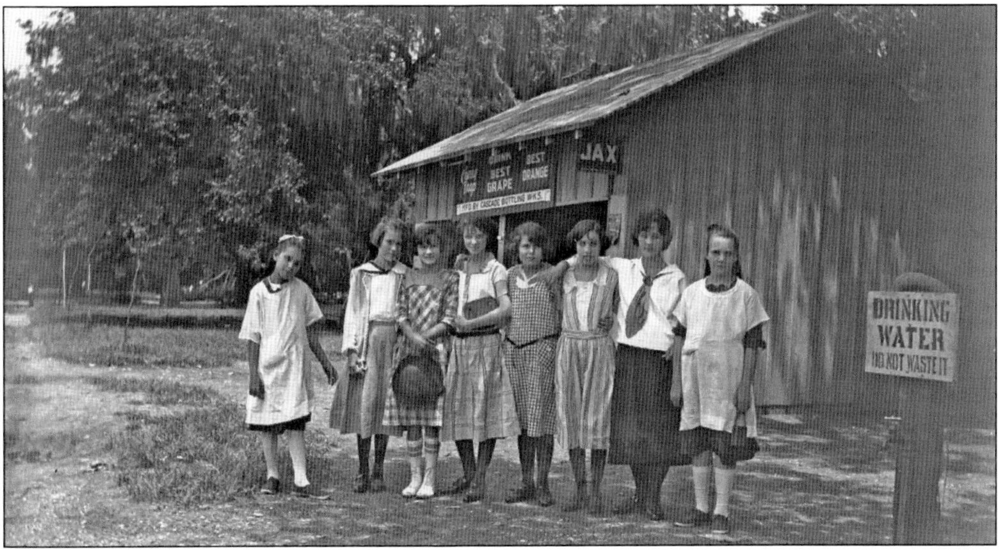

In 1922, twelve of the trees were marked with the names of local playgrounds, with each indicating a place for its children to gather before heading out to various areas of the park. By the end of the 1920s, the Annual Playgrounds Outing had become a tradition. In this 1925 photograph, girls pose in front a park refreshment stand offering Jax Beer, Best Grape, Best Orange, and Cherry Pop. The sign at right admonishes, "Drinking Water—Do not waste it." (LDL.)

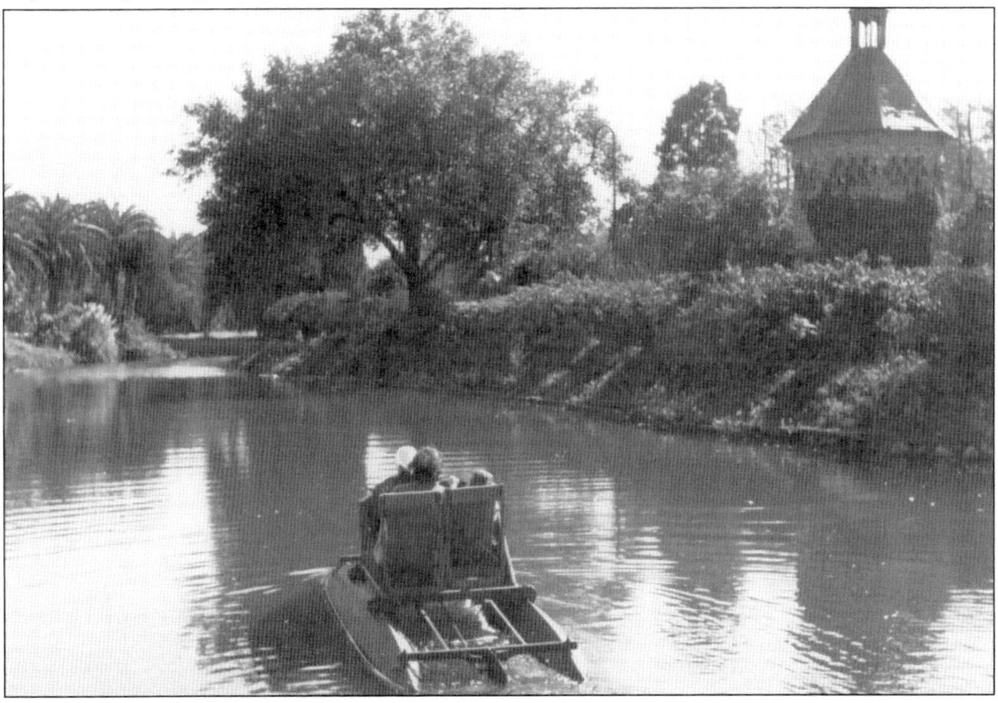

The original pigeon house was replaced in 1928 with a brick structure, seen above, which was given to the park by Felix J. Dreyfous in honor of his granddaughter Carol Vera Dreyfous. The new pigeon house was named "Colombier de Carole." Designed by Carol's father, architect F. Julius Dreyfous, the *pigeonniere* is located on Pigeon Island, near the Casino Building. It was refurbished in 2005 by descendants of Felix. This photograph was taken in 1941. (LDL.)

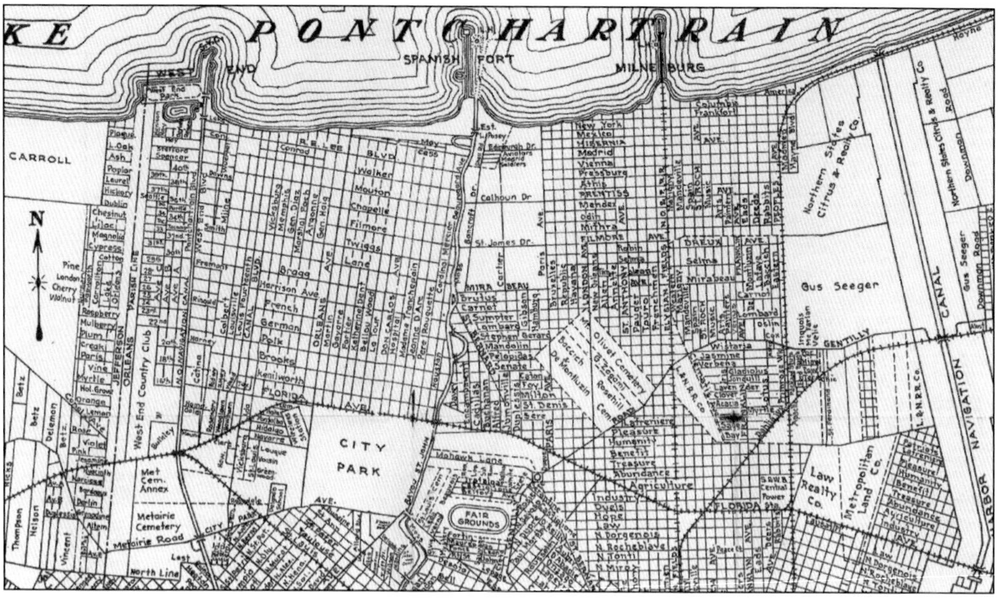

Here, on this 1924 map, the park's boundaries were Florida Avenue, Orleans Avenue, City Park Avenue, and Bayou St. John. By the end of the decade, the park had grown to include more than 900 additional acres, spreading from City Park Avenue to what was then the lakefront at Robert E. Lee Boulevard. These additional acres were former dairy land and marshland, owned primarily by the New Orleans Land Company. The area would be converted into streets, lagoons, golf courses, and the Couturie Forest. Below, Mendelson's band poses in front of the Casino. (Above, NA; below, LDL.)

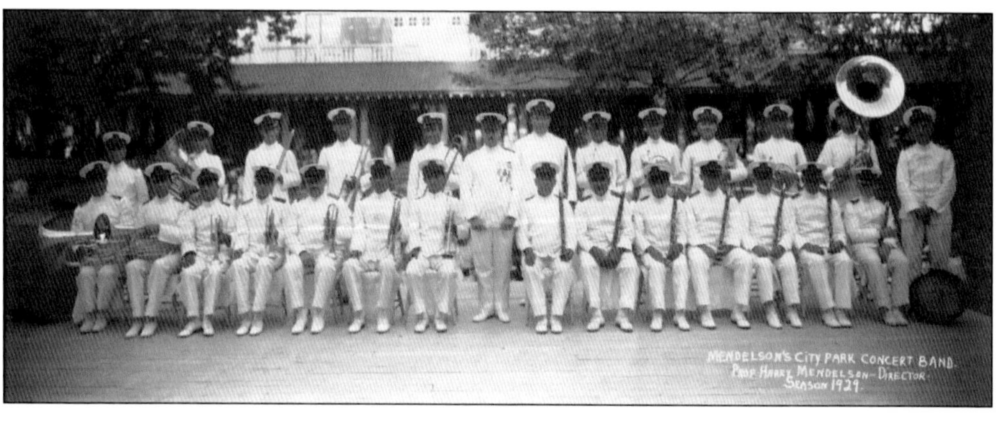

Four

The New Deal
1929–1939

The stock market crash of October 29, 1929, marked the beginning of the Great Depression.

Not much improved in the park thereafter until FERA (Federal Emergency Relief Administration), established in 1932, did a small amount of work. But when the WPA, established in 1935, came to the park, it became a different place—workers restored, renovated, improved, and added new buildings, bridges, and roads.

WPA artists and workers designed and constructed most of the existing brick buildings and Art Deco sculptures, reliefs, and flourishes on buildings, bridges, and fountains in City Park. Crew members also added new gates, lagoons, benches, shelters, the Administration Building, eight roads, eight bridges, baseball fields, a clubhouse and additions to the existing golf courses, new courses, a driving range, a caddy house, stadiums for football and baseball, athletic fields, and tennis courts with lights for night play.

Renovations, repairs, and improvements were made to Roosevelt Mall, the rose garden, the Casino, the Irby Pool, the Peristyle, and sculptures throughout the park. Popp Fountain was completed, three bridges rebuilt, City Park Avenue widened, Navarre Road paved, Lelong Avenue repaved, and Anseman Avenue landscaped. The swampy northern extension was drained, and the Couturie Forest was established. The lagoons were converted into a stream system with new drainage.

According to Mary Lou Widmer, as a child in the early 1930s, her neighborhood grocery store, a cement-floored H.G. Hill, located on City Park Avenue with traditional corner-store screened doors, took the place of the colorful business that preceded it in the Saux Building.

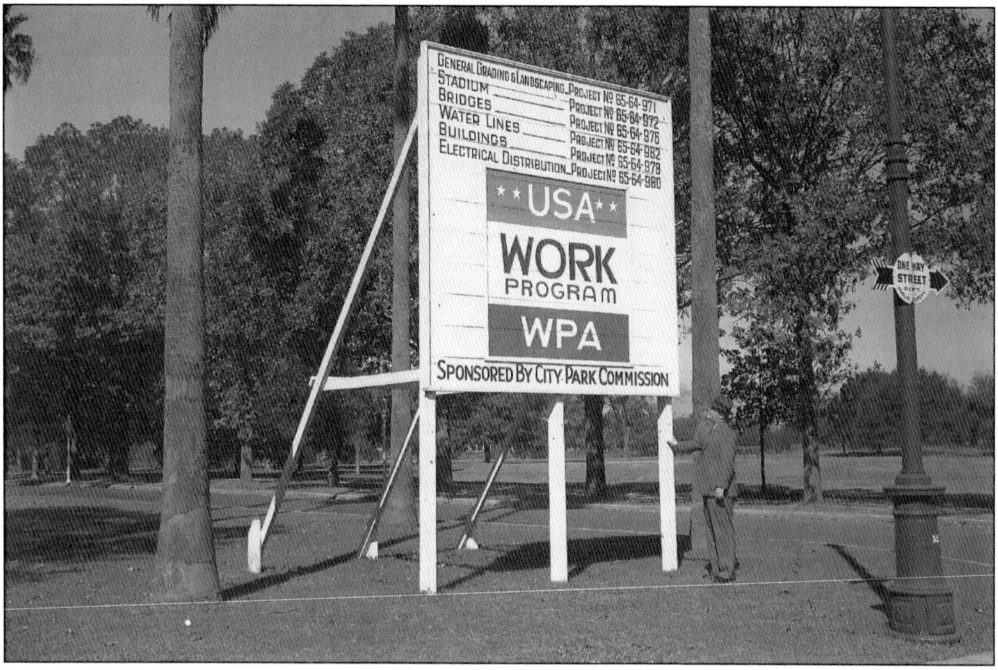

Signs, like the one seen in this 1937 photograph, could be found throughout the park during the 1930s when the WPA restored the old and built the new. Unseen improvements included land grading, new water lines, improvements to the existing electrical system, and the placement of electrical wiring through the new extension. (NOPL.)

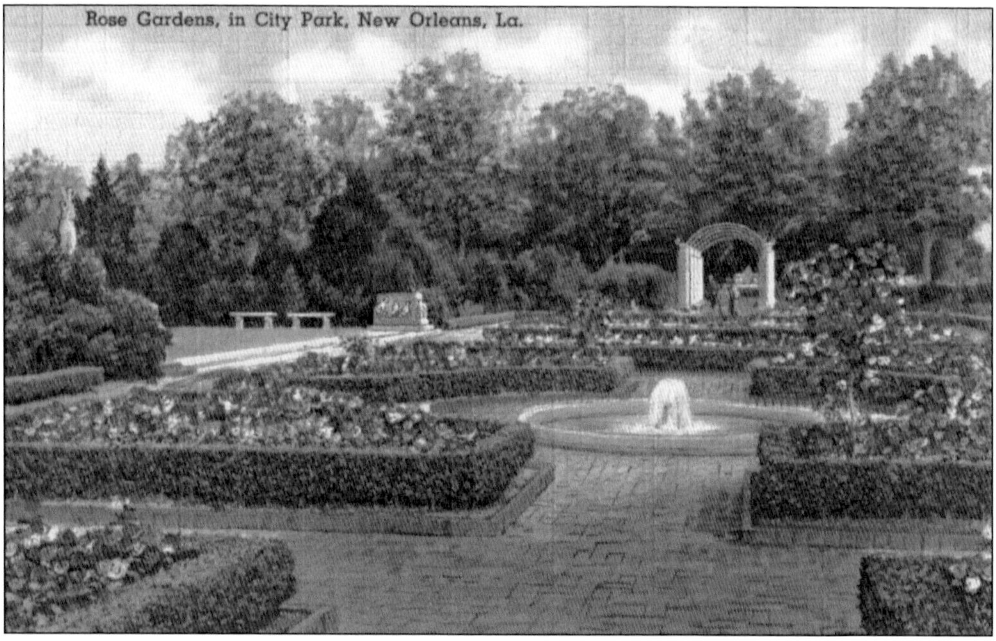

The WPA commissioned Enrique Alferez to create a sculpture and design gates, benches, and reliefs throughout the park. The Shriever Fountain in the City Park Rose Garden is shown in a 1930s postcard, which was prior to the installment of Alferez's *Water Maiden*. The *Water Maiden* can still been seen in the fountain today. (NOPL.)

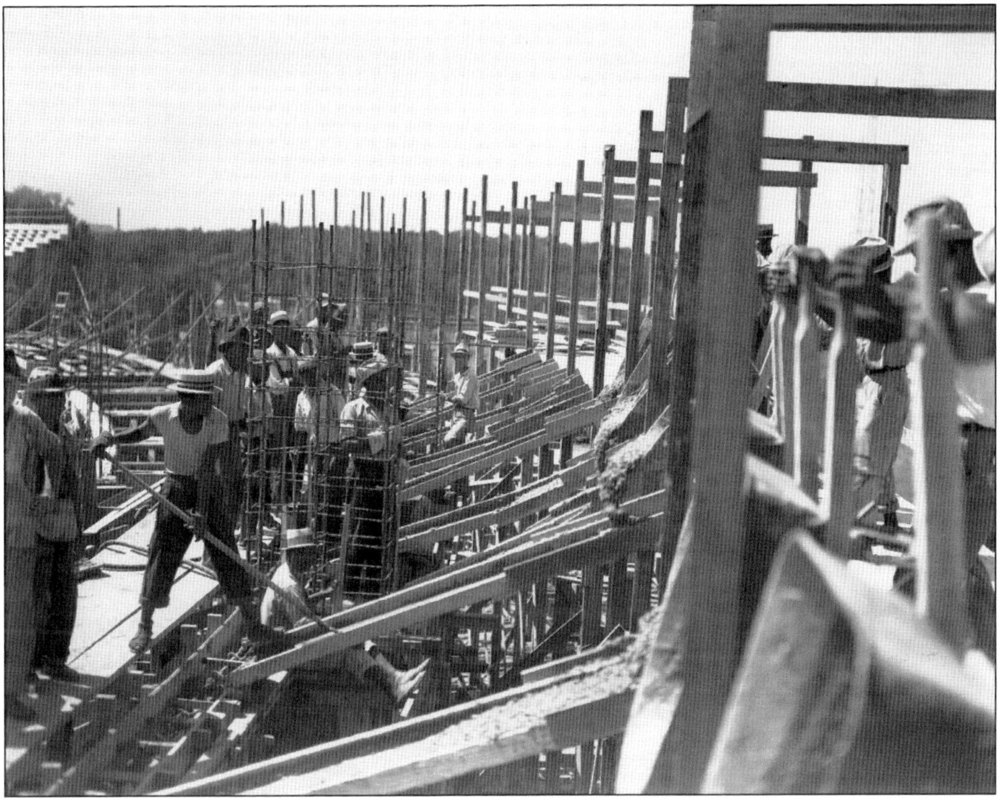

In 1935, workers are pouring concrete by hand while building the stadium, which will have 16 ramps and 26,500 seats. A WPA employee captioned this photograph as follows: "WPA-built stadium in New Orleans's mammoth City Park. The famous Sugar Bowl sports and football classics will probably be held here during the 1936–1937 holiday season." (NOPL.)

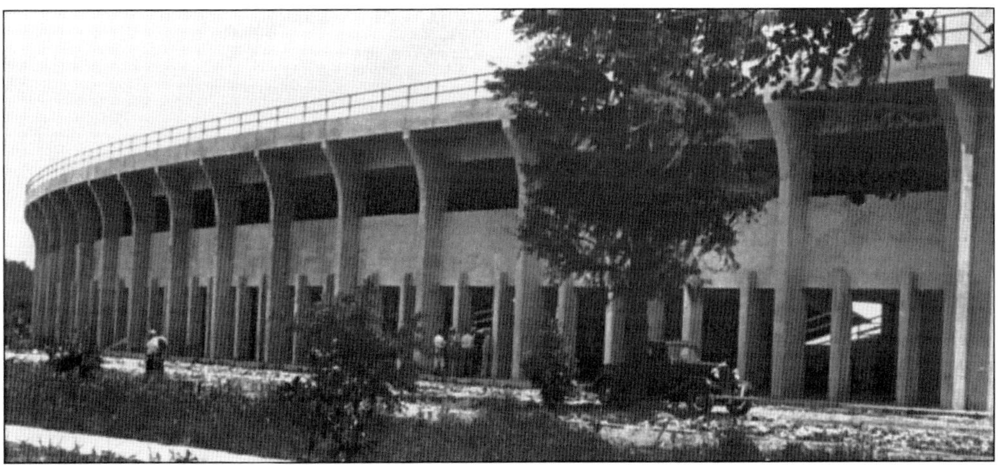

Dorothy Lamour sold war bonds here in 1942. Entertainers included Bob Hope (1944), Roy Rogers and Trigger (1959), and the Beatles (September 16, 1964). Home of the New Orleans Pelicans after their stadium was demolished in 1957 as well as host to the 1992 US Olympic Track and Field Trials, the stadium is pictured here in 1940. (NOPL.)

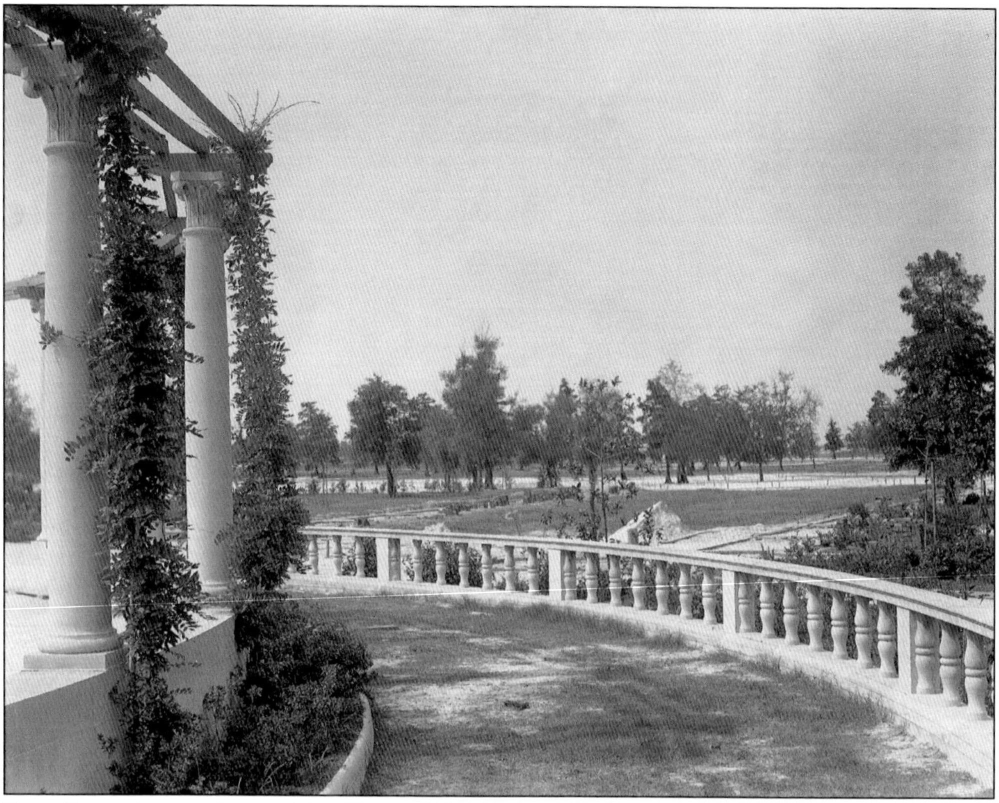

Popp Fountain was designed by Olmsted Brothers in the late 1920s after Rebecca Grant Popp donated $25,000 for a memorial to her husband, John F. Popp. Ionic columns reflect the taste of that era. Partially built by private contractors, it was dedicated in 1934. The WPA added tile walkways, landscaping, and the Art Deco fountainhead designed by Alferez. Here it is in 1936 in the new extension north of Harrison Avenue. (NOPL.)

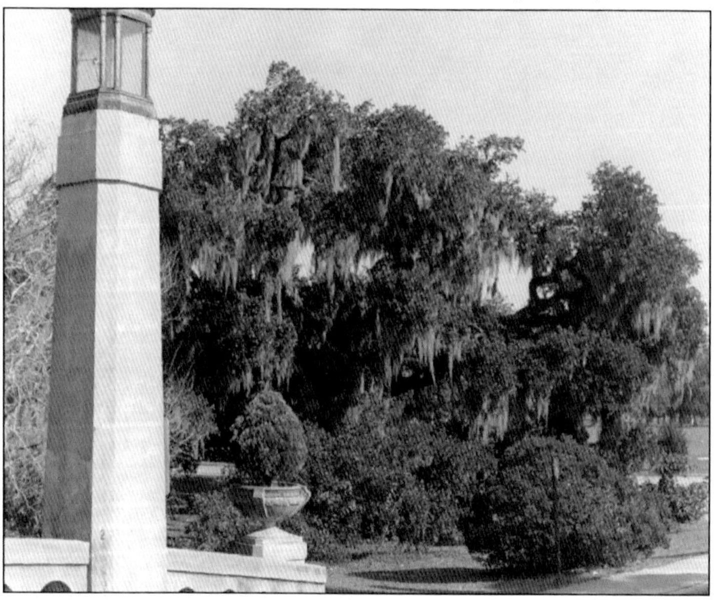

Here, extensive landscaping and the planting of palm trees as well as sidewalk and roadway repairs by the WPA had just been completed in the area of the park near the Dreyfous Bridge in 1937. (NOPL.)

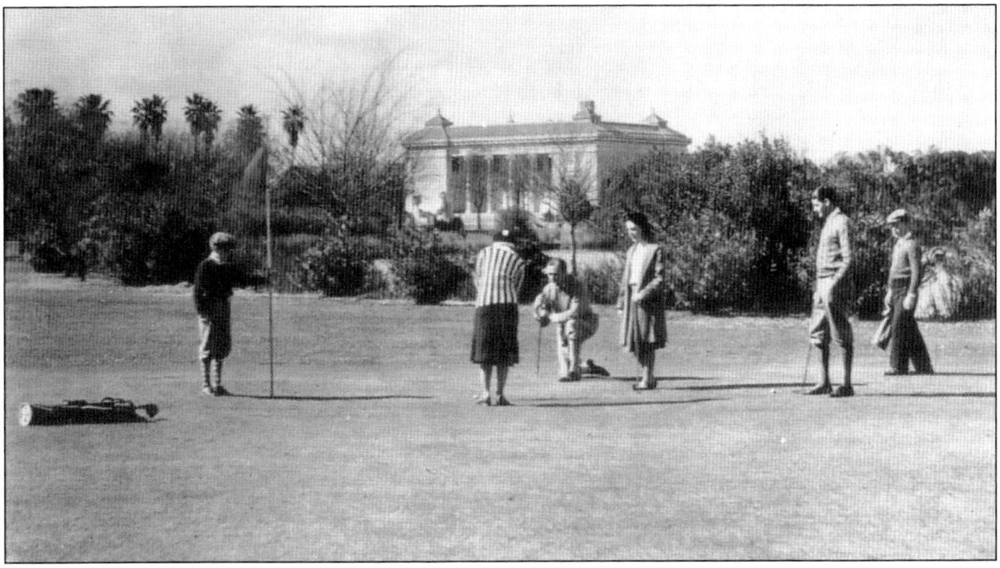

The new nine-hole golf course, completed in 1937, added nine holes to the original course. The WPA caption for this 1930s photograph reads, "Golf the year round. This course, in beautiful City Park, is one of the six evergreen golf courses in New Orleans on which play is continuous the year round." (LDL.)

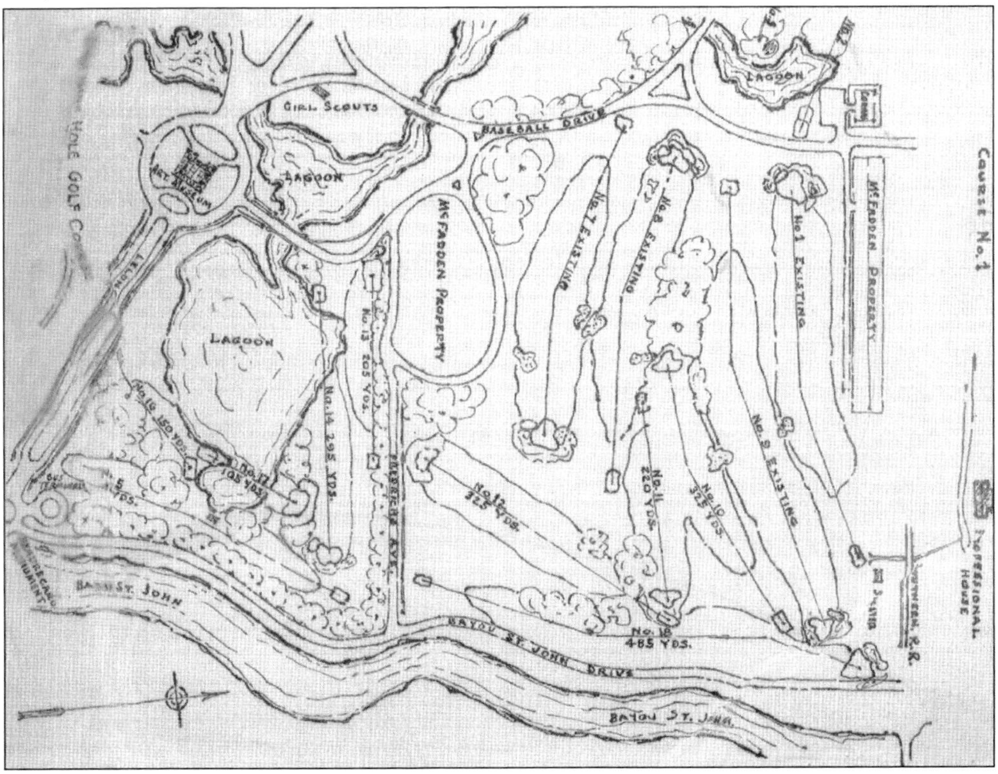

This diagram shows new and existing holes as they appeared after the WPA did general improvements to the park. This course, known as "the South Course," was closed in 2005 before Hurricane Katrina. (NOPL.)

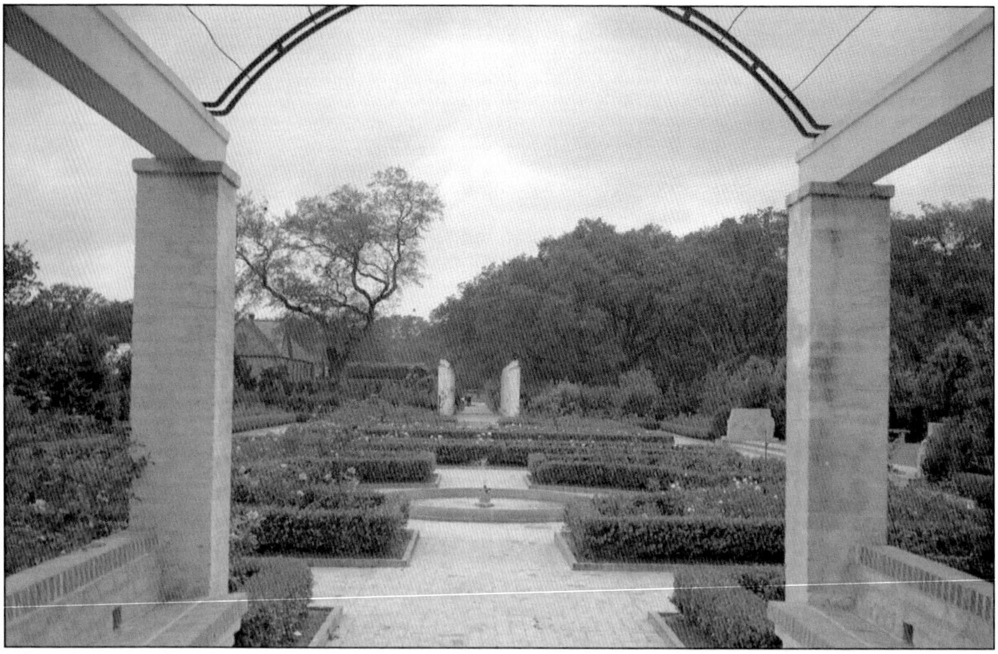

This photograph, taken in 1937, is of the now 10-acre City Park Rose Garden. After WPA work was completed, it was the first public classical garden in New Orleans and contained more Art Deco sculptures than any place in the city. Designed by Richard Koch and landscape architect William Wiedorn, it is used by modern brides who pose in this beautiful space before receiving guests at the Pavilion of the Two Sisters. (NOPL.)

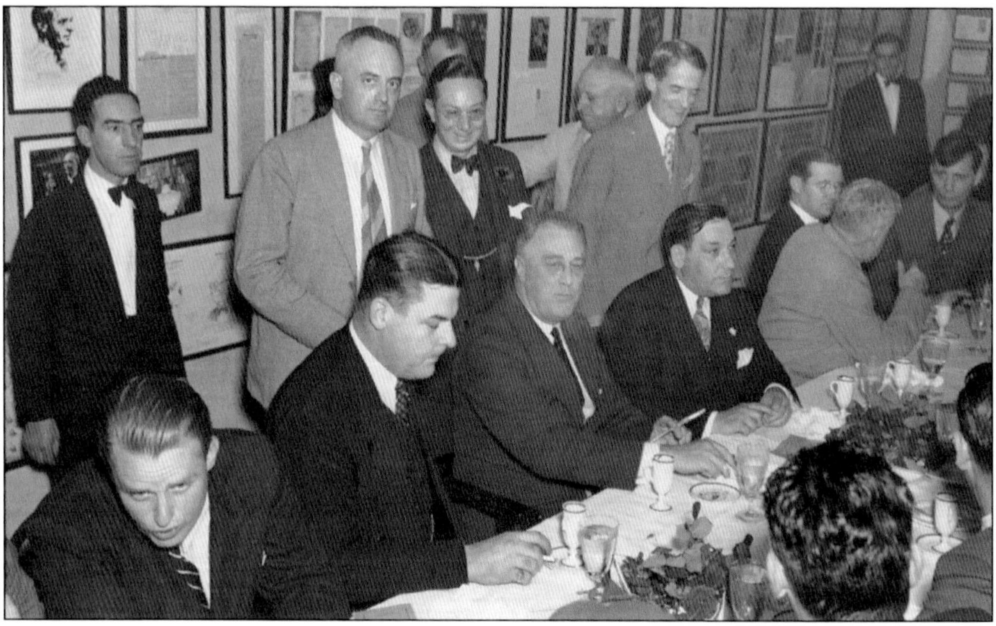

Pres. Franklin Roosevelt visited New Orleans in 1937 for the dedication of the WPA projects in the park. Federal funding of over $12 million allowed for the work and the employment of more than 20,000 people. During that trip, Roosevelt is pictured here dining at Antoine's with Gov. Richard Leche to his right and Mayor Robert Maestri on his left. (LDL.)

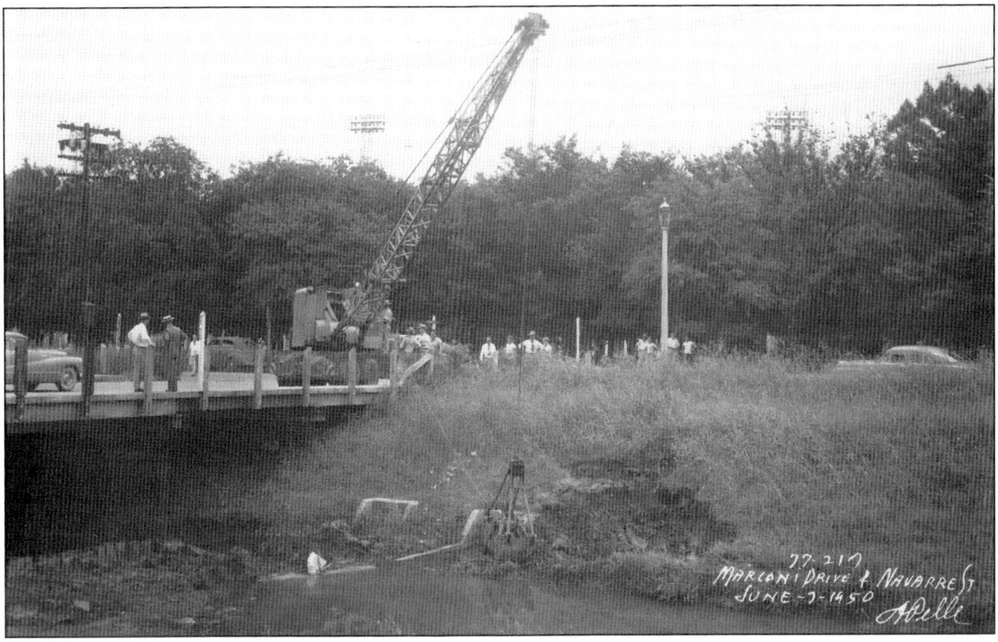

Christian Science Monitor reported on October 20, 1937, "100,000 trees have been planted in the extension of New Orleans's City Park on the 1,100-acre swamp in which alligators were hunted even after its purchase by the city for a park." In that year, Orleans Avenue, between City Park Avenue and Robert E. Lee Boulevard, was renamed Marconi Boulevard, which is pictured here in 1950. (LDL.)

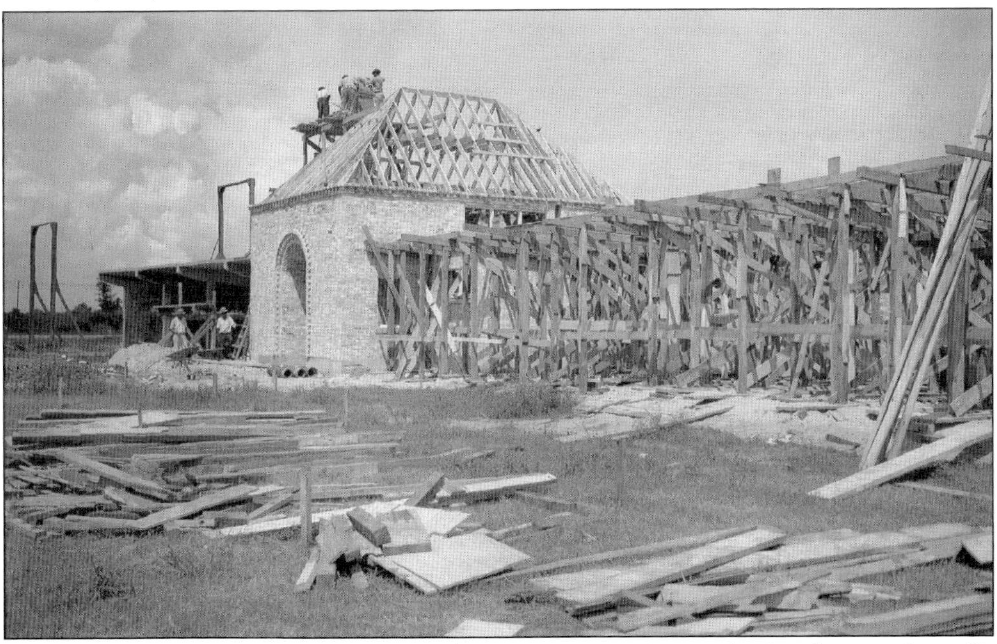

The driving range is under construction in this 1938 view. WPA notes for this photograph are, "It will have an Administrative Building, which will contain lockers and dressing rooms; refreshment room; six stalls, each of which will be 18 feet wide. The field will be equipped with four batteries of flood lights." (NOPL.)

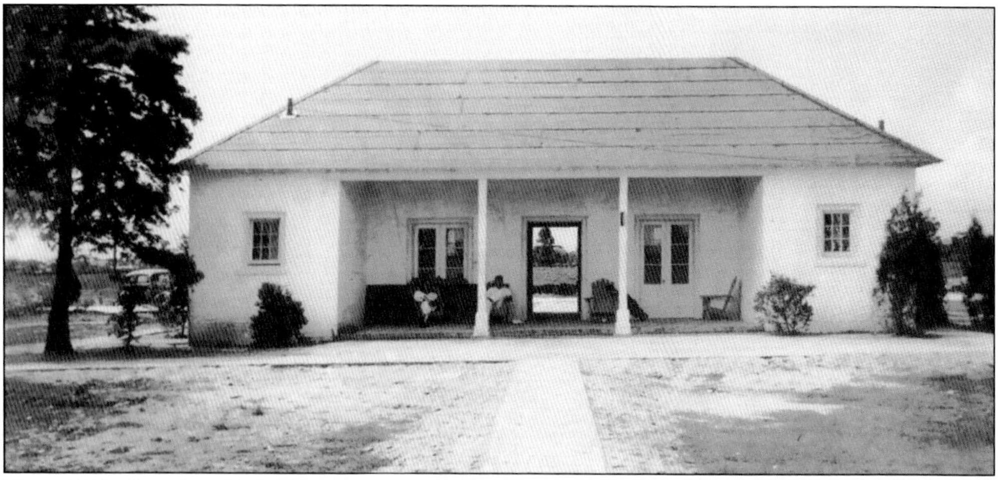

The old St. John's golf clubhouse is pictured above. Below, it is remodeled and surrounded by additional structures that contain a lobby, lounge, display shop, men's and women's locker rooms (increased from 75 to 250 lockers), a caddy house with a sound system connecting it with the clubhouse and a bulletin board maintained to display current news on golfing events throughout the country, and an outdoor recreational area—all at a cost of $85,000. The caddie house was able to accommodate up to 300 caddies. For the 1938 New Orleans Open PGA Golf Tournament, Mayor Robert S. Maestri donated $5,000 in prize money, and then $10,000 per year was donated until 1941, when dentist Herbert H. Meyer donated $5,000. The 1938 event attracted 10,000 spectators. The 1938 Crescent City Open was won by Lloyd Mangrum, who bested Sam Snead and Lawson Little. The park hosted the Crescent City Open until 1962. (Above, LDL; below, NOPL.)

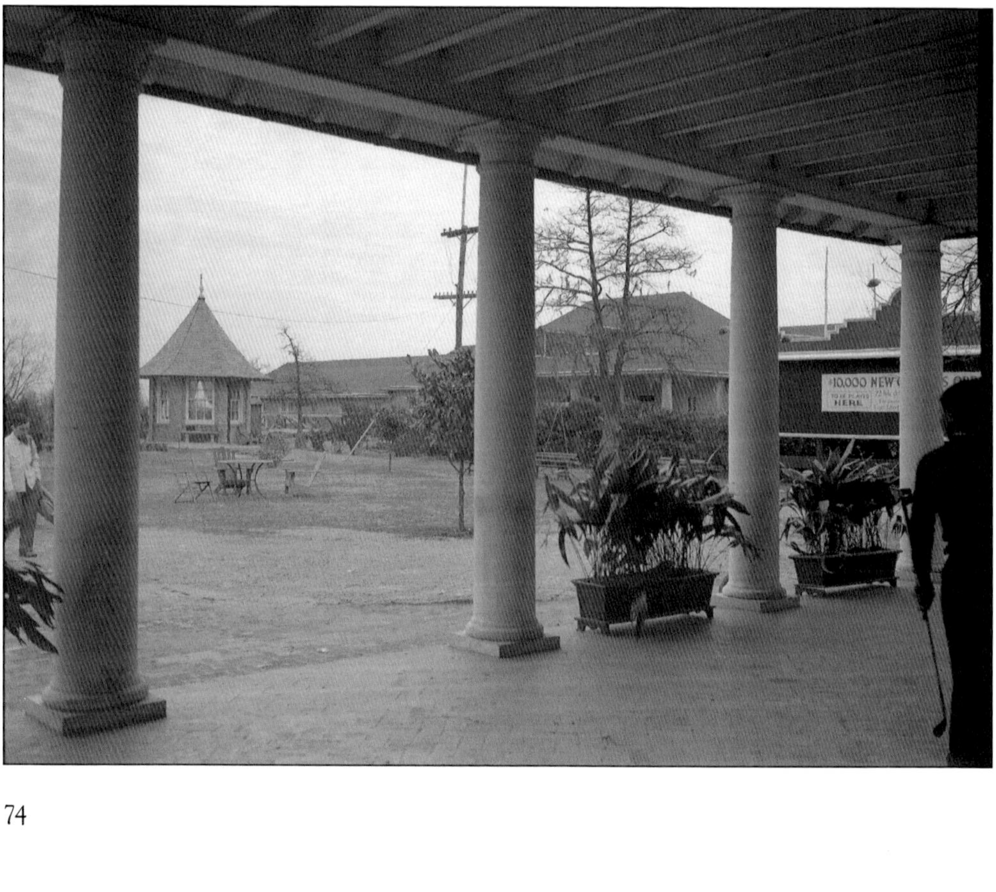

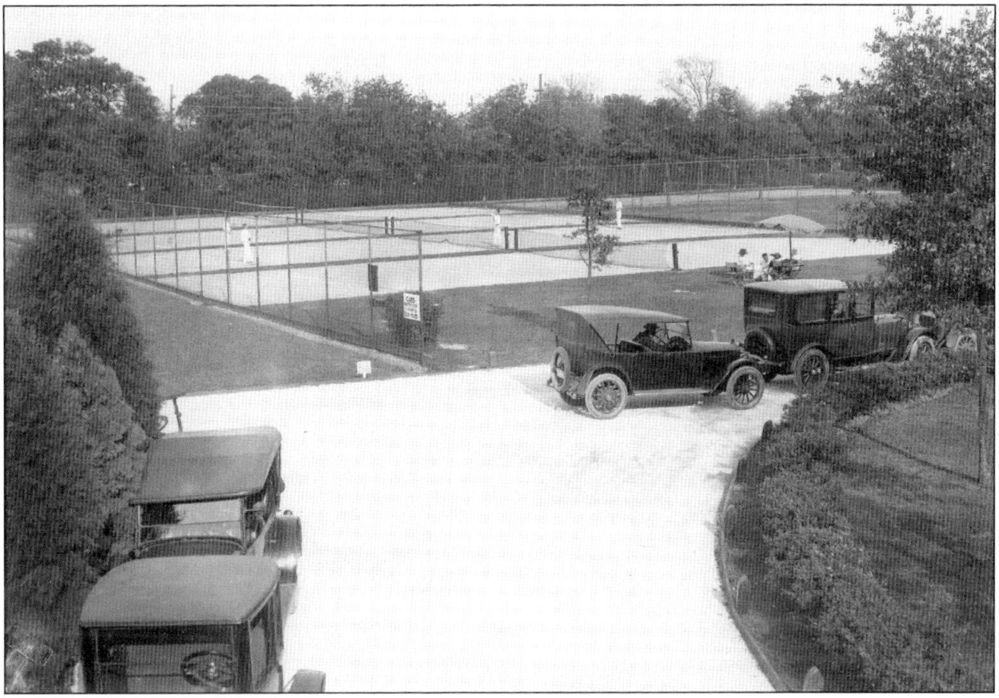

Noting the pace of WPA work around the tennis courts, the *New Orleans Item* reported on July 30, 1936, "This crew of WPA workers on the City Park project under Supt. Denis Flynn, yesterday broke the Louisiana record, and it is believed, the national record for laying sidewalk paving. In one day, they laid 700 lineal feet of 6.5-foot wide sidewalk." (LDL.)

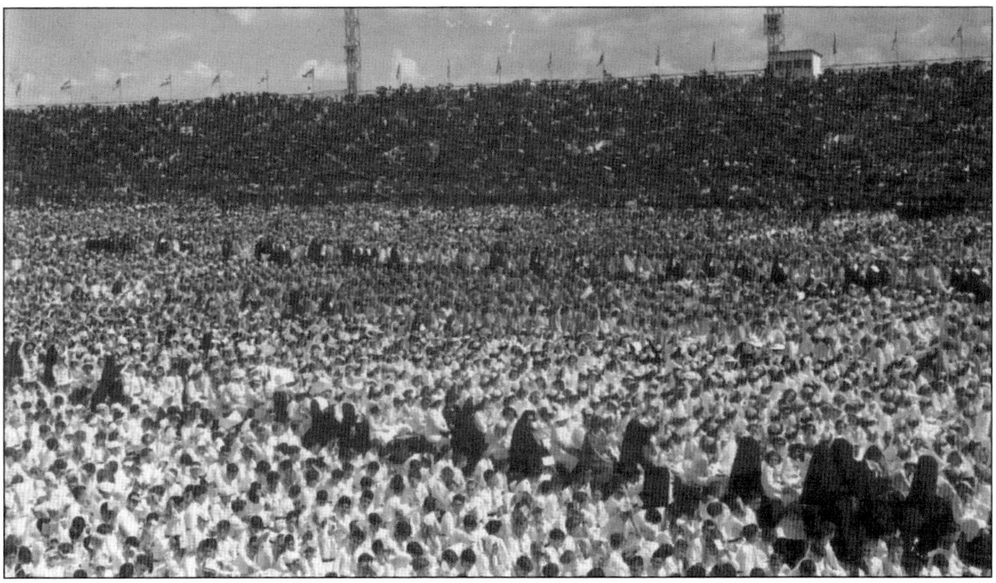

Pope Pius XI broadcasted the benediction of the Eighth Ecumenical–Eucharistic Congress via radio to the stadium filled to capacity. *St. Petersburg Times* reported on October 18, 1938, "There were 28 casualties—ranging from dogbite and fainting to a broken leg . . . during the mass, the most solemn and elaborate religious ceremony ever seen in this city. . . . Over 65,000 people were in attendance October 17th to 20th." (LDL.)

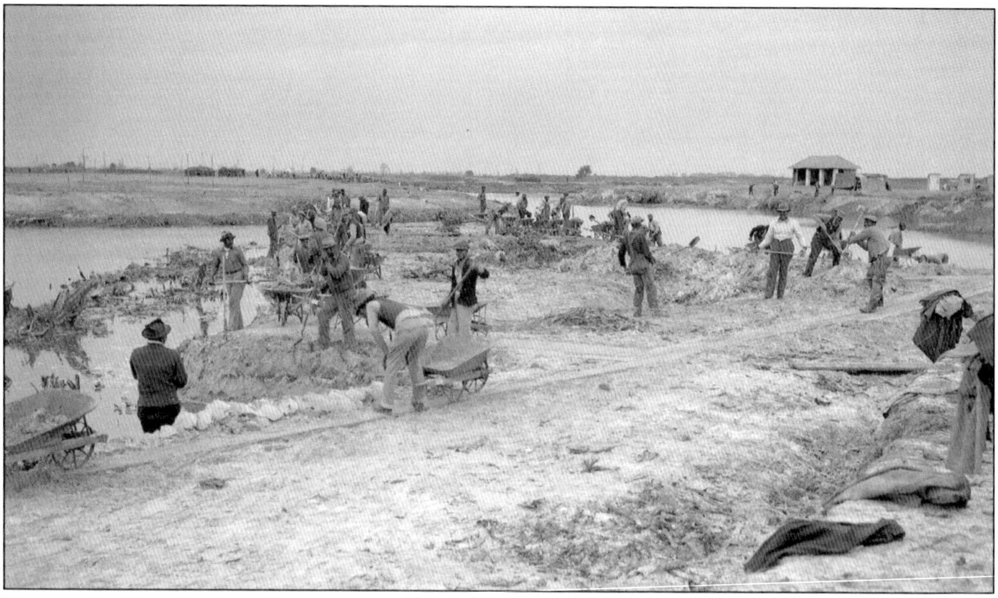

During the New Deal era, lagoons were dug laboriously by hand, as seen in this 1939 photograph. Other work with a human touch included landscaping, paving, building fountains, restoring old structures, Robert Tallant's writing of *New Orleans City Park, the First Fifty Years*, and the creation of glorious Art Deco designs. The hands of musicians were not neglected; they were employed by the WPA for concerts in the park. Below, the new McFadden Bridge (pictured in 1939) is replete with an Alferez-designed bas relief of workers plying their trades. (Both, NOPL.)

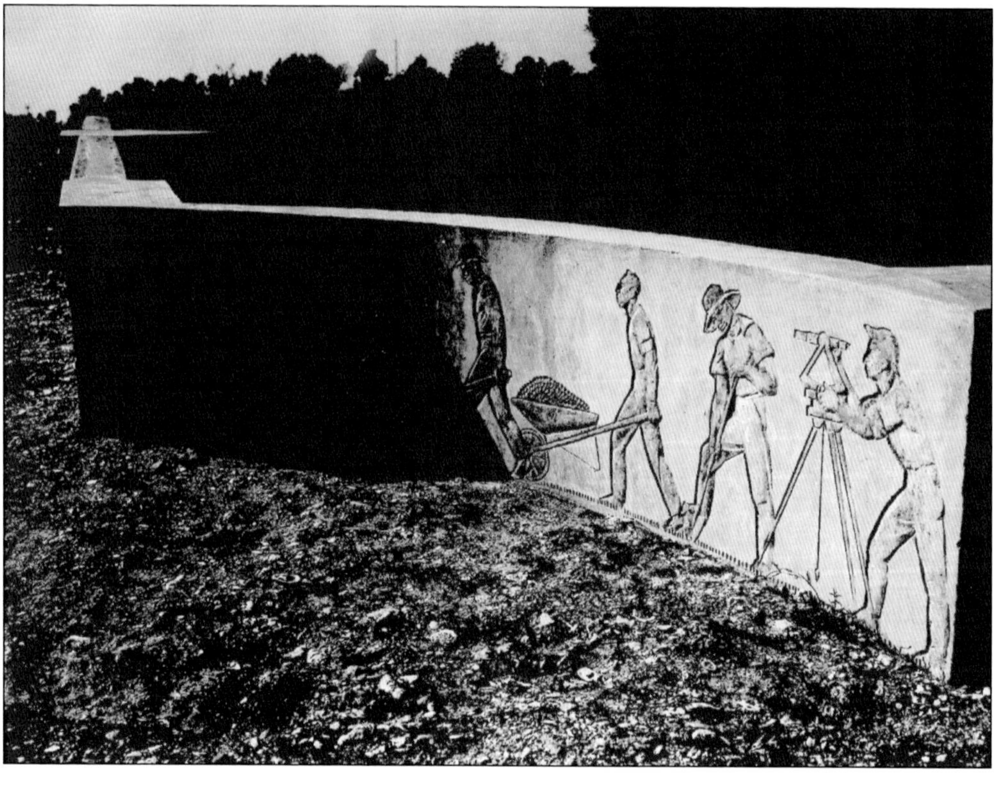

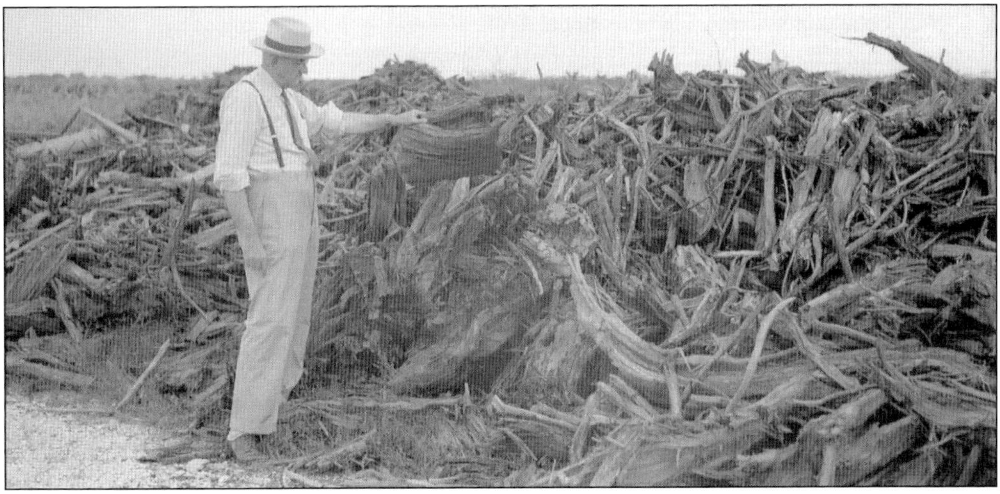

A 1928 ordinance ratified the purchase of the property known as the City Park Extension from the New Orleans Land Company, which totaled 900 acres of unimproved cypress swamp that reached to Lake Pontchartrain (roughly to what is now Robert E. Lee Boulevard). Though unimproved, many trees had been felled for timber. CPIA agreed to accept the land under the condition that the stumps be removed. This proved too costly and difficult for the company to undertake, so the land was returned to the park. This 1939 photograph graphically illustrates the scope of the endeavor. Eventually, WPA workers cleared the stumps, and the area became the location for the new golf courses and the Couturie Forest. The photograph below was taken in 1938 by Clarence John Laughlin and is titled *Invitation to Travel*. It features the park and the photographer reflected in the fender of an automobile. (Above, NOPL; below, LDL.)

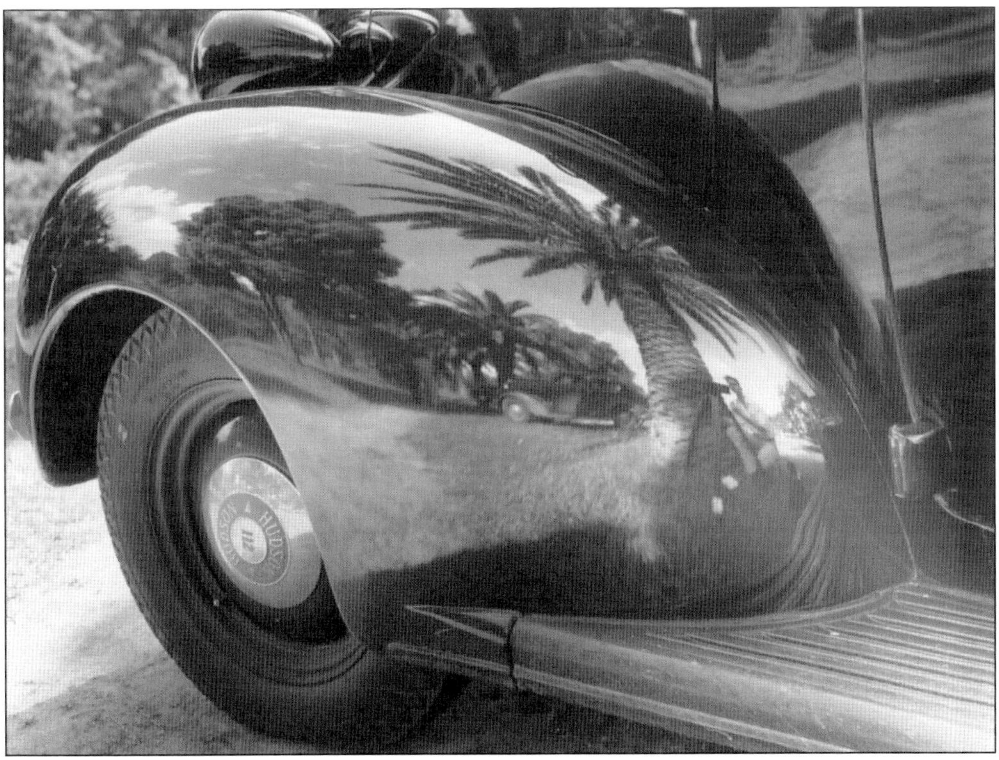

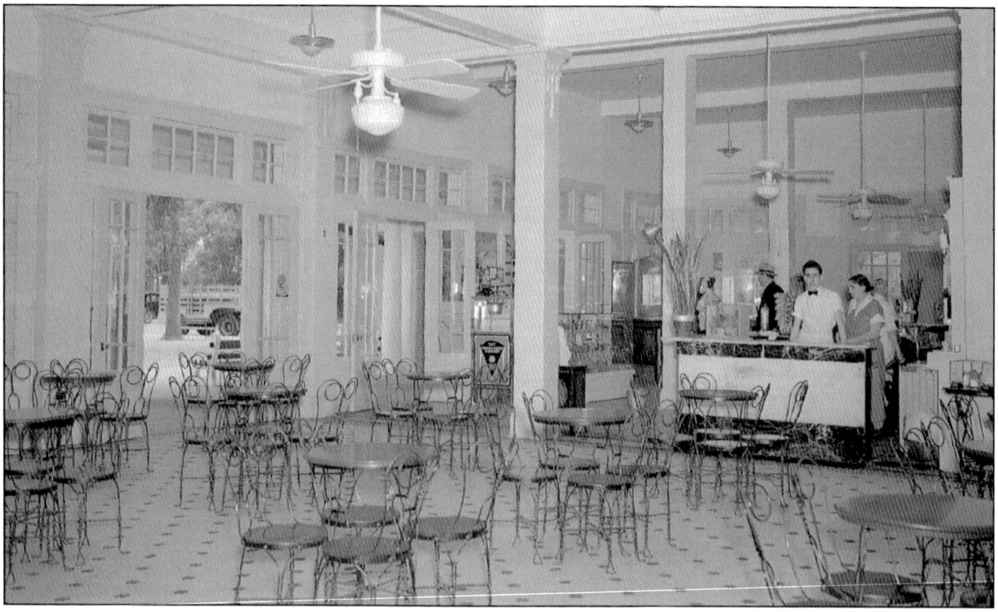

This is an interior view of the Casino in 1939 after WPA renovations. Generations of children and adults sat on the old-style, metal chairs to enjoy a cold drink, candy, a light snack, or ice cream inside the airy room, cooled by ceiling fans. Some paddled to the Casino on the adjacent Bayou Metairie in rented skiffs or rode there in the swan boat. (NOPL.)

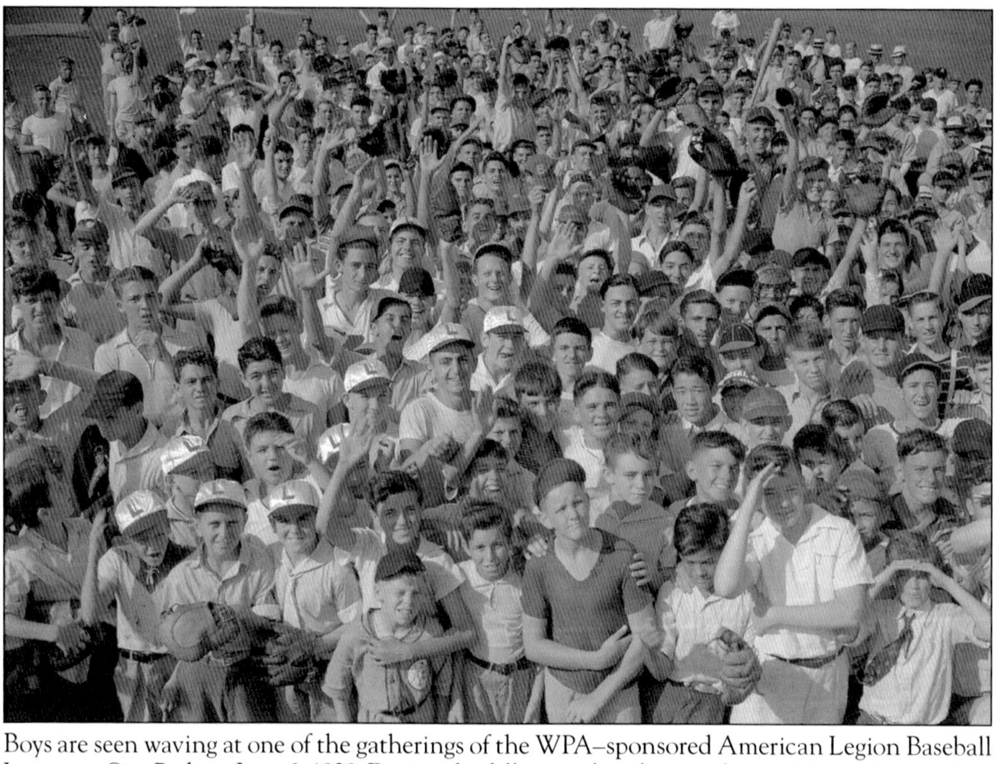

Boys are seen waving at one of the gatherings of the WPA–sponsored American Legion Baseball League at City Park on June 6, 1939. During the following decades, youth activities and attractions would become a major component of City Park's offerings. (NOPL.)

Five

Children and Friends 1940–2004

During this era, Storyland was new, children camped on Scout Island, and teenagers told horror stories of "Grunch Road" and "Mona Lisa Drive" (the park's lovers' lane) with its apparitions and Hookman.

Serious social issues were tackled. A 1949 Supreme Court decision prohibited segregation of the golf course and other facilities; Archbishop Joseph Francis Rummel canceled the biannual Roman Catholic observance of Holy Hour because park commissioners insisted on racially segregated seating in the stadium. CPIA fought full integration until 1958, when a final court decision mandated that "Negroes are now permitted to use all park facilities." According to the December 22, 1958, issue of *Times-Picayune*, the general manager stated, "We have exhausted every means to keep the park segregated."

Peggy Read, wife of Henry J. Read, recognizing that the lack of local and state funding had resulted in the park's disrepair, recruited volunteers to organize a fundraiser. From this effort, Friends of City Park was established in 1979. Peggy Read was its first president. Friends of City Park goal was to initiate programs and organize events to increase public awareness and support for the park. Its 3,000 members have raised millions through donations and major fundraisers, like Celebration in the Oaks, Lark in the Park, Ghosts in the Oaks, and Martini Madness. An oak tree has been named in appreciation of Peggy Read's contributions to City Park.

During the 1970s and early 1980s, the Saux Building operated as Parkway Tavern, a popular but by no means beautiful venue; there were even monkeys painted on the window transoms. In 1983, the building was placed in the National Register of Historic Places. After Jack and Martha Sands renovated it in 1985, they opened Tavern on the Park restaurant. In December 2003, Ralph Brennan opened Ralph's on the Park.

In 1971, despite protests and a lawsuit challenging the construction of highways through parkland, work began on the Interstate 610, which cut through the Couturie Forest. Excavation for the road resulted in a two-acre mound, located 60 feet above sea level. It is the highest earthen elevation in New Orleans; Audubon Park's Monkey Hill is 16 feet above sea level.

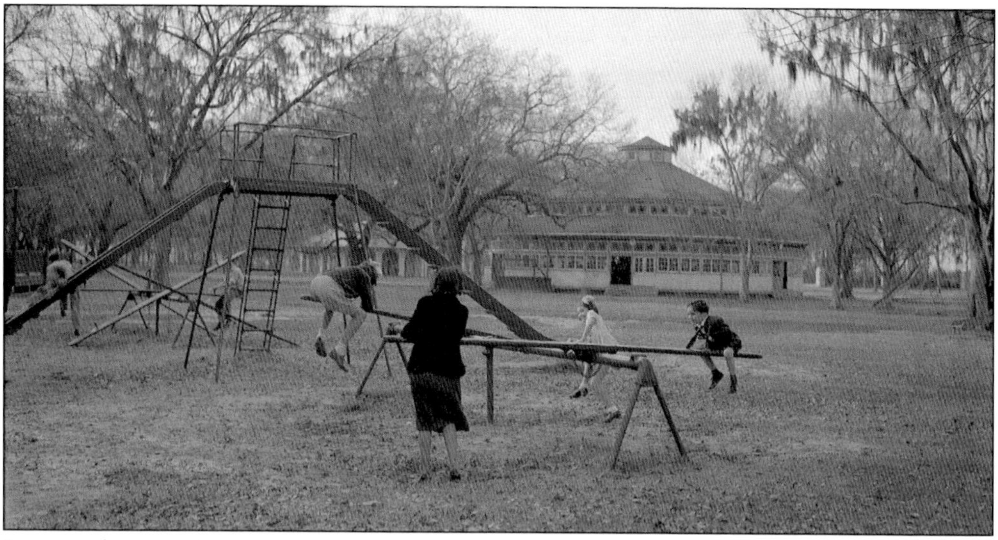

By 1940, the WPA had improved and beautified many playgrounds, one of which can be seen here in front of the carousel pavilion. Also in 1940, the record attendance of 34,345 in the stadium is thought to have been set during the Jesuit–Holy Cross football game, far surpassing the seating capacity of 26,500. Pictured below is the bandstand in 1941. The second of the pair of Dueling Oaks was uprooted during a hurricane in 1949. (Above, NOPL; below, HNOC.)

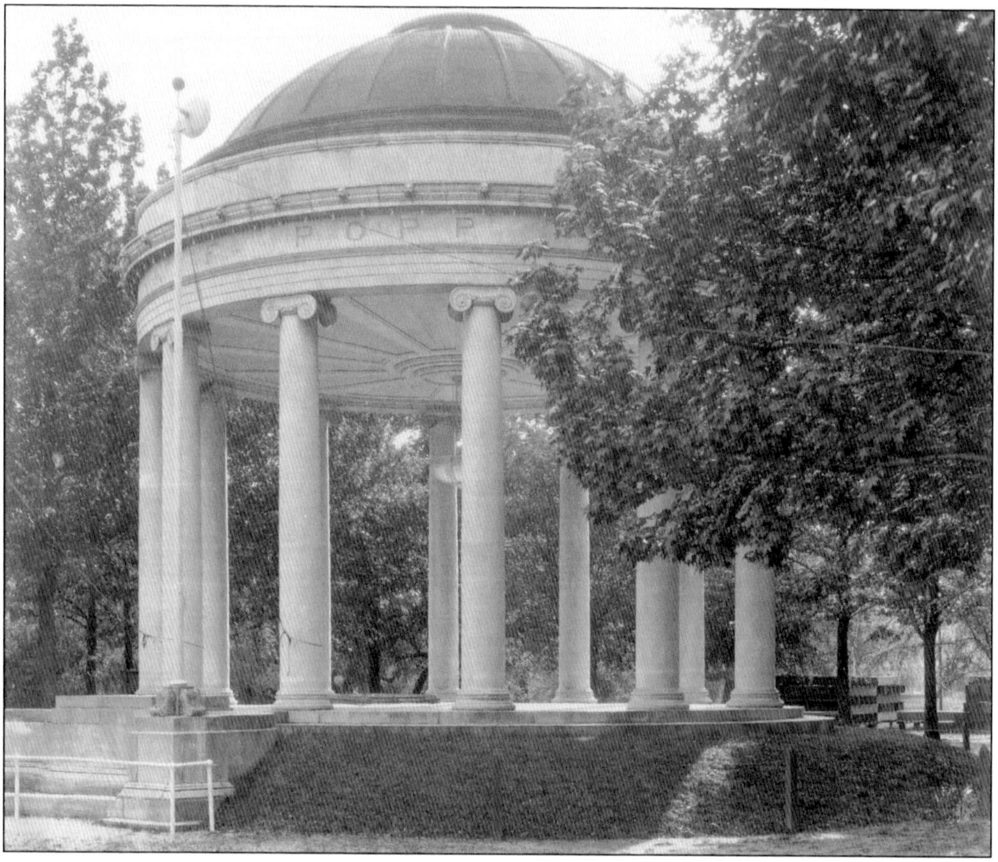

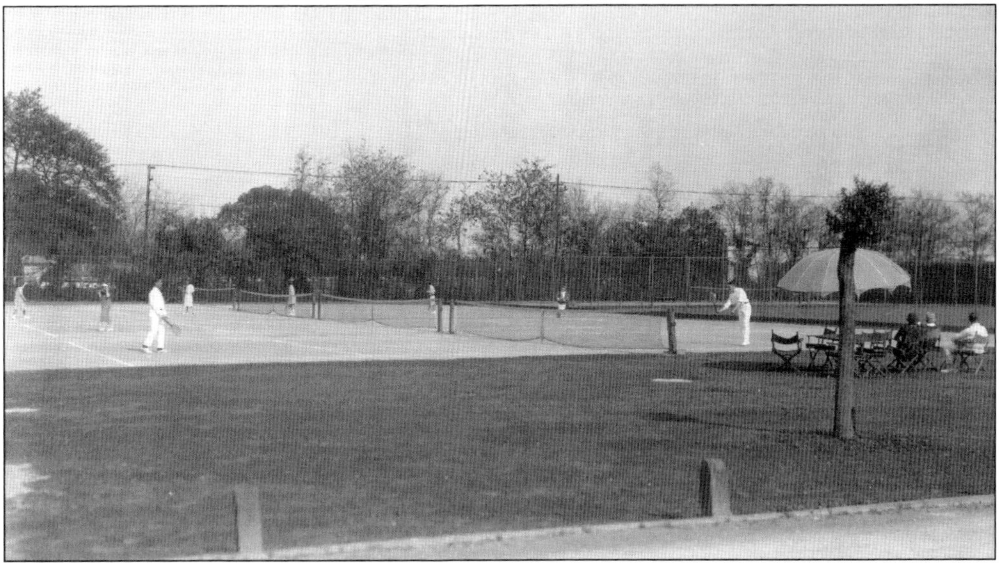

The WPA added tennis courts and a new tennis house and paved the surrounding area. The completed work can be seen in this 1941 photograph. Other recreational opportunities offered during the New Deal era included an 18-hole golf course that could be played for 50¢ and the first Big Bass Fishing Rodeo, initiated in 1946 and still held each spring. (LDL.)

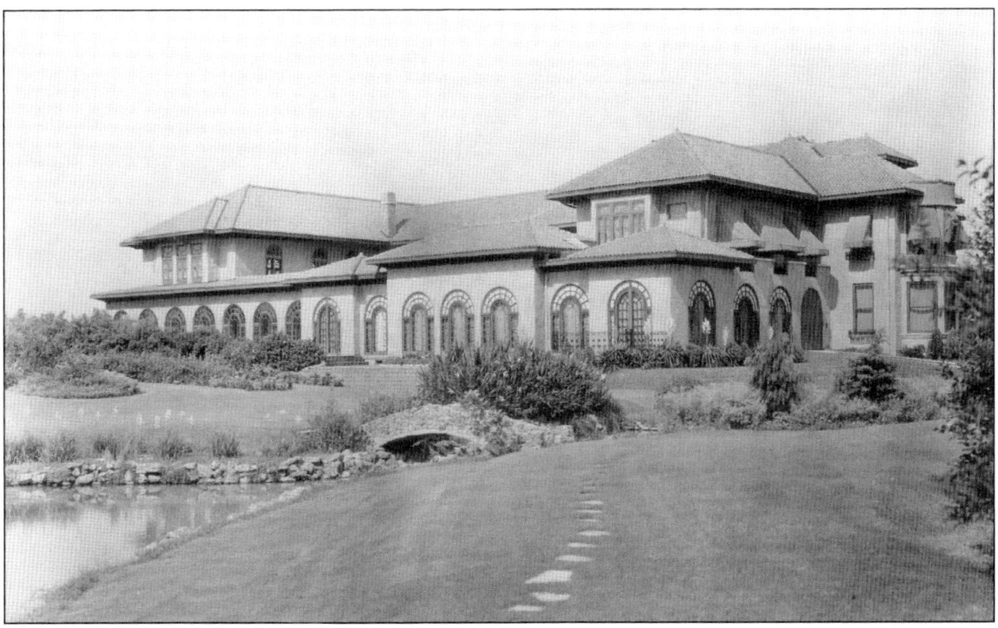

After McFadden sold his estate to the city, prospective uses included the mayor's residence, a convalescent home, a hospital, and a chicken farm. By 1949, Samuel Barthe opened a boys' elementary school in the mansion until the Christian brothers opened their academy for fifth-through seventh-grade boys in 1960. (LDL.)

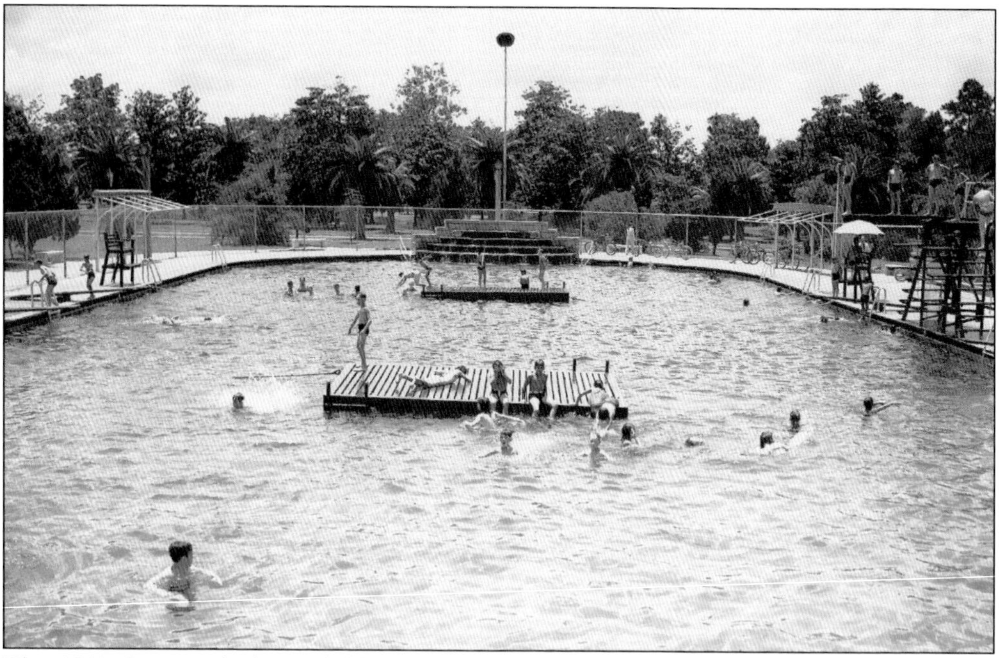

This 1941 photograph shows children playing in the newly repaired Irby Swimming Pool. As the WPA completed its work in the park, state director of the Public Works Reserve Allen J. Negrotto and City Park superintendent Marcel Montreuil began planning a five-year improvement program. (NOPL.)

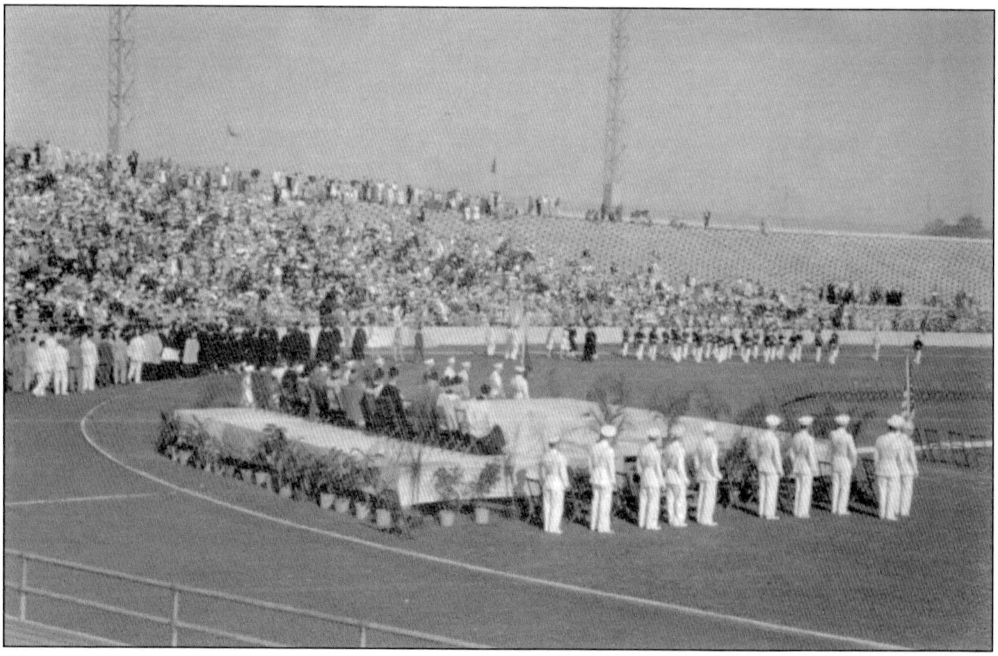

The Archdiocese of New Orleans's eighth annual celebration of Mary's Day (Mother's Day 1941) is viewed here. It was a gathering of clerics, sodalists, and students from 5 colleges, 14 high schools, and 64 parishes. Presided over by Archbishop Joseph Francis Rummel, the principal speaker was Rev. Leo Flood, pastor of Sacred Heart Church. (NOPL.)

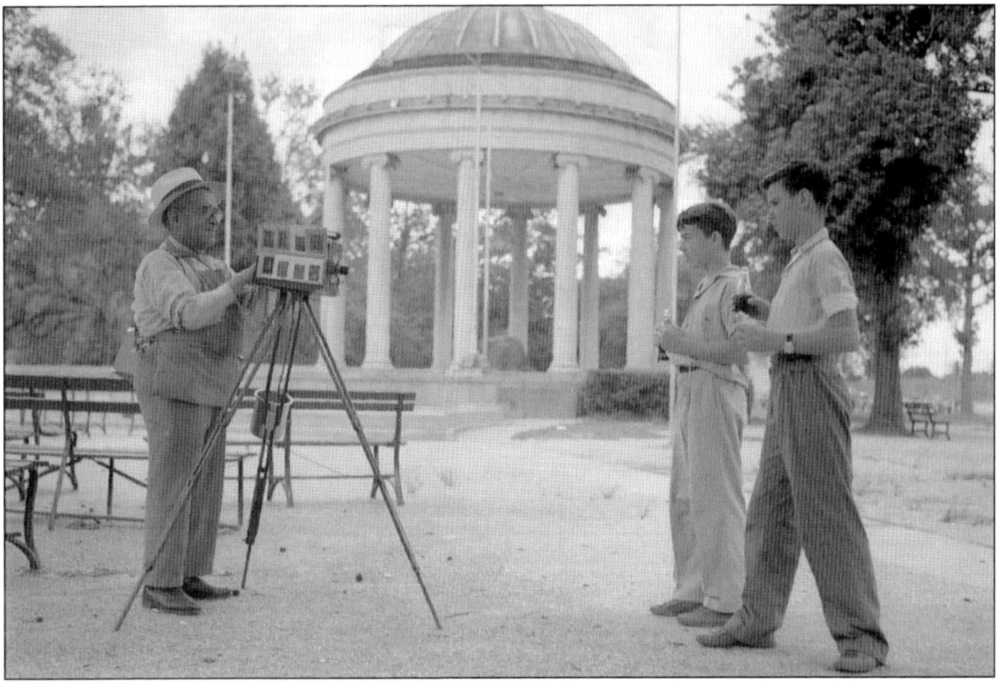

In 1942, someone snapped a shot of the man who photographed children in the park for generations. His was a familiar face to all who passed Popp Bandstand on their way to the Casino. Meanwhile, a few blocks away, Higgins Industries, Inc., was enlarging its World War II boatbuilding facility on City Park Avenue. (NOPL.)

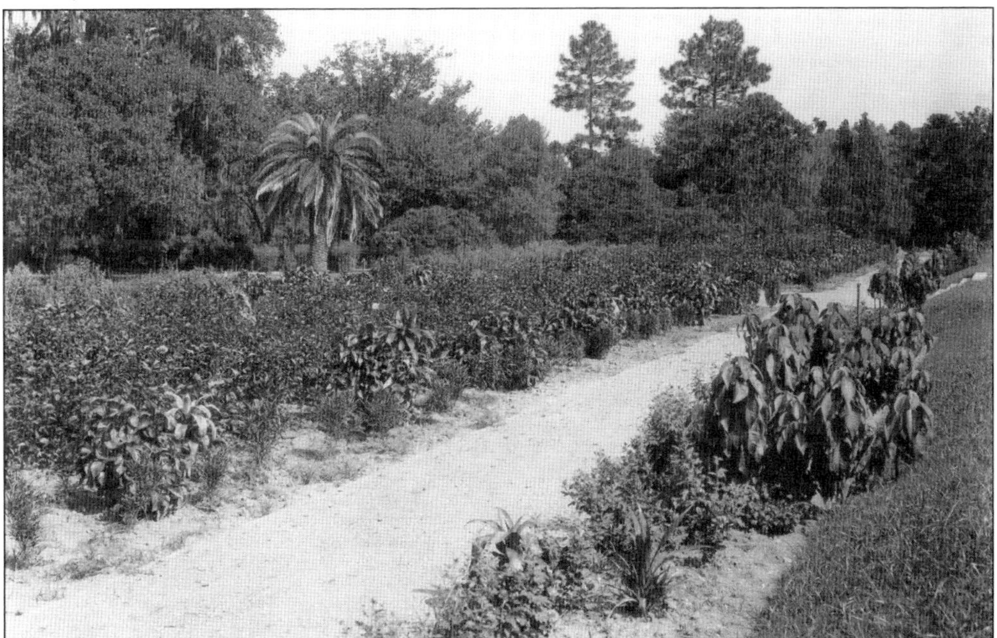

In 1942, the city completed the Floral Trail of over 35 miles of plantings along streets and in parks, making this one of the most colorful winter garden spots in the United States. The Floral Trail meandered through the park in this undated photograph. (LDL.)

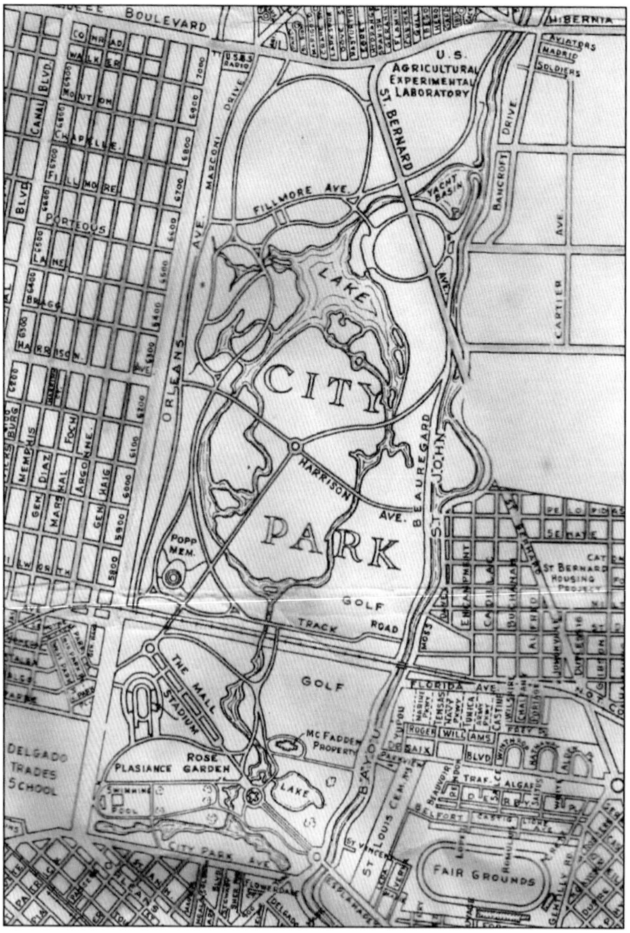

This 1940s map illustrates the park's features and boundaries after WPA workers cleared and developed the northern extension. Note that the yacht basin still existed along Bayou St. John and served to connect the park's lagoons to the bayou. Below is a 1950s view of the streetcar stop by the cemeteries near the end of City Park Avenue. (Both, LDL.)

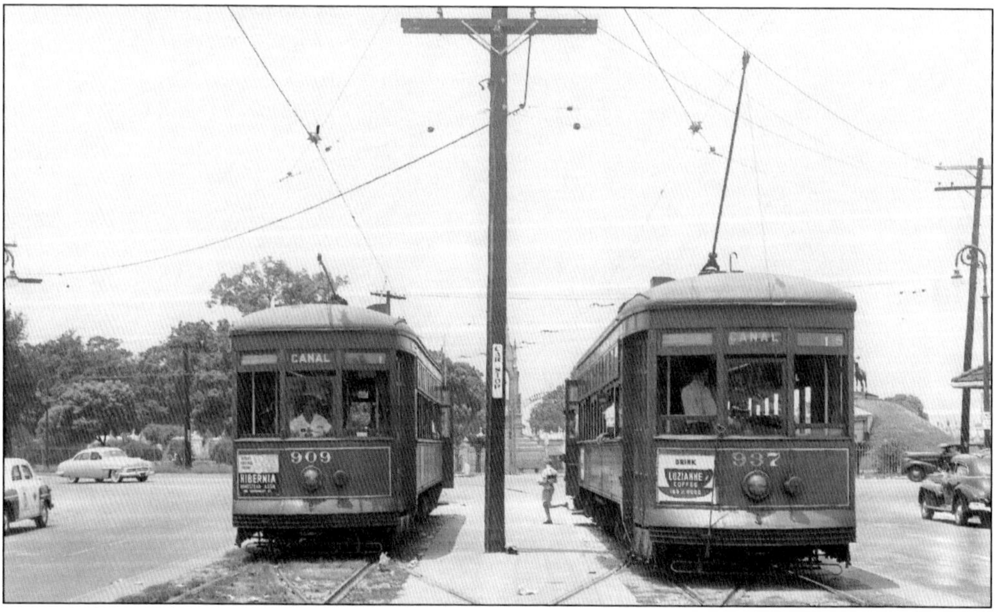

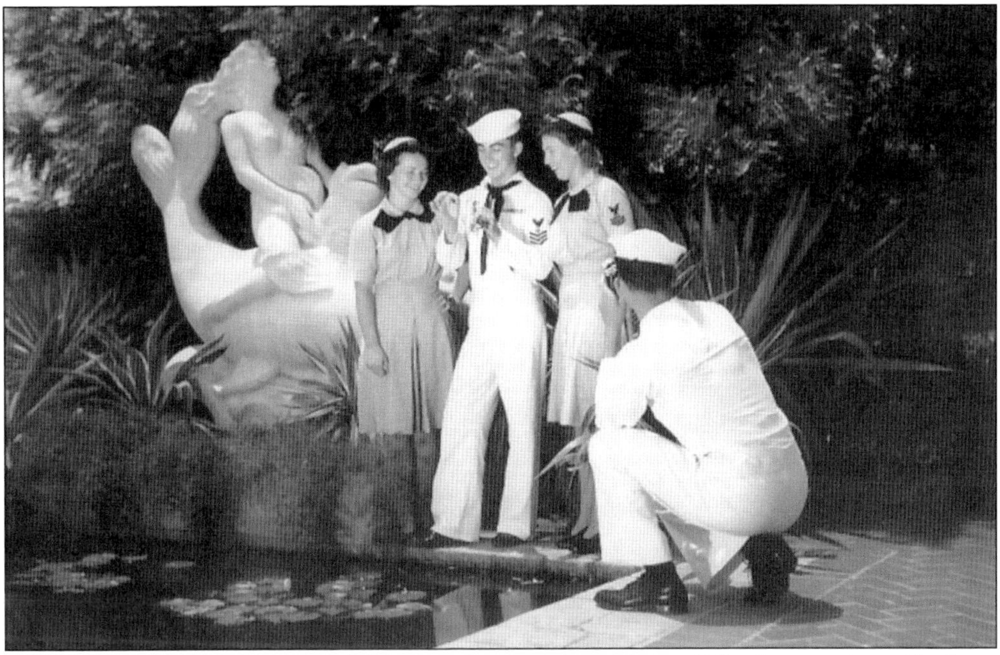

The Navy snapped and captioned this 1944 photograph as follows: " 'She loves me? . . . She loves me not?' Pharmacist's Mate 1st Class Jackie Welsh depetals a flower to settle an ageless question of romance, as Signalman 2nd Class Harold Howey records the event on film . . . All four are stationed at Naval Air Station, New Orleans, Louisiana." (NA.)

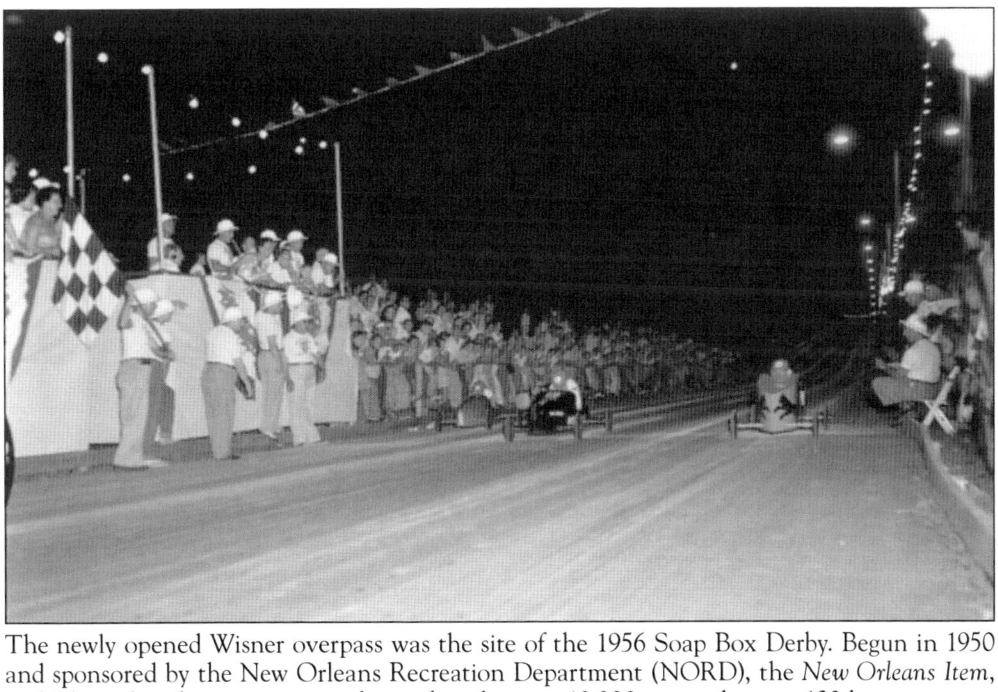

The newly opened Wisner overpass was the site of the 1956 Soap Box Derby. Begun in 1950 and sponsored by the New Orleans Recreation Department (NORD), the *New Orleans Item*, and Chevrolet, the races attracted crowds as large as 10,000 to watch some 130 boys compete. Fifteen-year-old Otto Potier won the Keating Trophy and a chance to compete in the national finals in Akron, Ohio. (NOPL.)

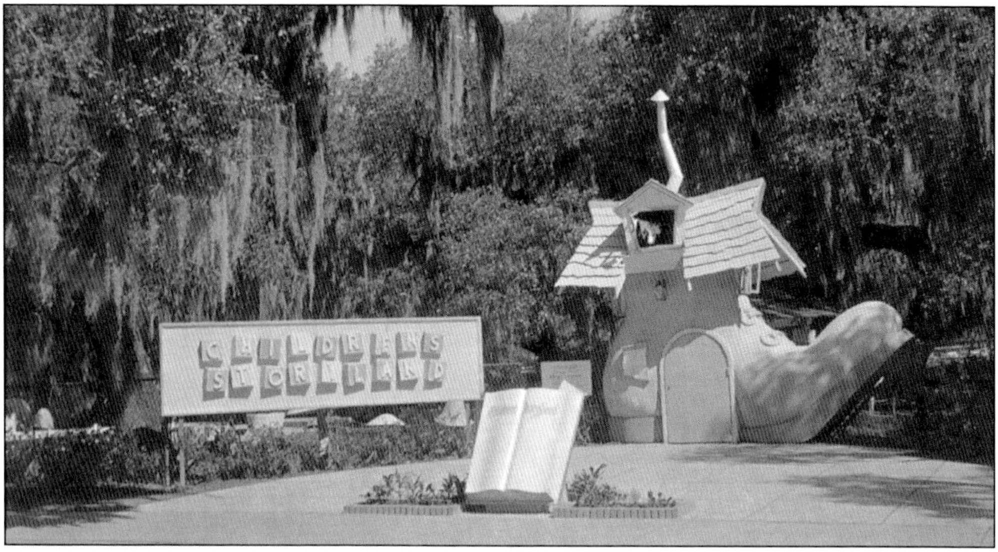

Storyland was opened in 1956 and was populated by nursery rhyme characters created by Blain Kern, with some hanging in the ancient oaks. This enchanting world of plaster and cement figures included Captain Hook and his ship, the Old Woman and her shoe, Pinocchio and the whale (with a gaping jaw to be walked into), Jack and Jill on their hill, Cinderella in her pumpkin coach (children could join her), King Cole in his castle, Red Riding Hood and the wolf, Hansel and Gretel, the Little Prince, Little Miss Muffet, Alice in Wonderland, the Three Pigs, Snow White, Hey Diddle, Diddle, and Humpty Dumpty (whose "wall" was Storyland's maintenance shop). Built adjacent to the Flying Horses at a cost of $25,000, Storyland attracted 500,000 visitors in 1958 when Park Amusement Company was managed by Frank Davis. It is seen here in 1960 (above) and 2007 (below). (DCM.)

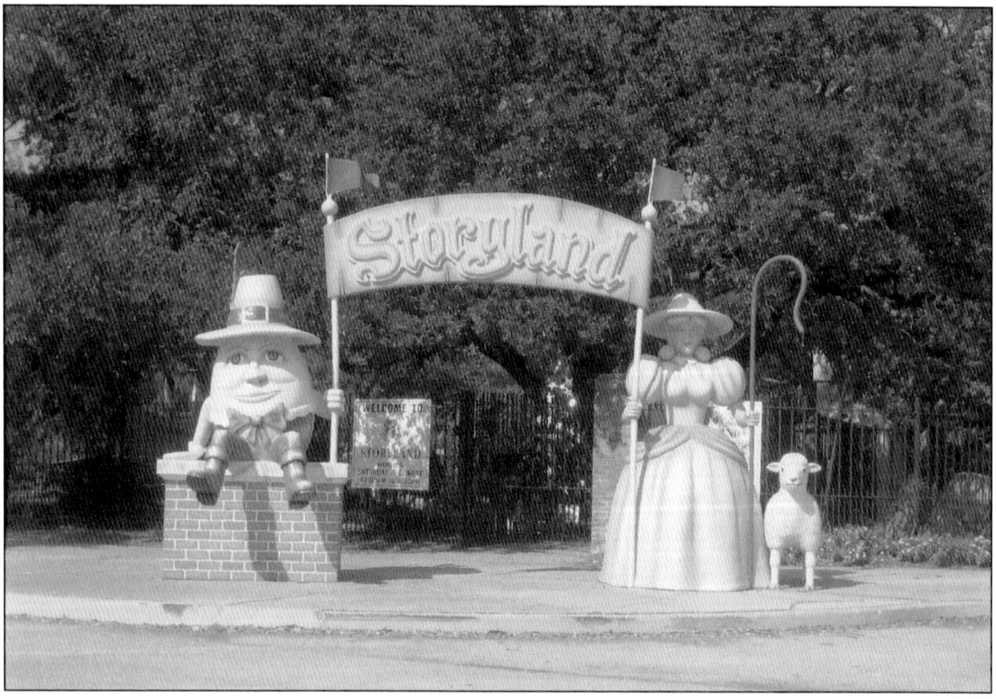

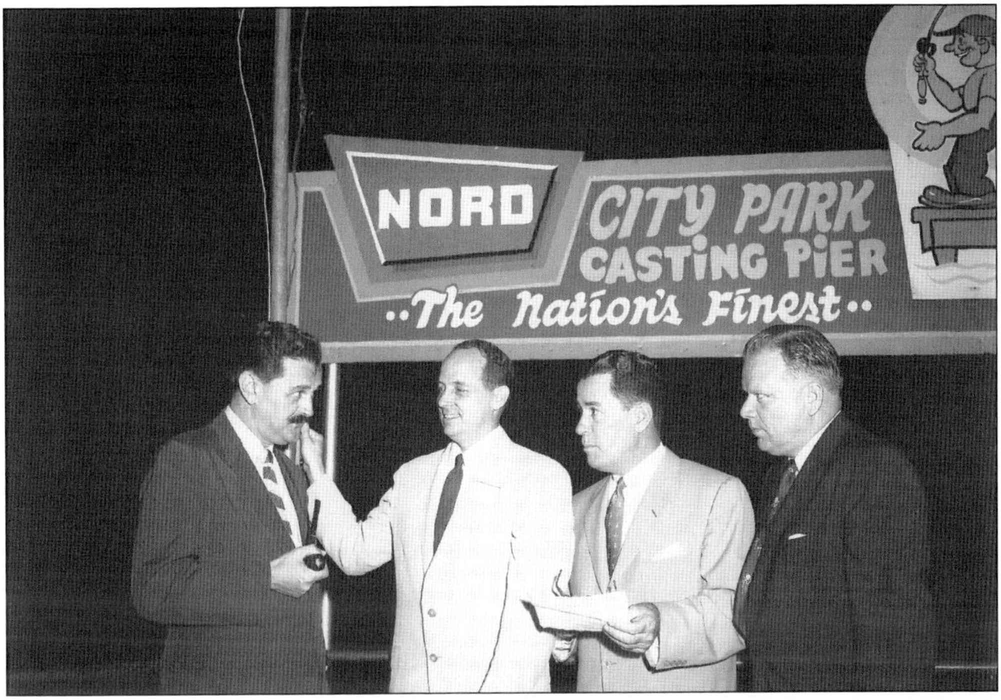

The New Orleans Recreation Department (NORD) Casting Pier was dedicated in 1955 with opening ceremonies, which included George Voitier, the first vice president of Dixie Casting and Fishing Association; Mayor DeLesseps Story "Chep" Morrison; L.J. Lautenschlaeger, director of NORD; and city councilman Glenn P. Clasen. (NOPL.)

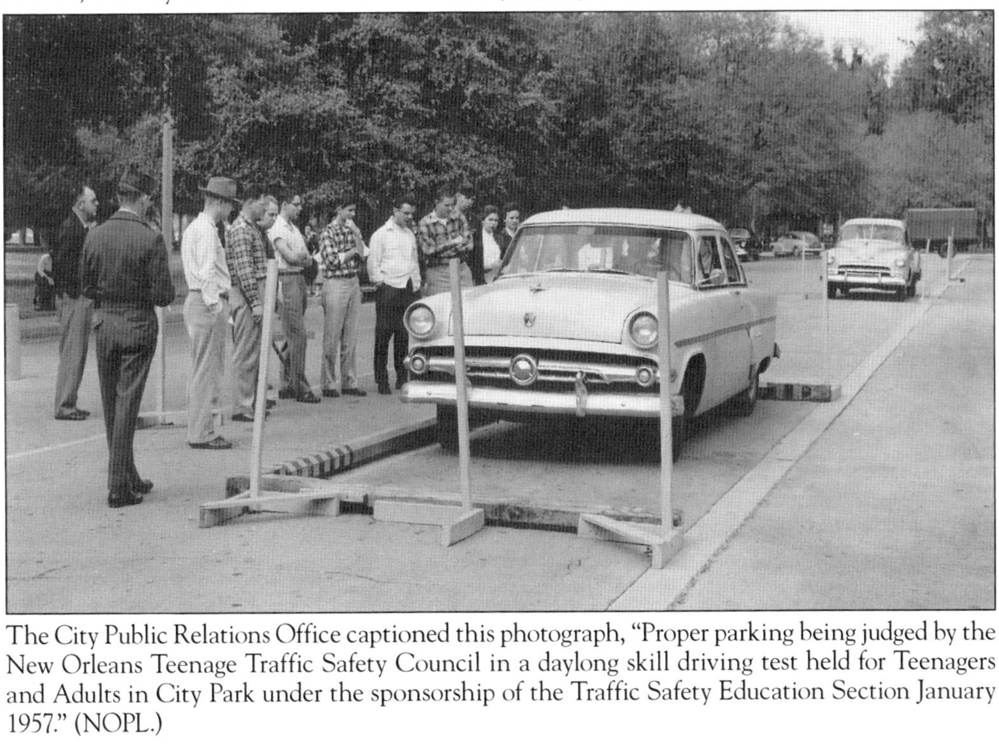
The City Public Relations Office captioned this photograph, "Proper parking being judged by the New Orleans Teenage Traffic Safety Council in a daylong skill driving test held for Teenagers and Adults in City Park under the sponsorship of the Traffic Safety Education Section January 1957." (NOPL.)

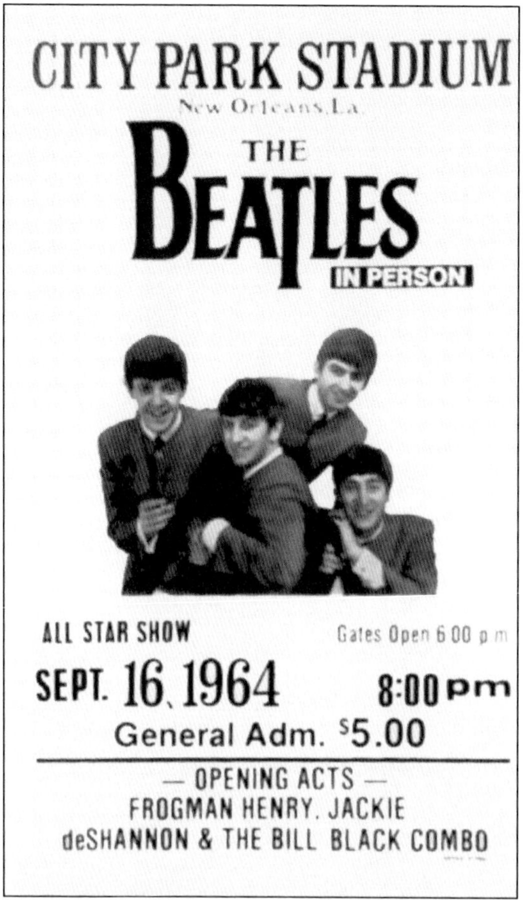

The stadium hosted the first American Football League (AFL) exhibition game held in New Orleans, organized by Jack DeFee and promoted by Dave Dixon, to demonstrate local fan support for major-league football. It pitted the New England Patriots against the Houston Oilers in 1962. The Beatles performed there on September 16, 1964, and in 1965, the stadium was renamed in honor of Frank "Tad" Gormley shortly after his death. Also renamed was the Delgado Museum, which became known as the New Orleans Museum of Art in 1971. Pan American Stadium was dedicated in 1973. In 1992, Tad Gormley Stadium was renovated to host US Olympic Track and Field Trials and Alerion Field was restored. The following year, the City Park Softball Quadroplex was built. The Botanical Garden Education Pavilion was designed, and the amusement area gift shop opened in 1993, followed by the Pavilion of the Two Sister in 1994 and the Lath House in 1997. (Author's collection.)

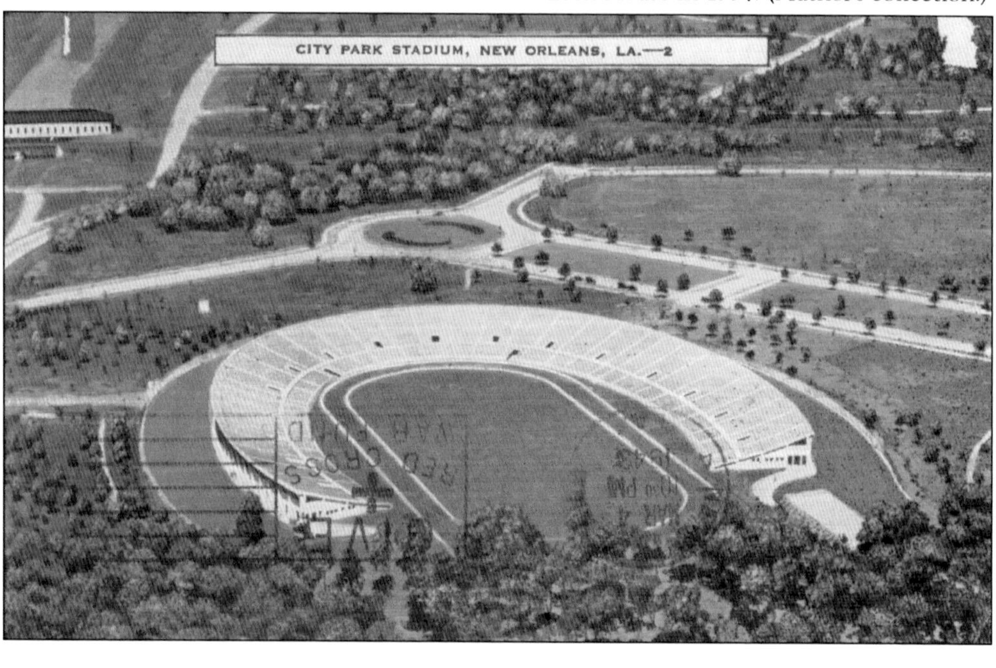

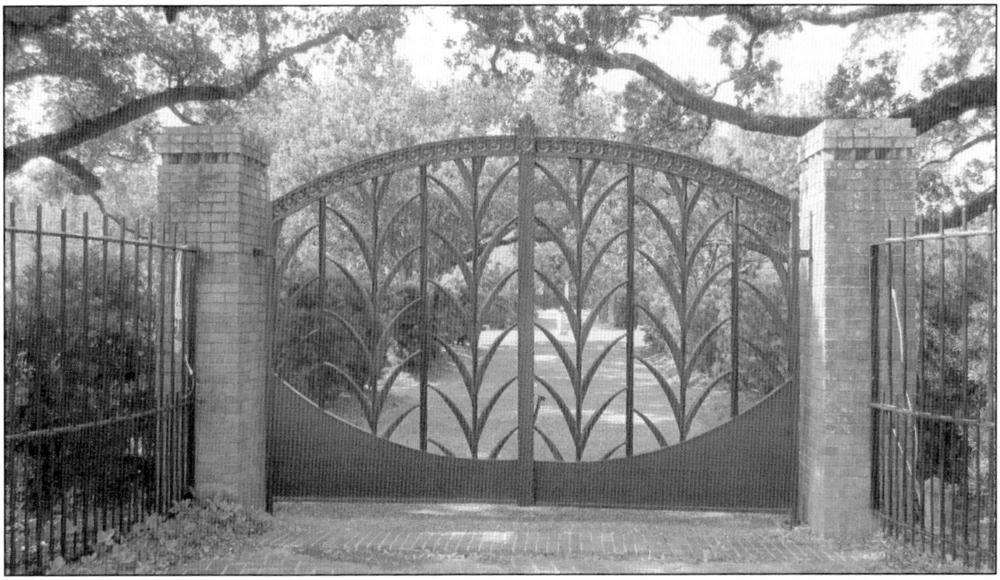

After Friends of City Park was established, its first major project was the 1982 enclosure and restoration of the rose garden, complete with 81-year-old Alferez's new Grass Gates (above) at the original main entrance to the garden. In 1984, Friends staged a Tribute to the Christmas Tree, which evolved into the beautifully magical Celebration in the Oaks. Celebration in the Oaks attracts 40,000 visitors annually. Storyland was restored by Friends in 1986, as was the carousel in 1988 when the amusement park gates (below) were constructed. In 1989, their efforts resulted in the restoration of the Peristyle. After Katrina, their volunteers took shovels and rakes in hand to clean up the park. The group, the City Park Improvement Association, which first sought to make the park a nicer place, celebrated its 100th anniversary in 1991. (Both, DCM.)

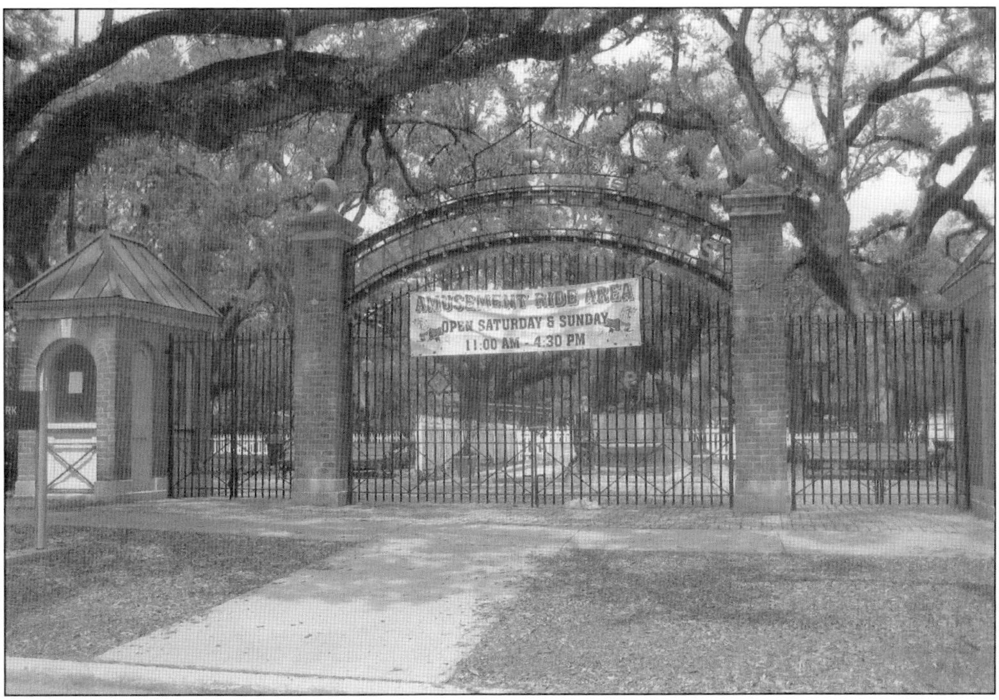

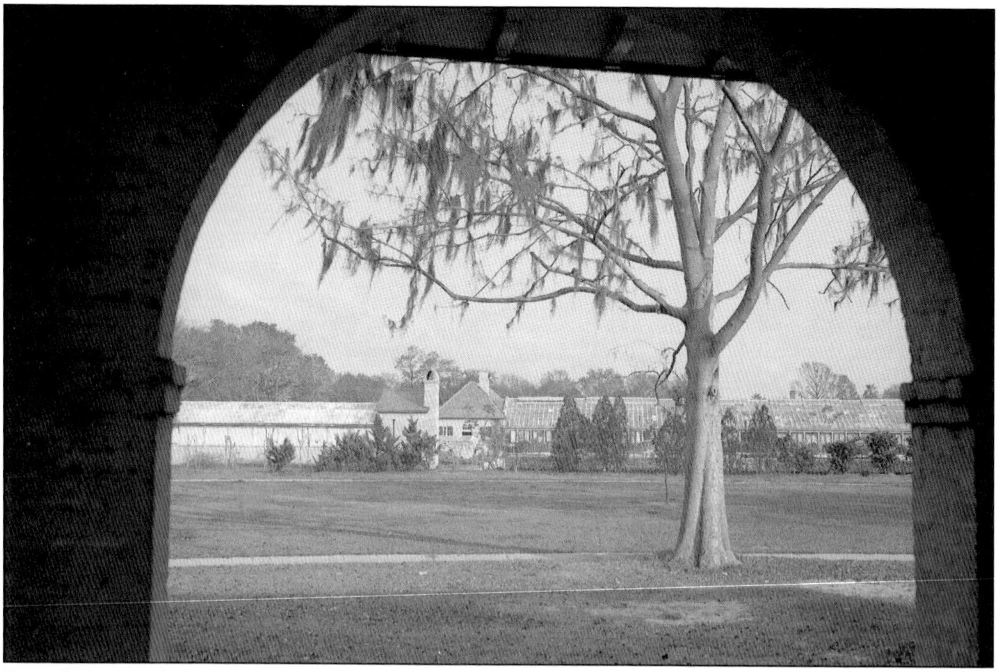

Friends restored the Casino Building (below) in 1998 and Popp Fountain in 1999. In 2000, the Couturie Forest Nature Trail and Arboretum project was completed, a natural turf system was installed in the stadium, and Tiger Woods conducted a clinic for local young people at Bayou Oaks. The hothouse, seen above in 1940, was converted in 2002 into the Conservatory of the Two Sisters, where, from under the 40-foot dome's reception area, one can enter either the living fossil or tropical rainforest wings. In 2003, the five-acre Sidney and Walda Besthoff Sculpture Garden, a gift from the Besthoff Foundation, opened its gates to 60 20th-century works by American, European, Israeli, and Japanese artists valued in excess of $25 million. (Above, NOPL; below, DCM.)

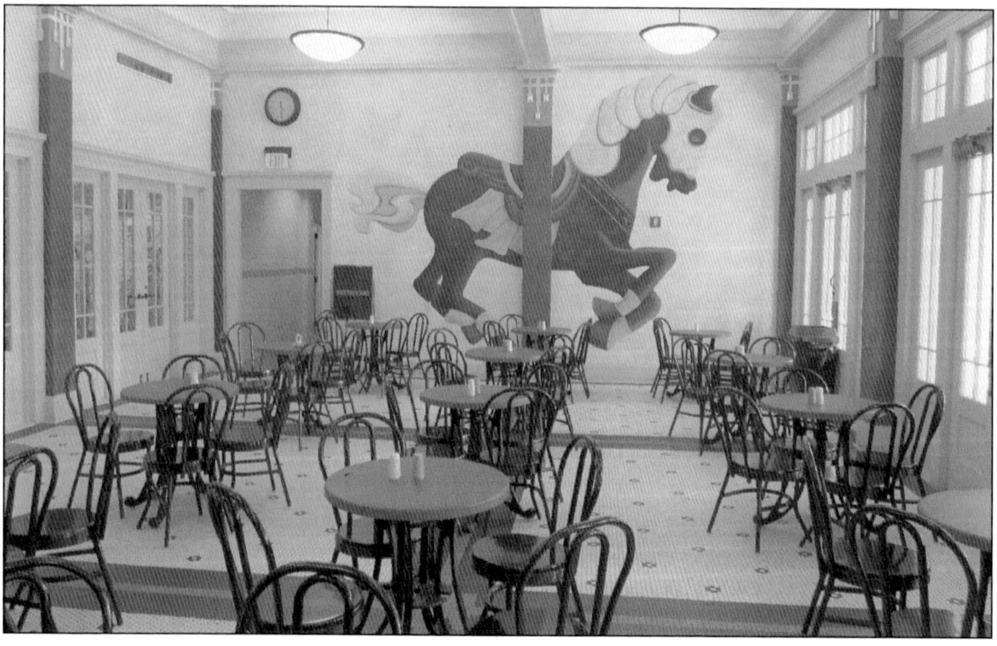

Six

Rebirth 2005–2010

On March 29, 2005, the board of commissioners approved City Park 2018, a master plan for improvements over the next 13 years. Its completion would coincide with the 300th anniversary of the city of New Orleans. On August 29, 2005, Hurricane Katrina made her unwanted and devastating arrival. A look at the park in the weeks that followed broke the hearts of many, but CPIA never lost sight of the plan; it is being implemented as written before Katrina.

The park's recovery has been made possible by civic, business, and private contributions of blood, sweat, tears, money, and hard physical work. Thousands of people, New Orleanians and volunteers from around the world, came to its rescue. While still a bit on the mend as this book was completed, City Park is once again a jewel.

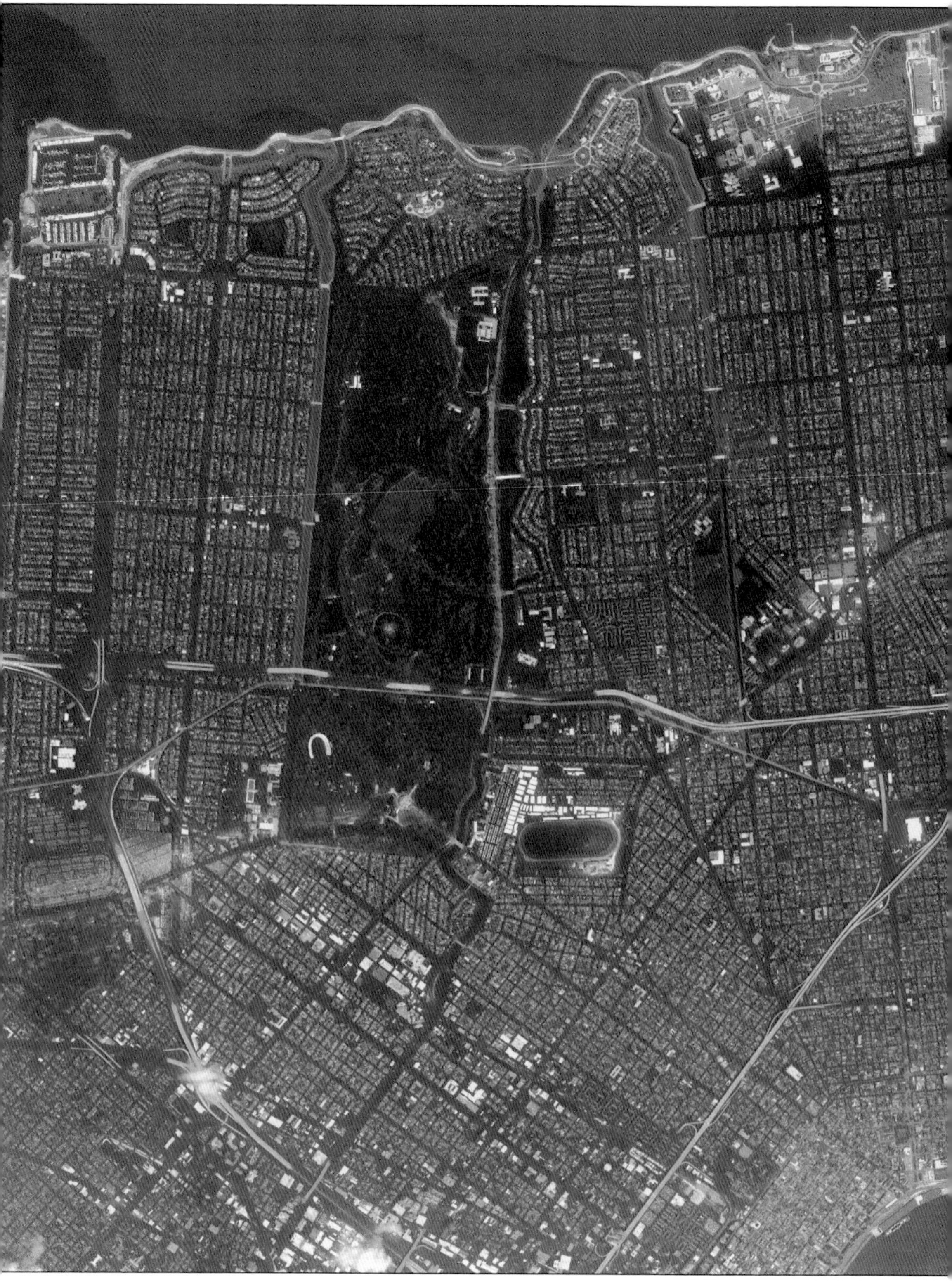

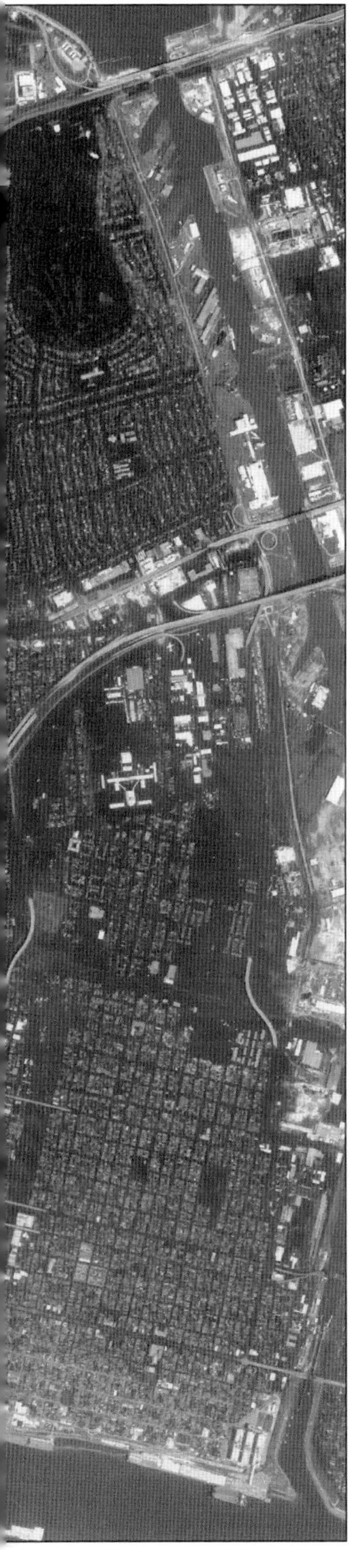

In the days immediately following Katrina, flooding from poorly engineered levees and canal walls devastated 80 percent of the city. Floodwater up to eight feet deep in sections of the park sat for as long as three weeks. The inundated park, surrounded by the flooded city, can be seen in the center of this NASA photograph. Damage to the park was massive, including the damaging of 122 buildings, 2,000 trees, grass, and 2,000 varieties of plants from around the world. About 90 percent of the park was flooded, sustaining $43 million in damages. Operations at the park ceased, and the staff was laid off. (NASA.)

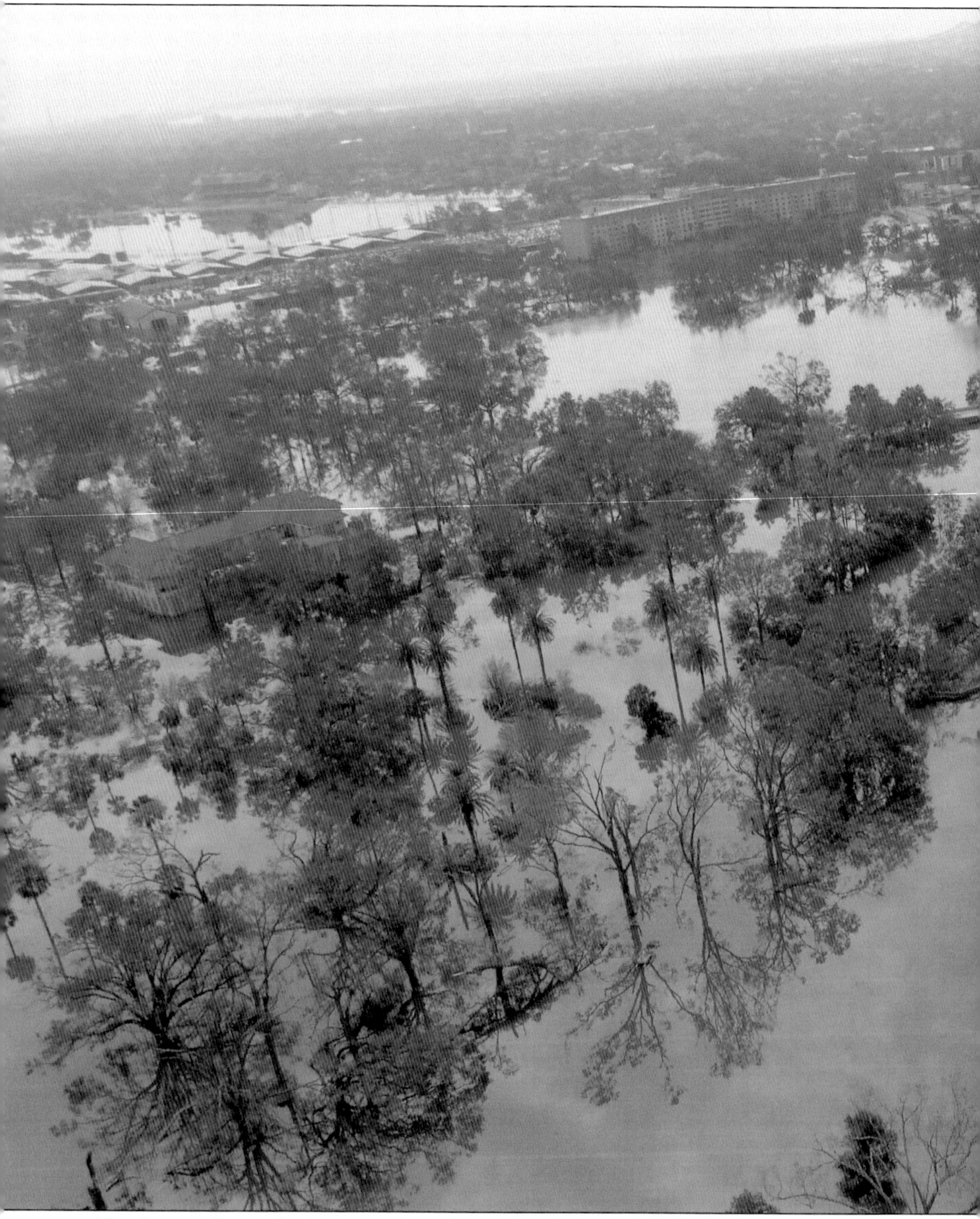

Flooding in the garden by as much as three feet for up to two weeks killed the plants there. Over 1,000 trees died in the floodwaters—over 1,000 more were toppled or extensively damaged by wind. The loss of electrical power to run air-conditioning and automatic watering systems resulted in the loss of orchids, stag-horn ferns, bromeliads, and other plants in the hothouses and

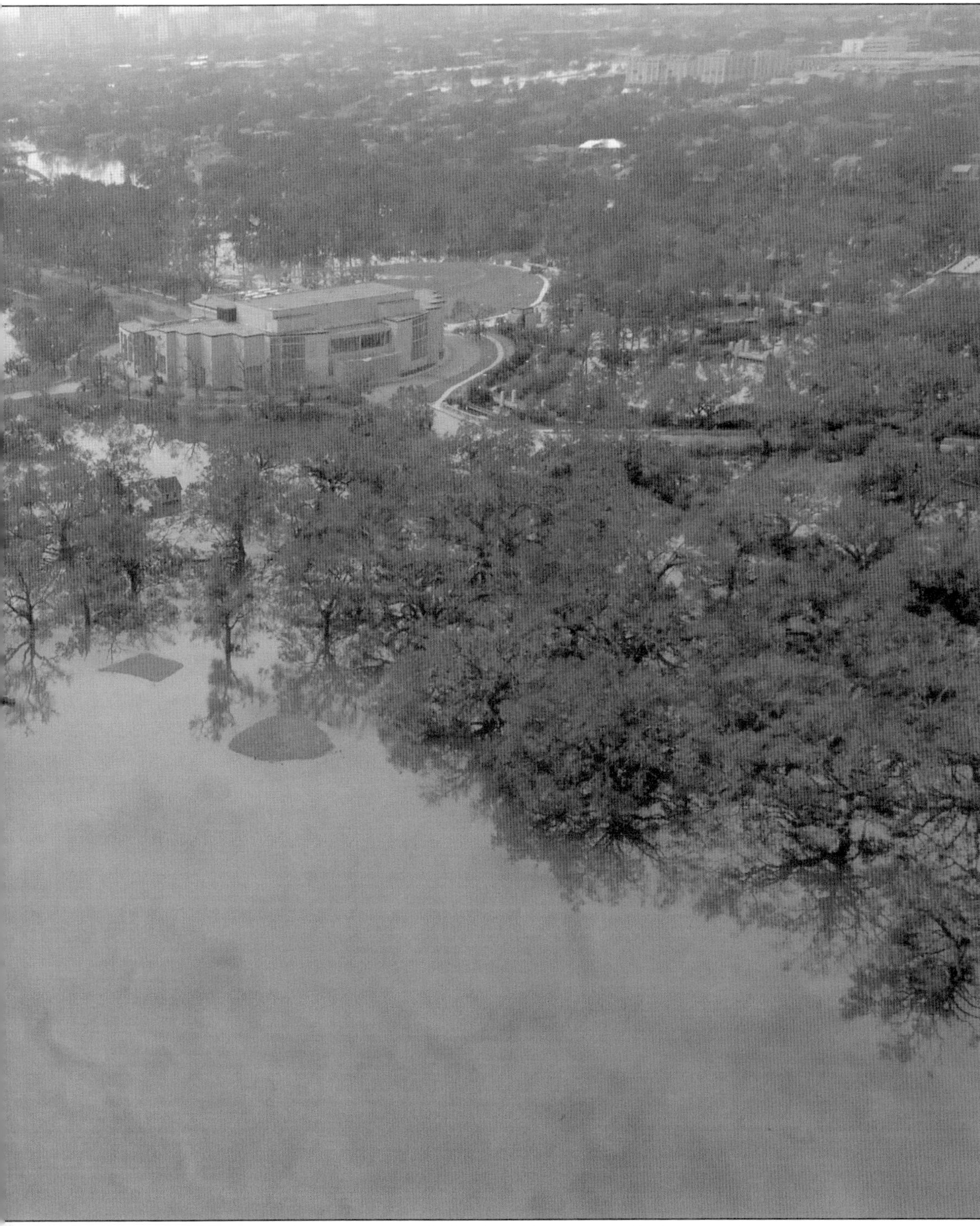

conservatory. Saltwater made its way from Lake Pontchartrain to kill most of the grass, tender vegetation, and many large magnolia trees. Archives were lost, records soaked, and computers ruined in the Administration Building, which sat in four feet of water. (FEMA.)

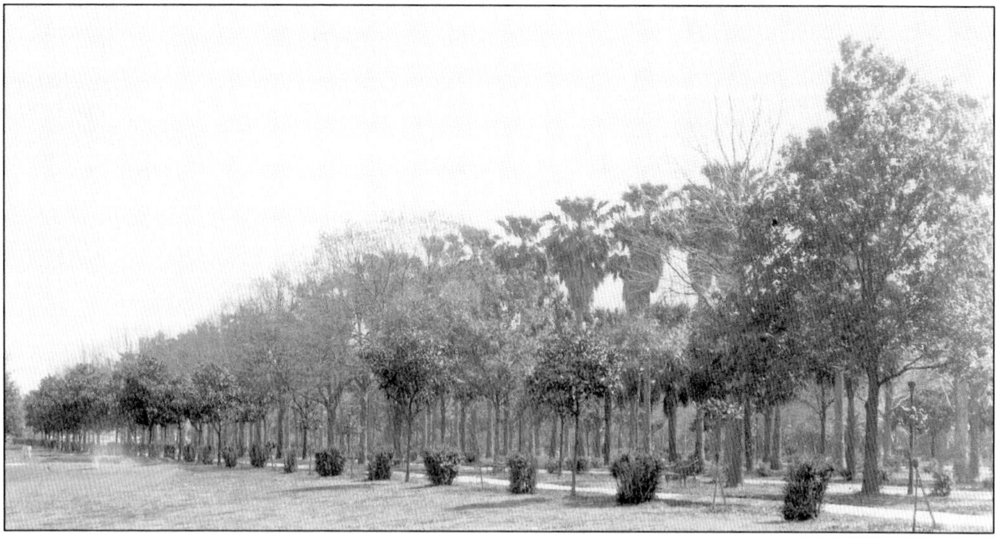

The rebirth of City Park post-Katrina during the early years of the 21st century in some ways parallels the improvements undertaken by the WPA decades before. Above, one can see young plantings along Lelong Avenue during the 1930s. Below, approximately the same view in 2007, the avenue is seen leading to the museum with newly planted trees again. (Above, LDL; below, DCM.)

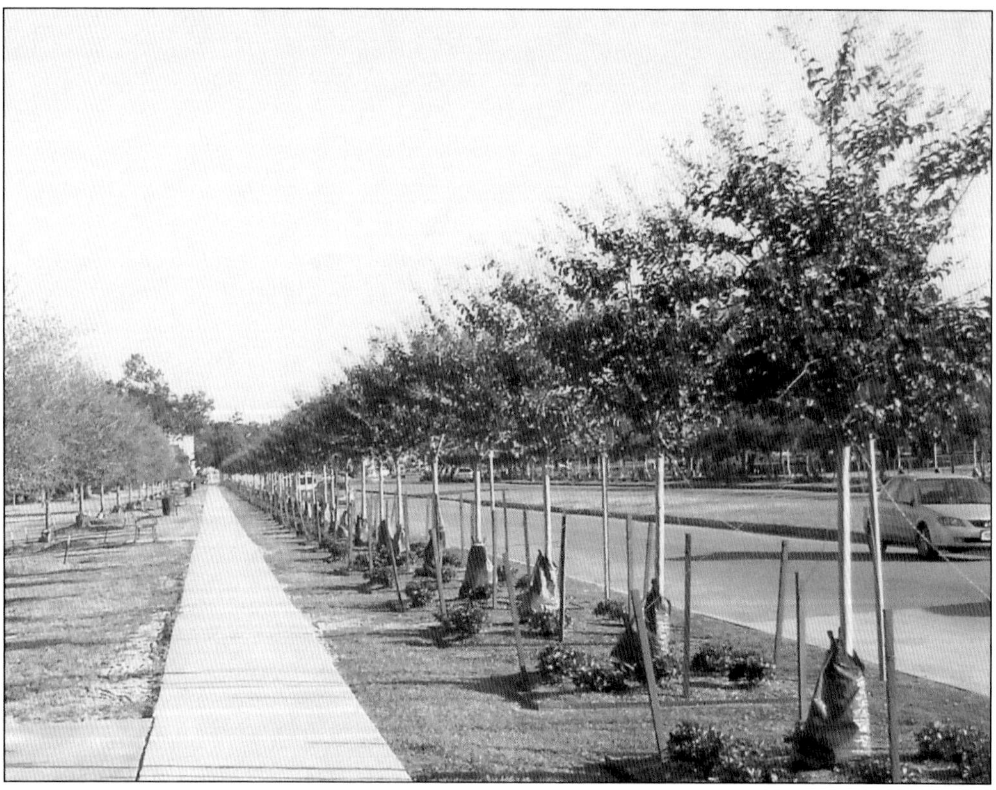

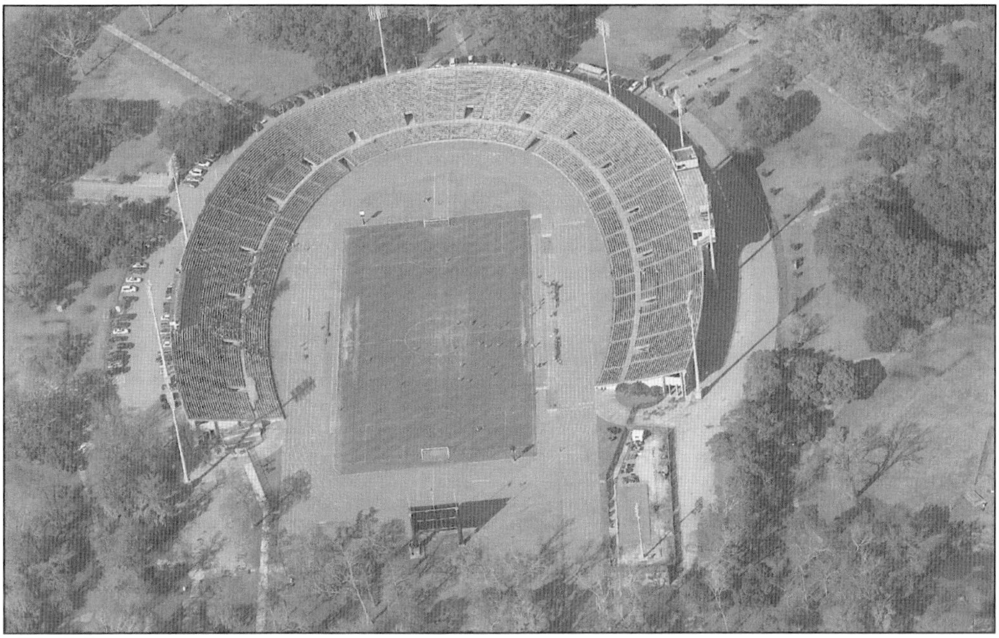

Supplies, vehicles, and pieces of equipment were destroyed, including tractors, bucket trucks, end-loaders, bush hogs, and golf carts. Most of the grass on the three golf courses was dead. Only the crossbars rose above the floodwater on the field of Tad Gormley Stadium, seen here before and after Katrina. The stadium remained structurally sound but required major work to repair the electrical system and the field. In the Couturie Forest, the mature trees in the 62-acre arboretum were downed, and the protective shade-rim, over-story structure was lost, allowing invasive plants to thrive. Walking trails were damaged, as were the homes of wildlife and more than 100 species of migratory and resident birds. (Both, PI.)

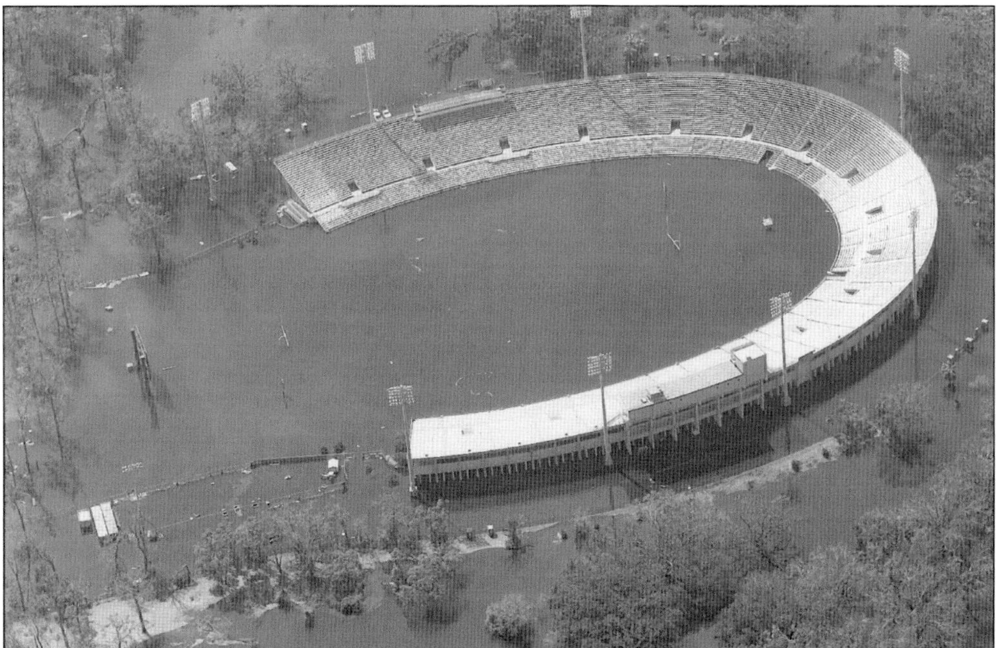

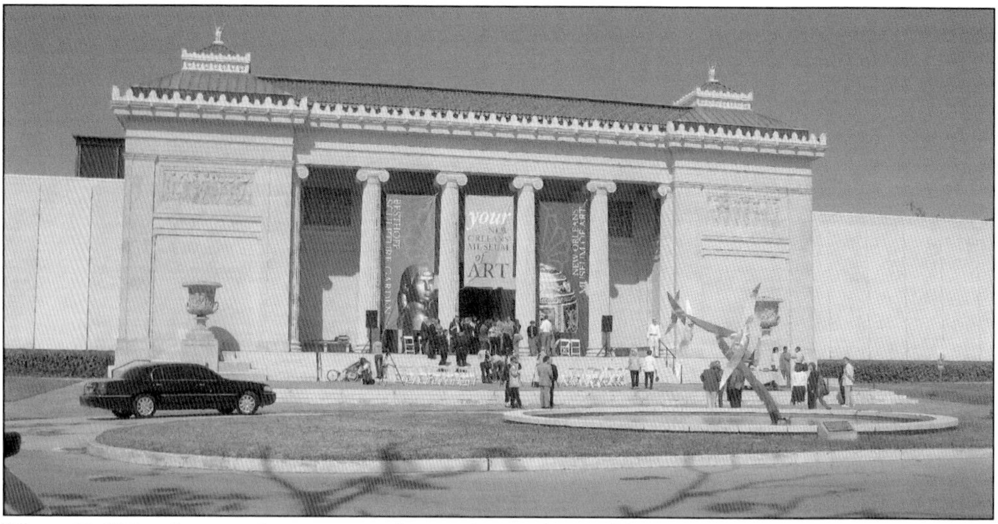

"Over 13,000 volunteers have invested over 66,000 hours (the equivalent of 32 people working full time for one year) to help restore the park. The cash value of their donated hours totals $1.2 million. They have picked up trash, removed tree limbs, painted fences, strung lights, potted plants, dug holes, entered data, you name it—they have done it," said City Park chief development officer John Hopper. Pictured is the reopening of the museum in March 2006. (DCM.)

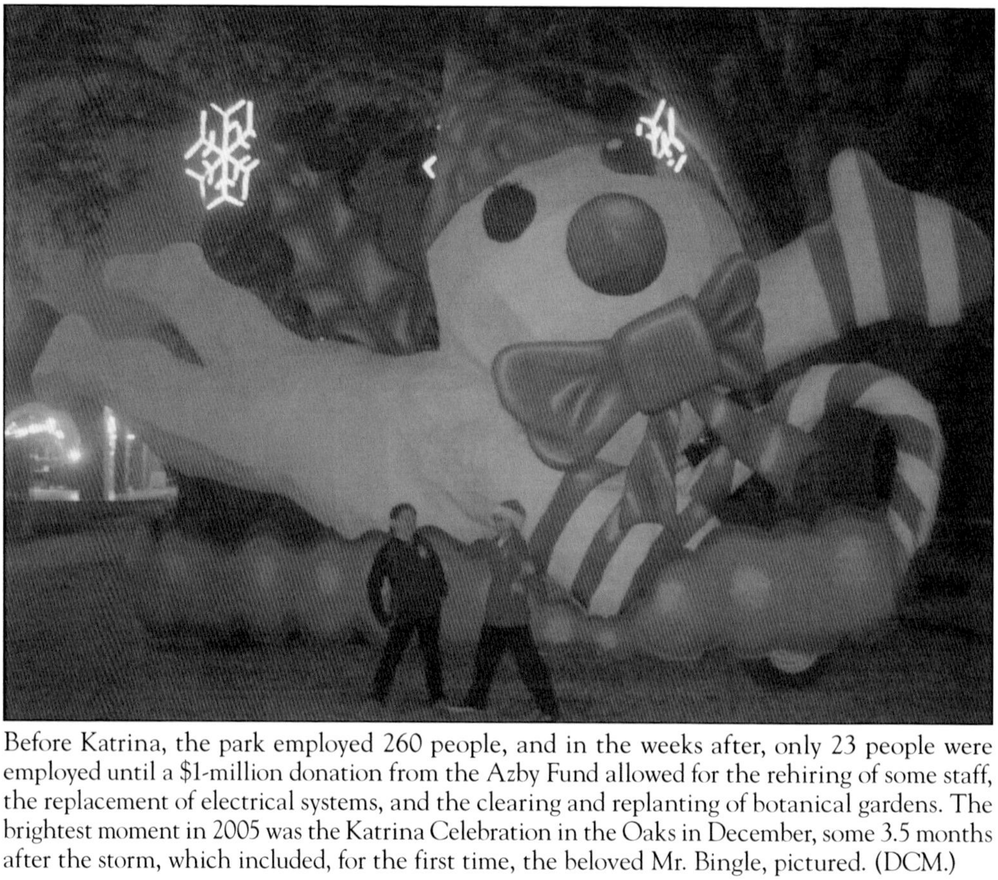

Before Katrina, the park employed 260 people, and in the weeks after, only 23 people were employed until a $1-million donation from the Azby Fund allowed for the rehiring of some staff, the replacement of electrical systems, and the clearing and replanting of botanical gardens. The brightest moment in 2005 was the Katrina Celebration in the Oaks in December, some 3.5 months after the storm, which included, for the first time, the beloved Mr. Bingle, pictured. (DCM.)

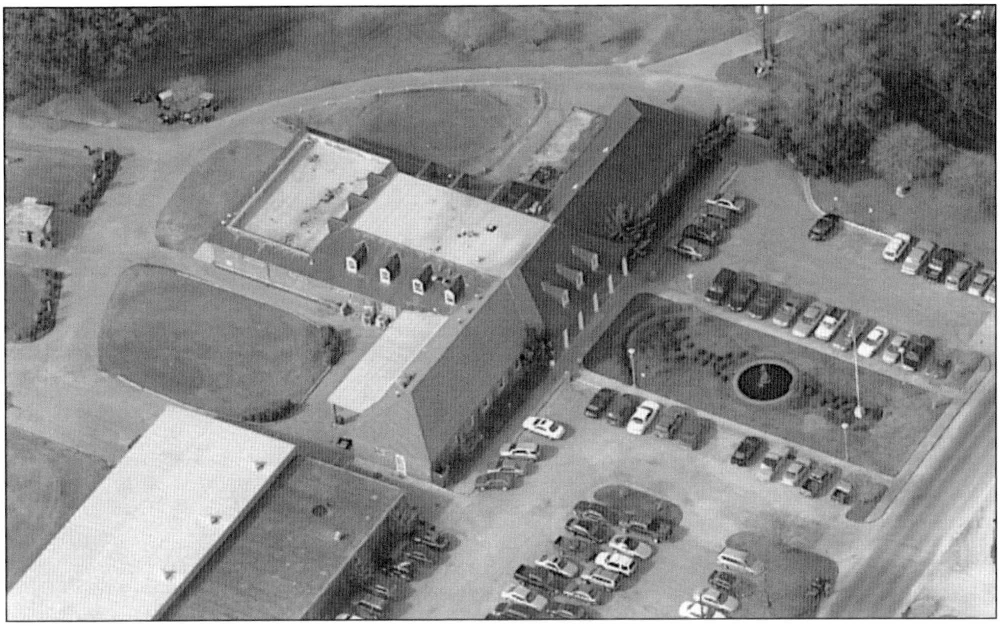

All amusement park rides sustained major damage. The Hyams Fountain was swamped with fallen branches and unwanted vegetation. The golf clubhouse, shown before and after the hurricane, was flooded and later demolished. But in 2005, some tennis courts reopened. In August 2006, *Runner's World* reported that many water fountains and streetlights were still not working, but the park's roads were clear. The New Orleans Botanical Garden reopened to the public, and its facilities were again available for functions beginning on March 4, 2006, a little over six months after Katrina. "Thanks in large part to volunteers and donors from throughout the United States and worldwide," read an article in the *Time-Picayune*. (Both, PI.)

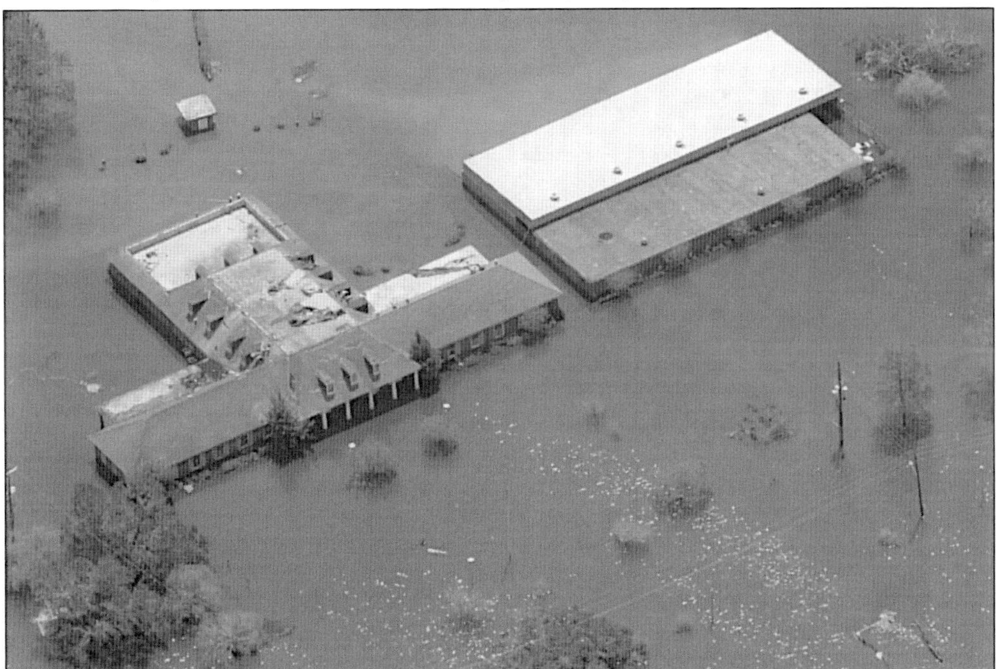

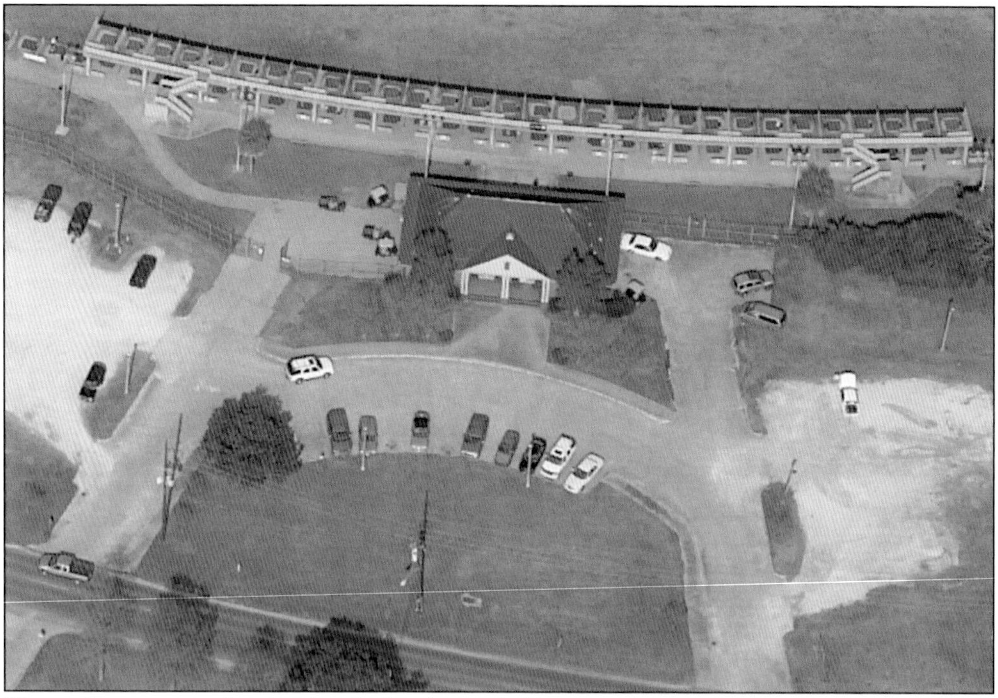

The stadium reopened in 2006 with the playing field renamed Reggie Bush Field after the Saints' football star donated $80,000 for its repair so that high school teams could play there again. The first post-Katrina event was the Louisiana High School Athletic Association (LHSAA) game on September 21, 2006, pitting the Brother Martin Crusaders against the Higgins High Hurricanes. The stadium has been party venue for the 10-kilometer race Crescent City Classic since 2000; the party was even hosted here in the March following Katrina. The year 2006 brought the reopening of the driving range, shown before and after Katrina; Storyland; and Carousel Gardens Amusement Park, which only ran during Celebration in the Oaks that year. (Both, PI.)

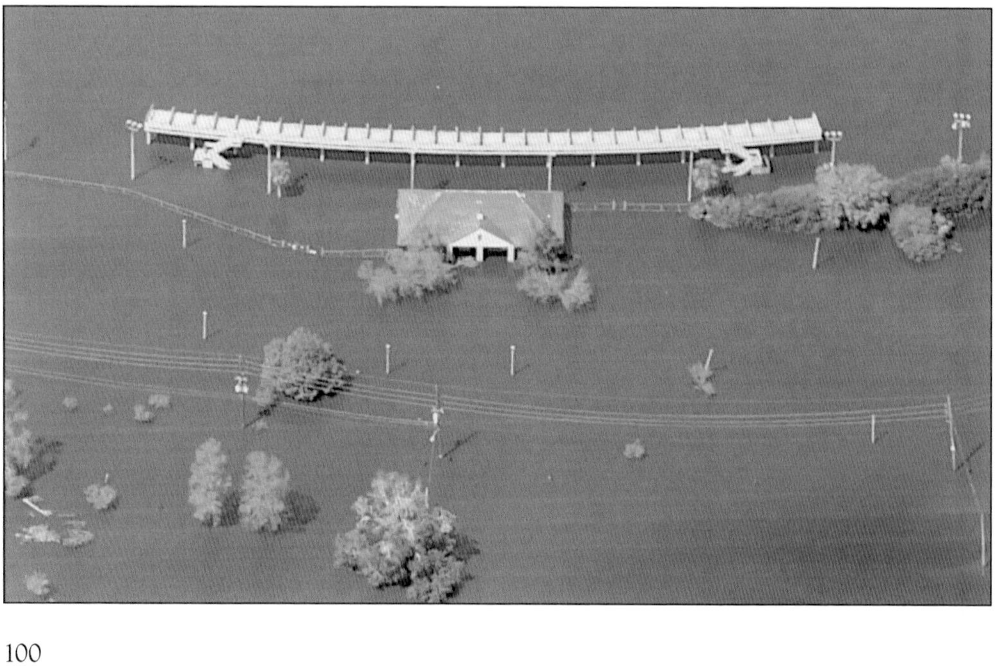

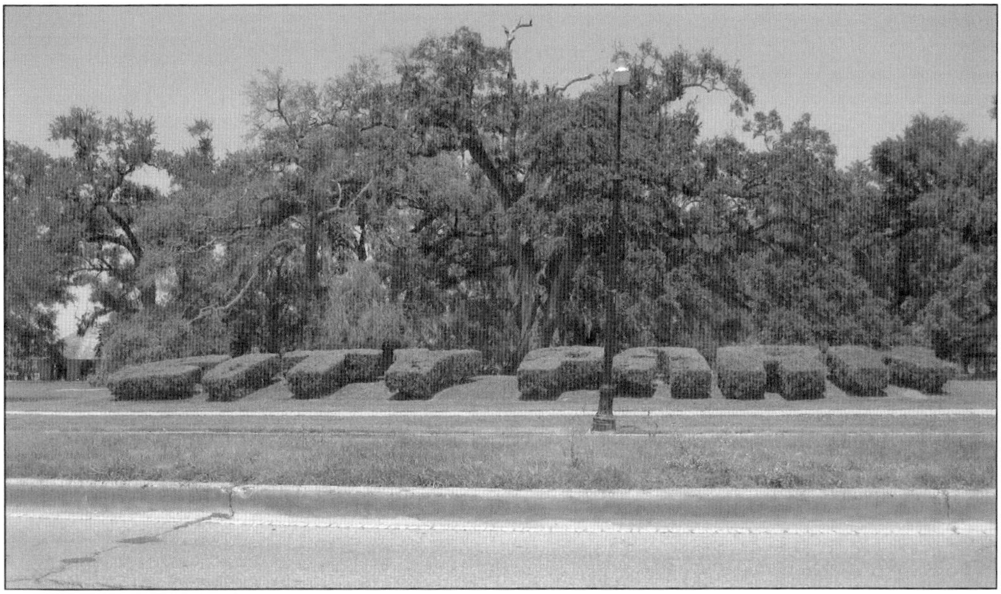

"In many ways City Park is like the little engine that could," said *New Orleans City Business* when reporting the story in 2006 of the inaugural post-Katrina train ride by first graders of Our Lady of Divine Providence School along the 2.5-mile route. Square D–Schneider Electric donated the engine and ADA-accessible coach. Pictured is the topiary along City Park Avenue in 2007. (DCM.)

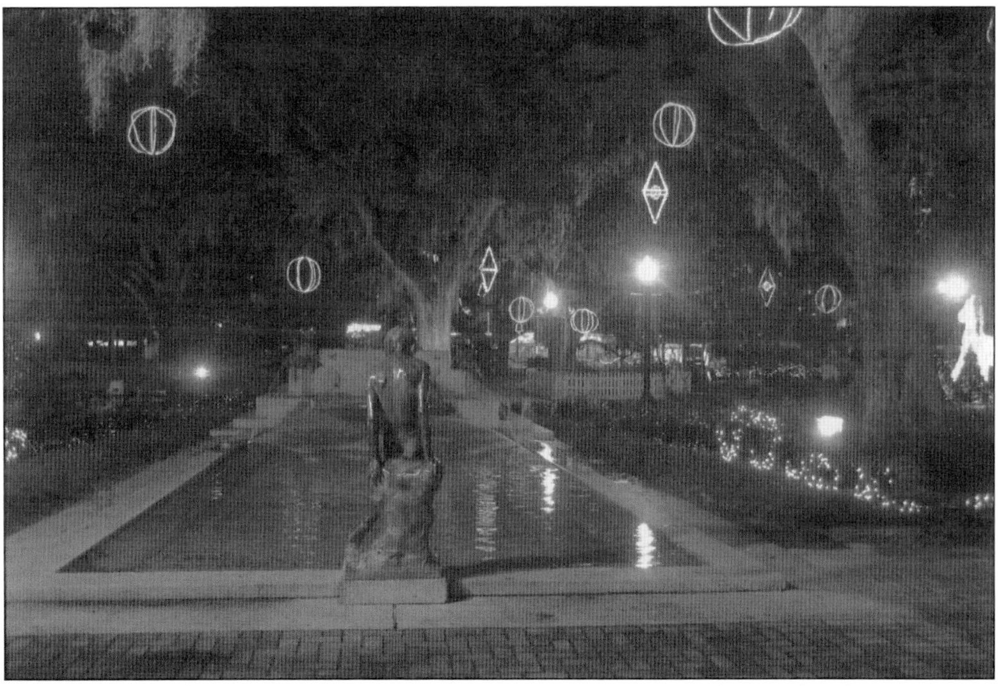

After more than $3 million worth of improvements, including several new rides, the amusement park resumed seasonal operations on Saturday, March 3, 2007, about 18 months after the storm. A post-Katrina marker is located just inside the entrance gates of the Carousel Garden Amusement Park indicating that "floodwaters from Hurricane Katrina on August 29, 2005, reached the bottom of this sign." (DCM.)

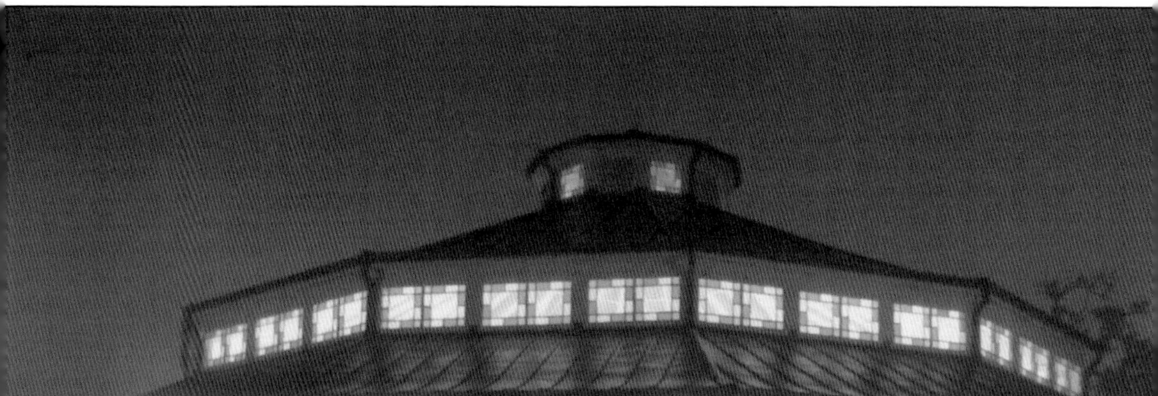

The Schoen Fountain and golf clubhouse were demolished in 2008. In that year, the park continued its $46.8-million recovery. New sidewalks along City Park Avenue and 19 construction and renovation projects, including the restoration of Pan American Stadium, were undertaken. In 2009, public support for the park amounted to approximately 19 percent of the total operating budget. Although the park received support from the city, it did not receive operating funds from the state. The state did, however, supply operating assistance. So, the park was left with the prospect of raising 81 percent of the operating funds through self-generated revenue. The master plan for the park was on track. It had already raised $64 million of the $140 million that was required by the plan, and thus, Friends was awarded a $50,000 grant to restore Couturie Forest. In 2010, the Mercedez Benz Corporation funded landscaping around the new Administration Building. For the December 2010 Celebration in the Oaks (pictured), 70 tons of man-made snow delighted New Orleans children in City Park. (DCM.)

Seven

The People behind the Names

Donors, Benefactors, and Patrons

City Park's first benefactor, the man who gave the property to the city, is memorialized only with a solitary tree, the McDonogh Oak, which was not named for him until 70 years after his gift was given. Born in Baltimore of Scotch-Irish descent in 1779, McDonogh came to New Orleans as a young man and began building his fortune trading molasses, sugar, hides, pig iron, and indigo. He then became a planter and amassed great wealth in cotton and real estate, buying huge tracts of unimproved property. McDonogh was a founding member of the American Colonization Society, which reportedly provided passage for 18,000 slaves to the Liberian Republic. In 1842, McDonogh oversaw the shipping of 80 slaves who were able to "buy" their freedom after work credited to their accounts equaled their market value.

A staunch believer in the value of education, most of McDonogh's assets of approximately $3 million were bequeathed for the building of schools. His will stipulated, "That it be permitted annually to the children of the free schools to plant and water a few flowers around my grave." He was buried in his native Baltimore, but the children of New Orleans honored him for many years by bringing flowers to his memorial in Lafayette Square.

From McDonogh's gift of the land to the funding of $1 million in 2005, along with countless donations from modest citizens, the park would not be the place it is today had not generous New Orleanians opened their hearts and their pocketbooks.

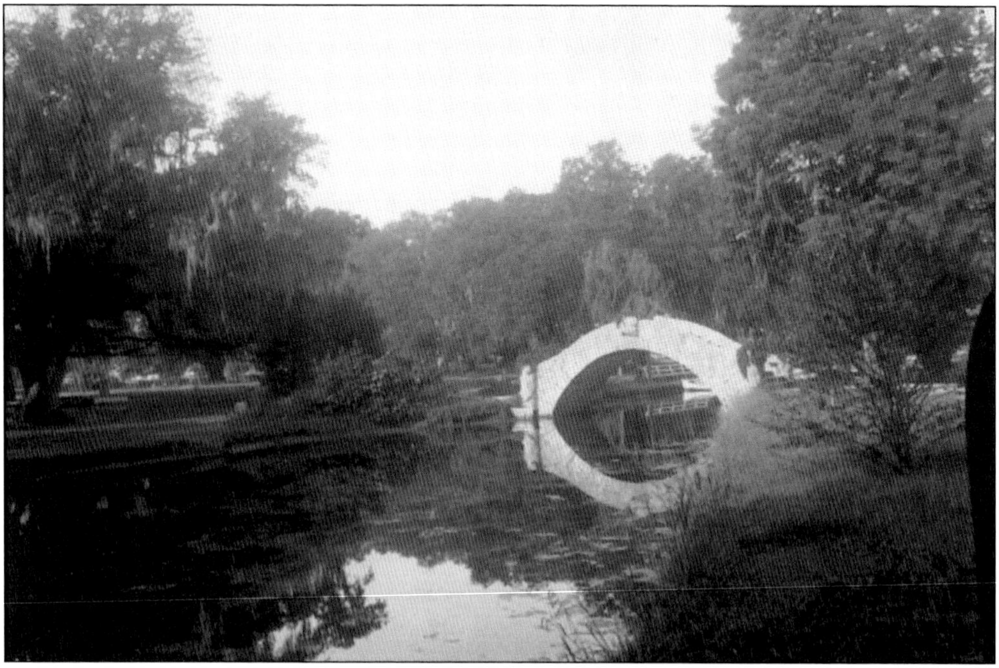

This bridge was built with a donation by Angele Langles. Her memorial in Metairie Cemetery, shown below, is marked only with "Angele Marie Langles—105 LA 39." Angele and her widowed mother, Paulina Costa Langles, were lost at sea in the North Atlantic on July 4, 1898, aboard the French steamship *La Bourgogne*, which had left New York for La Havre, France, two days prior. The ship was broadsided in heavy fog by the ironclad British sailing ship *Clomartyshire*. Both mother and daughter had willed their considerable fortune to one another. Family members contested the wills but begrudgingly and by court order erected the monument. "105 LA 39" is the docket number of the Supreme Court of Louisiana decision on April 23, 1900, which mandated that the monument be built with funds from the estate. (Both, LDL.)

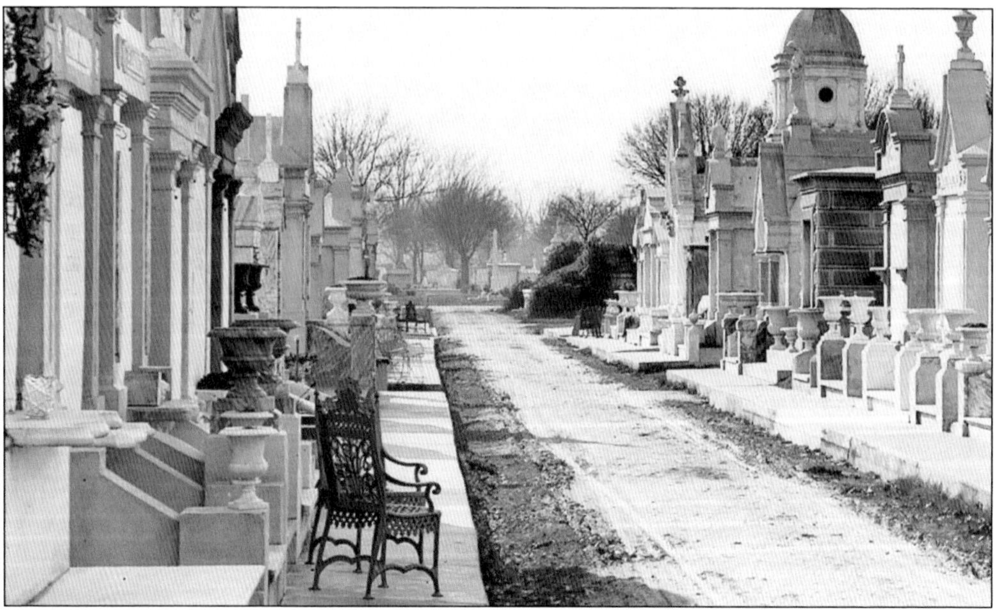

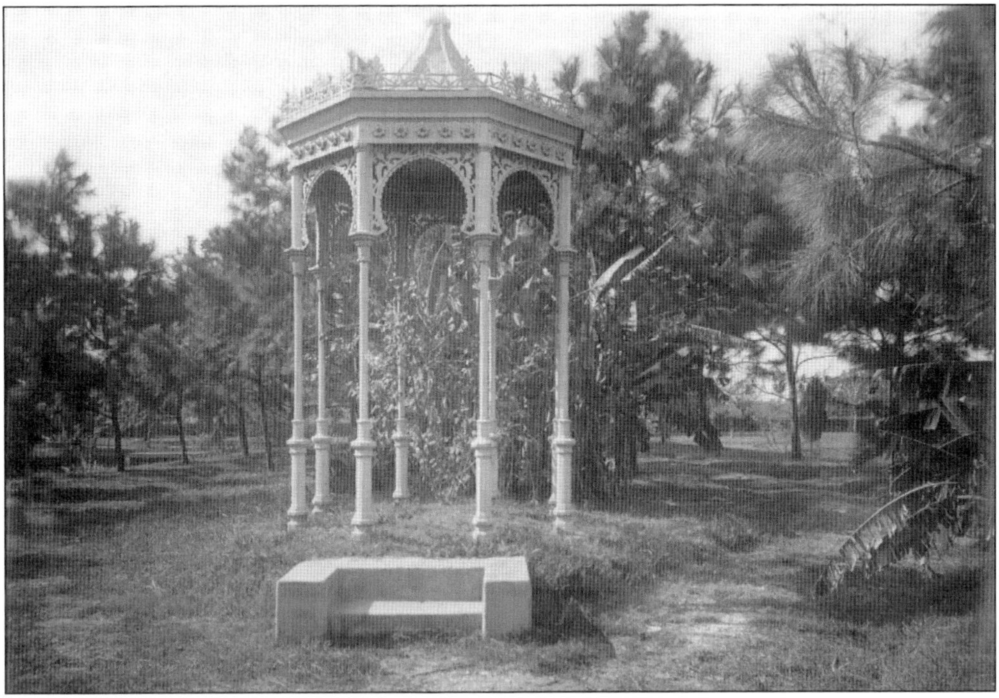

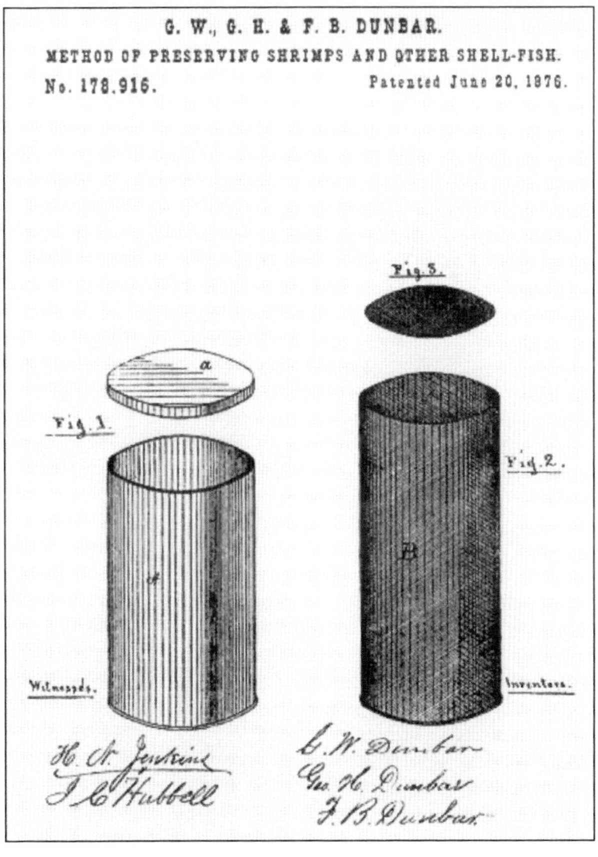

In 1904, Francis B. Dunbar donated a pavilion, shown above, that was located along Bayou Metairie. Restored in the 1980s, it now serves as the storyteller gazebo in Storyland. In 1876, George W. Dunbar with his sons Francis and George invented a new process for preserving shrimp and other shellfish. They became the largest packers south of Baltimore with US sales and foreign markets in France, England, Germany, and Mexico. The company won the Silver Medal of Merit at the Paris Exposition of 1878, an award from the International Fisheries Exhibition in London in 1883, and was recognized in the New Orleans World's Fairs of 1884–1886. G.W. Dunbar's Sons was established in 1865 at No. 3 Tchoupitoulas along with two canneries "in the suburbs." The company packed gulf shrimp and oysters, turtle, ready-to-eat Barritaria shrimp, fruit syrup, figs, and other semitropical fruits distilled in French cordials. (Both, NOPL.)

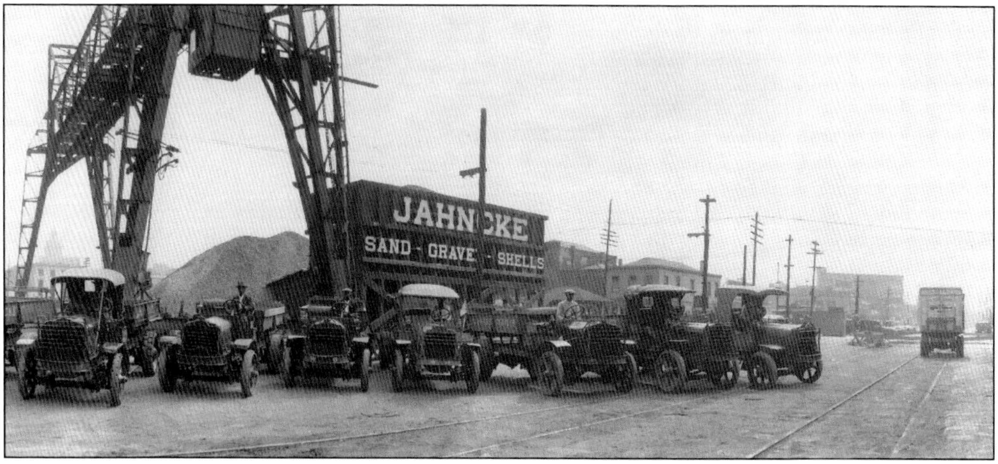

The Jahncke name is prominent in City Park and can be found in the following locations: on the gift shop, built in 1993 by Jahncke Architects, Inc.; on the fountain across from the Casino Building, donated in 1961 in memory of Walter F. Jahncke; on the plaque in the rose garden, honoring architect Douglass V. Freret by his wife, Ruth Jahncke Freret, in 1982; and on the fountain, dedicated in 1912 to Fritz Jahncke by his sons. Jahncke advocated developing the New Basin Canal, commonly called "Jahncke's Ditch," where he built Jahncke Service, Inc. The company hauled Lake Pontchartrain sand and shells to the city at 81 Howard Avenue, shown in 1924; note the Hibernia Bank Building in the distant left. Along with shipping and brick-making businesses on the Tchefuncte River, Jahncke was an original board member of Jax Brewery, an advocate for the establishment of the Sewerage and Water Board, and member of the Southern Yacht Club. His sand and shells built many streets and sidewalks in New Orleans. (Both, LDL.)

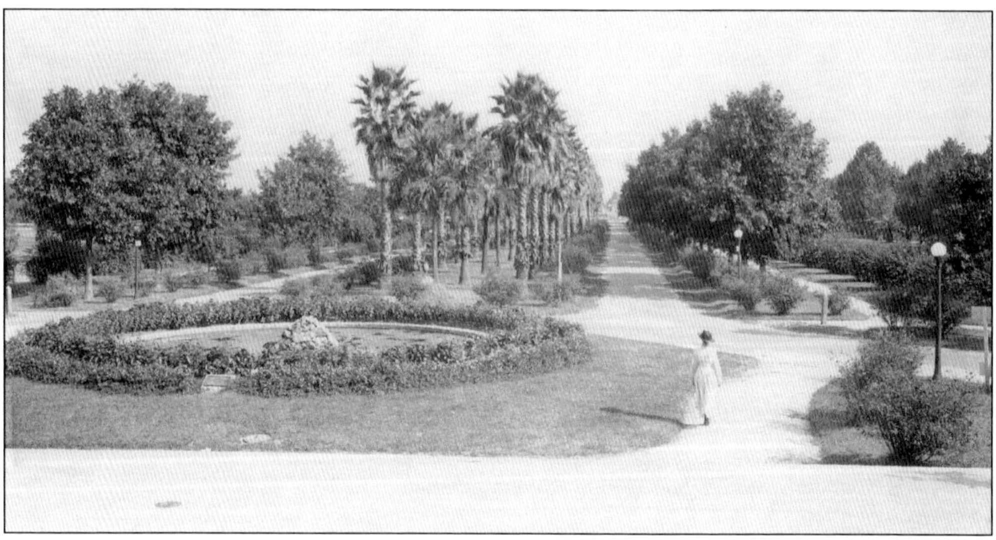

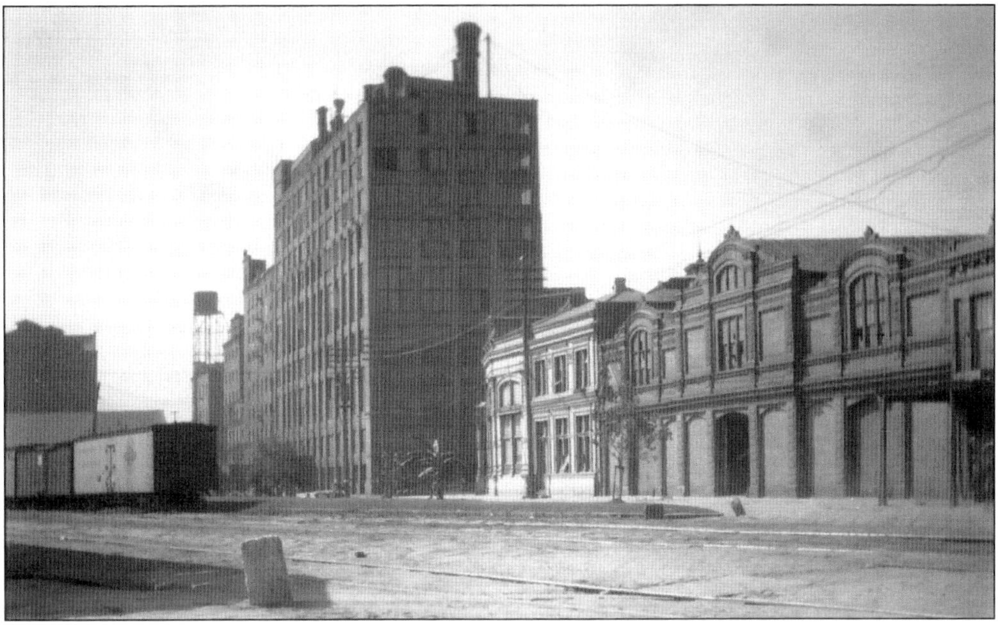

"Presented to the people of New Orleans by Isaac Delgado MCMX," reads the lintel over the main entrance to NOMA. Delgado's only stipulations were that the museum be under the control of a group of three or four members from the City Park Board and of an equal number from the art association, that a room be set aside for his own collections, and that the museum be "a temple of art for rich and poor alike." A native of Jamaica, Delgado made his fortune in sugar, acquiring a wealth of land and businesses, including Delgado and Company on Bienville Street, seen here on the right in 1920, located at the river and near the present-day aquarium. He was well known as a benefactor of the arts, medicine, and education; the Delgado School is pictured below. When the museum opened on December 16, 1911, Delgado could not attend the dedication because he was aged and ill. Isaac Delgado died the following month on January 4, 1912. (Above, NOPL; below, LDL.)

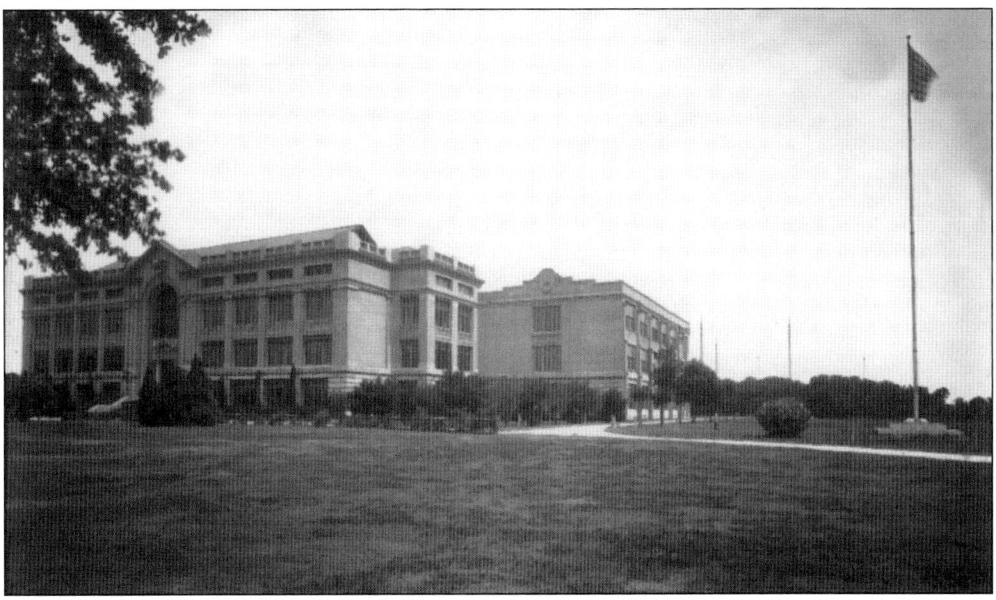

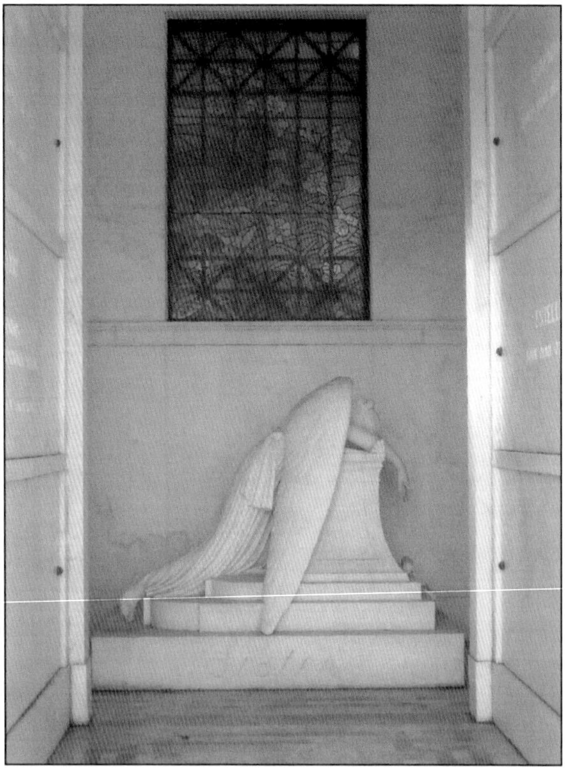

Sarah Lavinia Todd Hyams died in New York in September 1914 while returning from a European tour to collect artworks for her collection. She bequeathed her jewels, valued at $30,000, or $500,000 today, for the building of identical fountains and wading pools in Audubon and City Parks (see page 61) and her art collection to the Delgado Museum. Her name is also known for the beautiful Hyam tomb in Metairie Cemetery, which includes the "Angel of Grace." (DCM.)

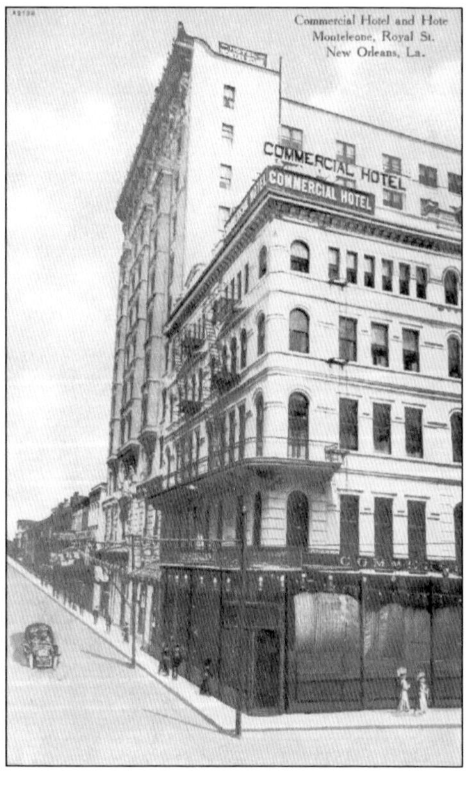

The Monteleone Gate (see page 58) was donated by Antonio Monteleone, park commissioner in 1913, who had owned a shoe factory in Sicily before coming to New Orleans to open a shoe shop in the French Quarter. By 1888, he employed 100 workers to produce 500 pairs of shoes per week. In 1886, he purchased the 64-room Hotel Victor, which became the Hotel Monteleone, pictured here in 1910. (LDL.)

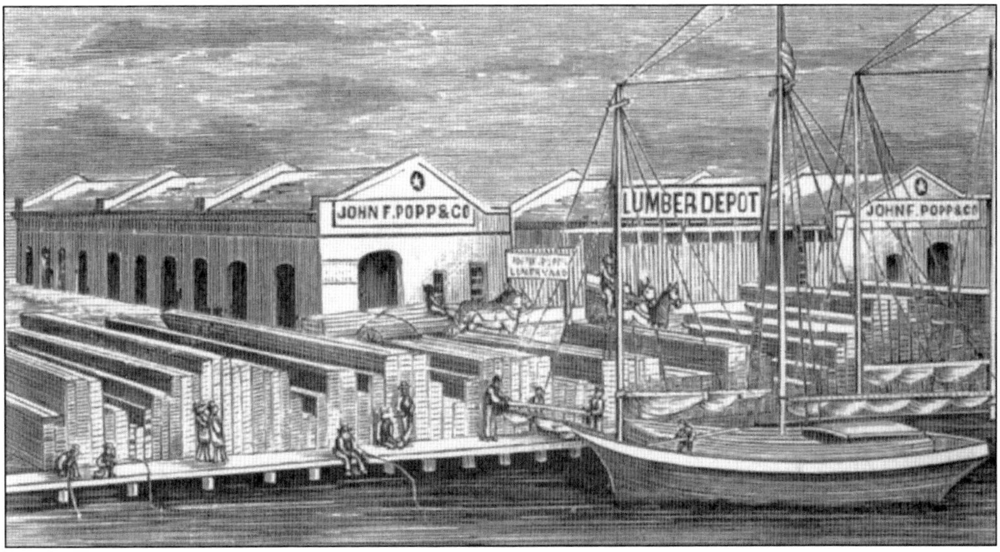

The Popp name is memorialized twice in the park, on the bandstand (see page 59) and on the fountain (see page 70), which would not exist if not for the generosity of Mr. and Mrs. John F. Popp. The Popps were present at the dedication of bandstand; John died shortly afterward. Pictured is the John F. Popp and Company lumber dealership and manufacturers depot on the New Basin Canal in an 1888 engraving. (LDL.)

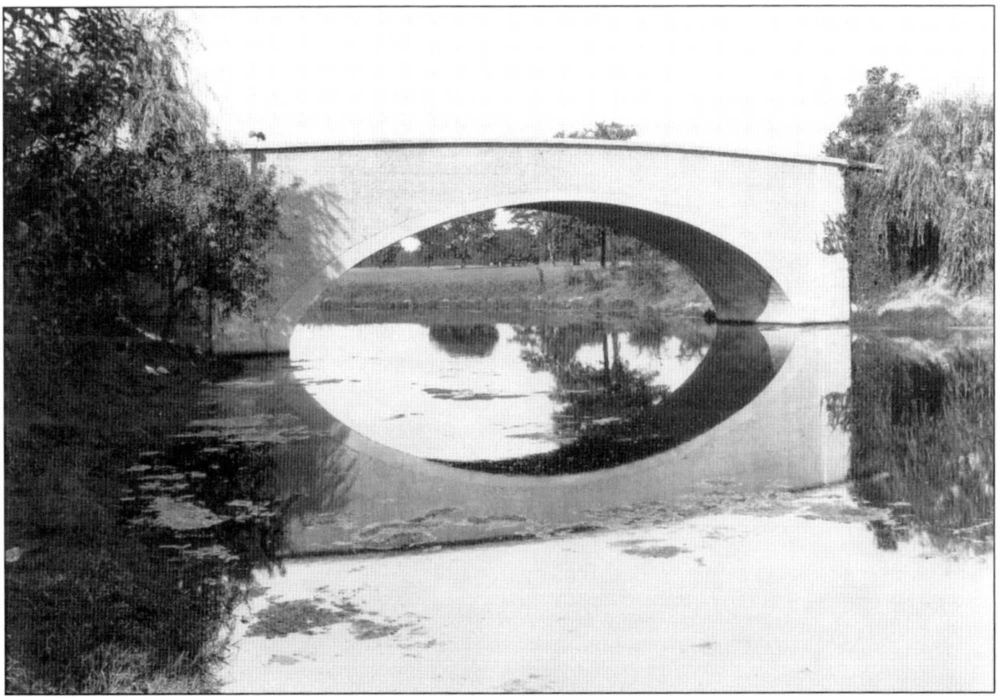

"Dedicated to Victor Anseman for his great devotion to the park 1842–1904," states the 1928 plaque on the Anseman Bridge (see page 48), which was replaced by the WPA with this structure. Anseman Avenue (see pages 50 and 72) was also named in honor of the man who, as a child living on rural Metairie Road, loved growing different types of plants so much that he became a professional florist. (LDL.)

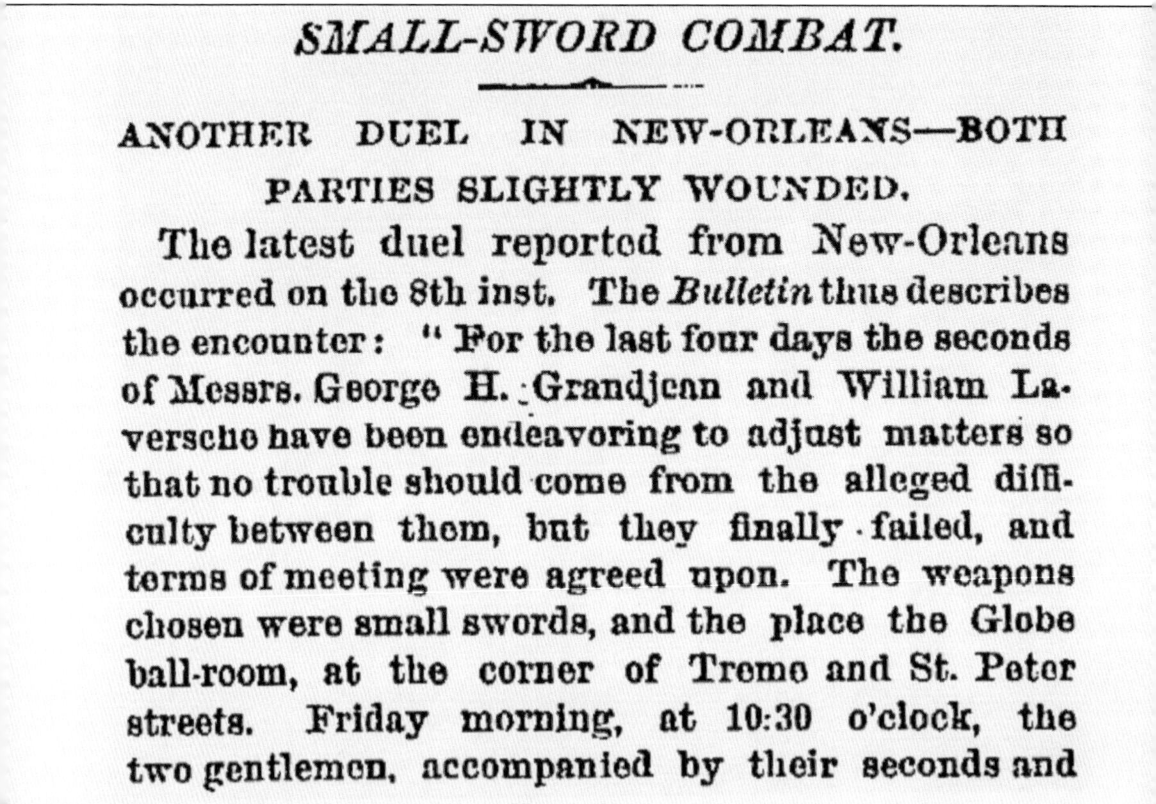

SMALL-SWORD COMBAT.

ANOTHER DUEL IN NEW-ORLEANS—BOTH PARTIES SLIGHTLY WOUNDED.

The latest duel reported from New-Orleans occurred on the 8th inst. The *Bulletin* thus describes the encounter: "For the last four days the seconds of Messrs. George H. Grandjean and William Laversche have been endeavoring to adjust matters so that no trouble should come from the alleged difficulty between them, but they finally failed, and terms of meeting were agreed upon. The weapons chosen were small swords, and the place the Globe ball-room, at the corner of Treme and St. Peter streets. Friday morning, at 10:30 o'clock, the two gentlemen, accompanied by their seconds and

The *New York Times* report of May 17, 1874 (above), continued as follows: "Surgeons met and after the usual preliminaries both took their positions. As they put themselves *en garde* they were calm and collected . . . They got to work . . . and rattle of the foils made the scene dramatic in the extreme. Mr. Laversche was wounded in the stomach and Mr. Grandjean in the shoulder . . . A parley was held, and the friends of both parties being satisfied, the wounded men left their posts . . . The cause of the difficulty was a dispute a few nights ago in a club room about some private matter . . . Both gentlemen are doing well today, and their hurts will only inconvenience them for a short time." Grandjean was about 18 years old at that time, but 64 years later, a plaque was placed on a bridge (see page 50) in City Park reading, "Memorial to George H. Grandjean C.E. [Civil Engineer] Park Commissioner 1892–1900 Designer of original Lagoons." Grandjean also served as United States deputy land surveyor. (*New York Times*.)

In 1938, Francis Thomas "Tad" Gormley became the athletic director of City Park after a distinguished career beginning in 1908, which was when he worked with athletes at the Young Men's Gymnastic Club. From 1921 until 1923, he served as the head men's basketball coach at Louisiana State University, posting a 25-11 record. He was a trainer at Tulane and Loyola, a coach for the 1932 US Olympic Track Team, an official in the New Orleans Prep School Athletic League, and a football and basketball referee. In 1962, Gormley was inducted into the National Athletic Trainers Association Hall of Fame and into the Louisiana Association in 1990. Upon his death in 1965, the stadium was named for him. He was also the man who originated what would become the annual New Orleans Turkey Day Race. Tad Gormely is pictured here in 1923. (Right, LOC; above, DCM.)

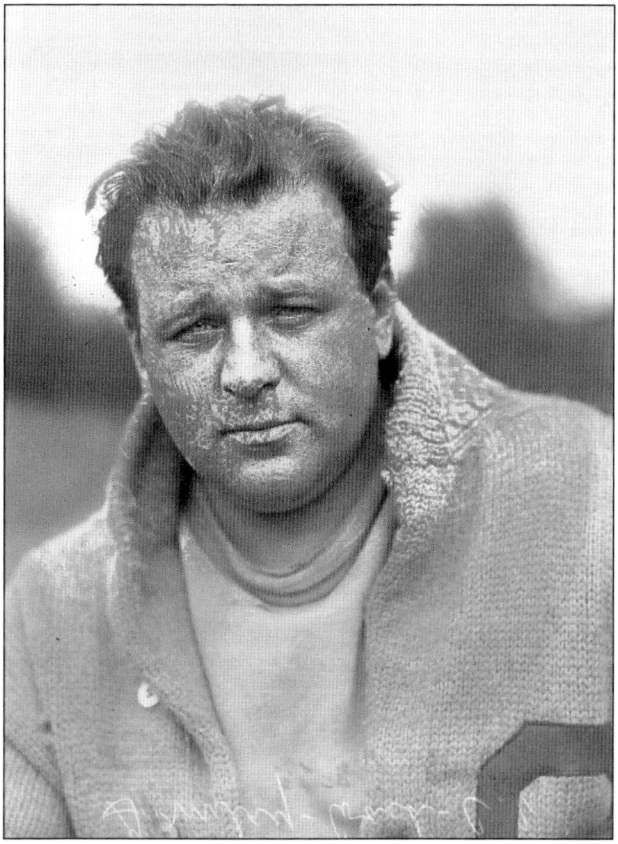

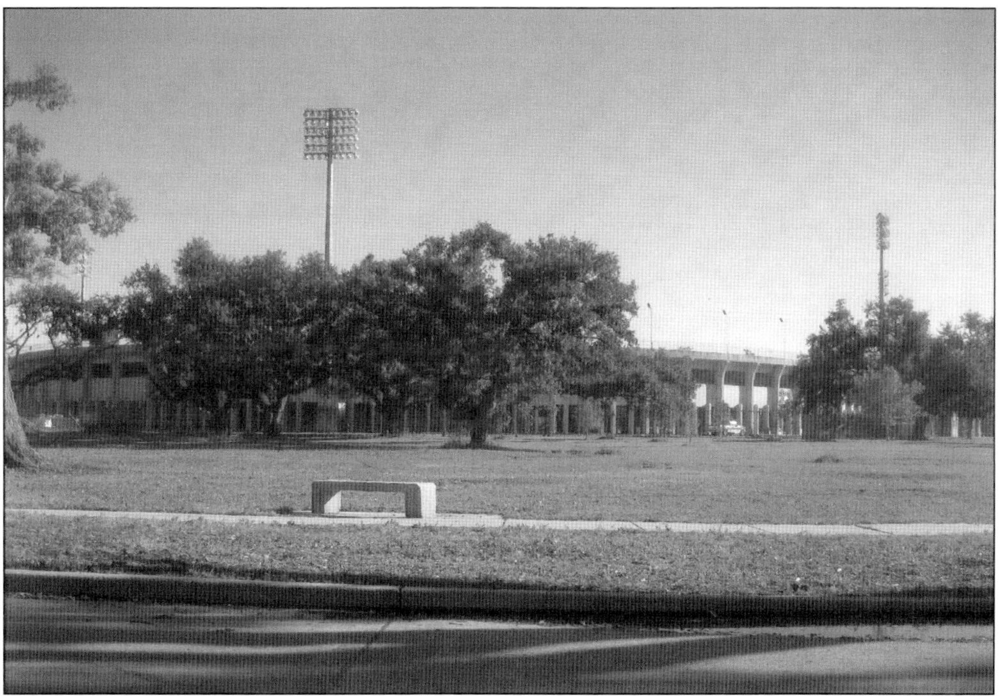

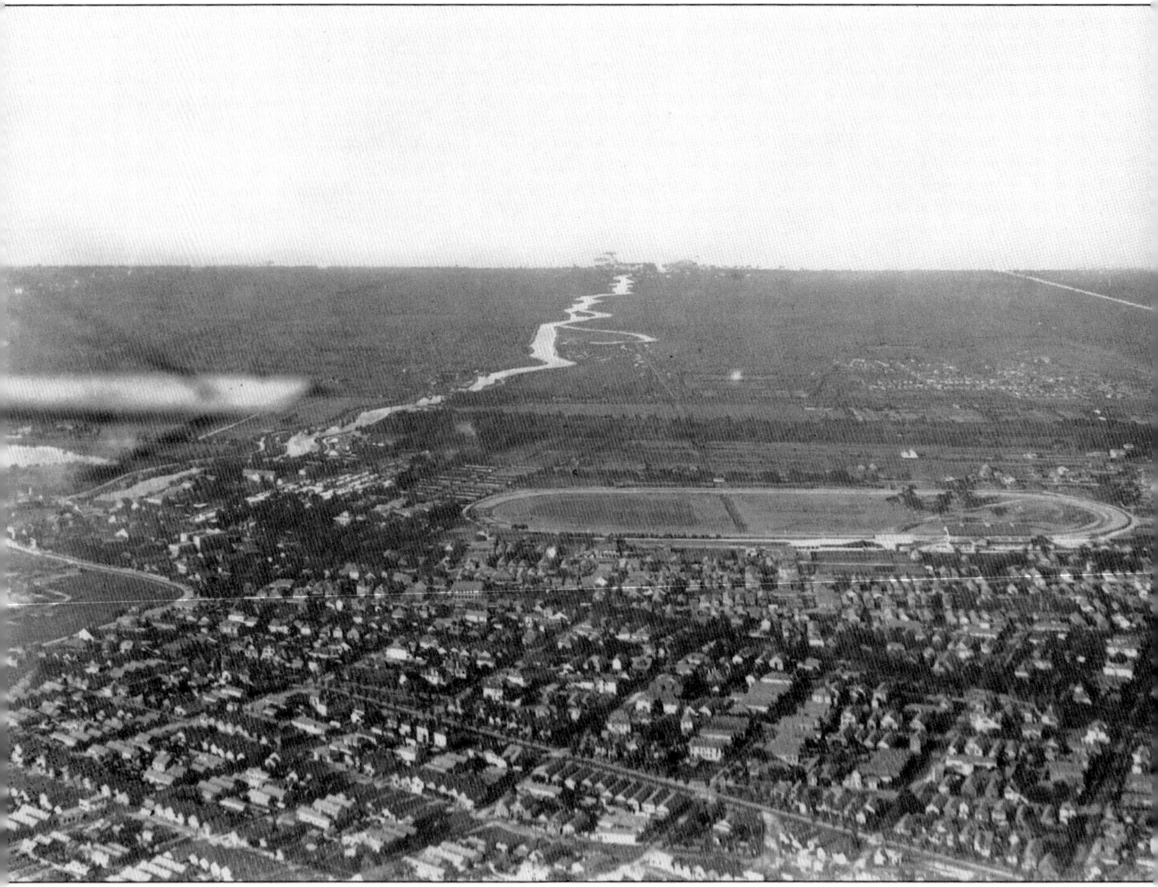

A marker north of Harrison Avenue in the center of the park recognizes a 1938 bequest of $43,231.88 by Rene Couturie, who was an importer of wine, liquor, and other luxury goods, as well as director of Acme Homestead Association and an active member of Elks. He was a colonel in the Washington Artillery in 1893 and a park board member. He was married to Louise Braughn, the 1887 Queen of Rex, who died in 1896. The widower later became involved with Lilian Lorraine. In 1915, Lilian's mother called for Rene's arrest and sued him for, among other things, promising then refusing to wed her daughter after giving her gifts, including jewelry his wife had worn while Queen of Carnival. The sensational story ran in the *Times-Picayune*, which called him a "prominent New Orleans society man," as Couturie contested and finally settled the case. The 33-acre Couturie Forest was designated as a community arboretum in 1939 when 6,000 trees were planted. Pictured is a 1941 aerial view with the forest in the distance. (LDL.)

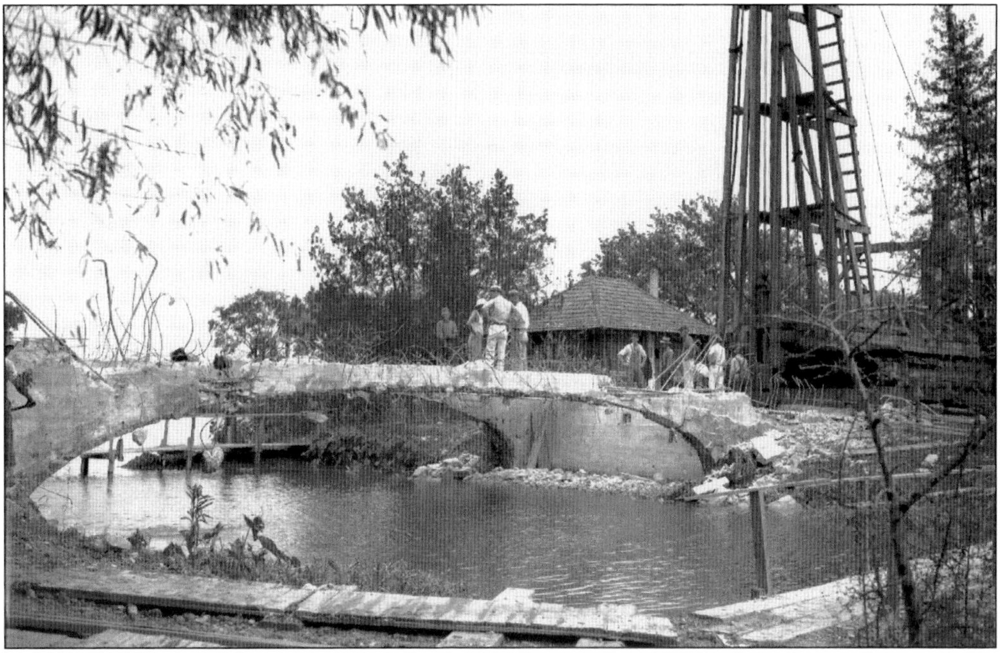

William Harding McFadden (see pages 57 and 58) donated this stone bridge that leads from his home to the traffic circle near the museum, which is seen being dismantled and replaced by WPA workers in 1938 (see page 84). He also designed and donated the Arts and Crafts–style Girl Scout Cabin during the 1920s. It is located behind the museum, near the Grandjean Bridge. (NOPL.)

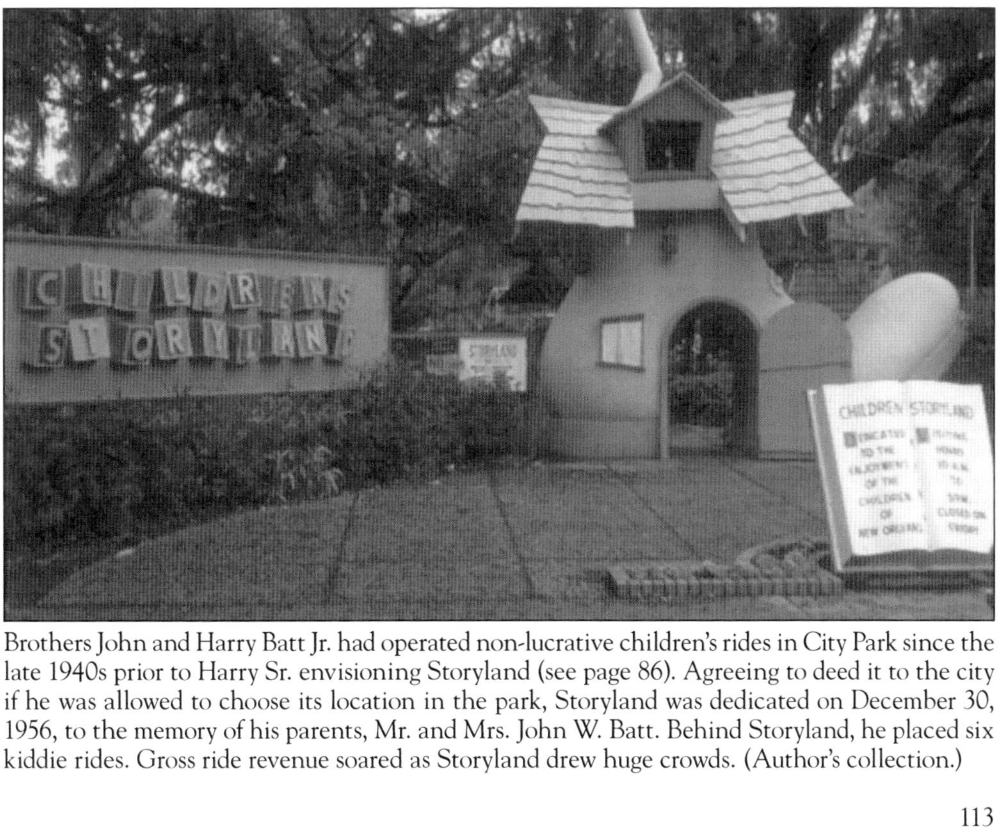

Brothers John and Harry Batt Jr. had operated non-lucrative children's rides in City Park since the late 1940s prior to Harry Sr. envisioning Storyland (see page 86). Agreeing to deed it to the city if he was allowed to choose its location in the park, Storyland was dedicated on December 30, 1956, to the memory of his parents, Mr. and Mrs. John W. Batt. Behind Storyland, he placed six kiddie rides. Gross ride revenue soared as Storyland drew huge crowds. (Author's collection.)

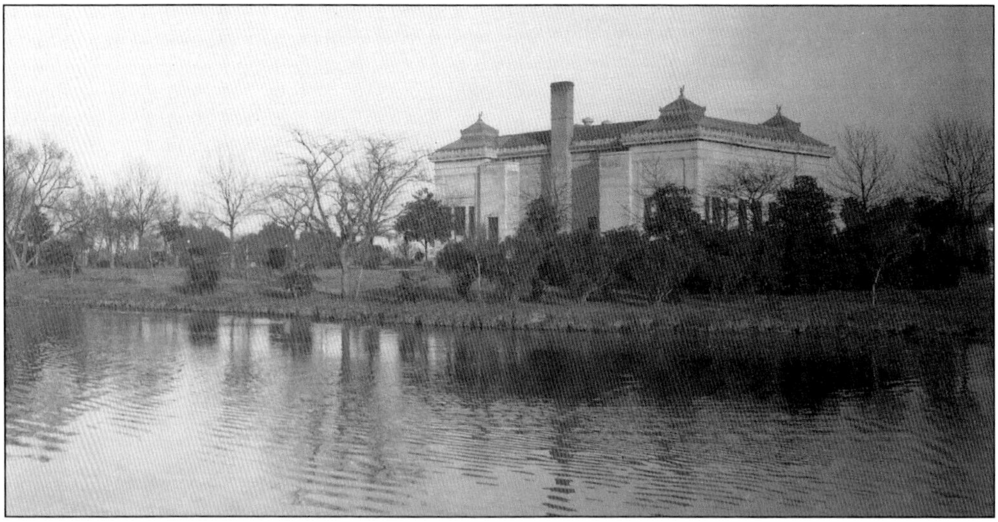

One Collins C. Diboll Circle is the address of NOMA. The street is named for the New Orleans–born architect who designed Loyola University buildings, St. Henry's Church, Our Lady of Lourdes Church, Academy of the Sacred Heart, Holy Ghost Catholic School, and St. Joseph's Academy, among other New Orleans landmarks. He restored St. John's Church and St. Louis Cathedral. Collins Cerre Diboll (1868–1936) was a member of the Vieux Carre Commission Advisory Board and partner in the firm of Diboll, Owen, and Goldstein. The Collins C. Diboll Foundation has contributed millions of dollars to community projects in Southern states. The road circling the museum can barely be seen in the 1920s view, shown above, but is apparent in the 1954 photograph of museum plans. (Both, LDL.)

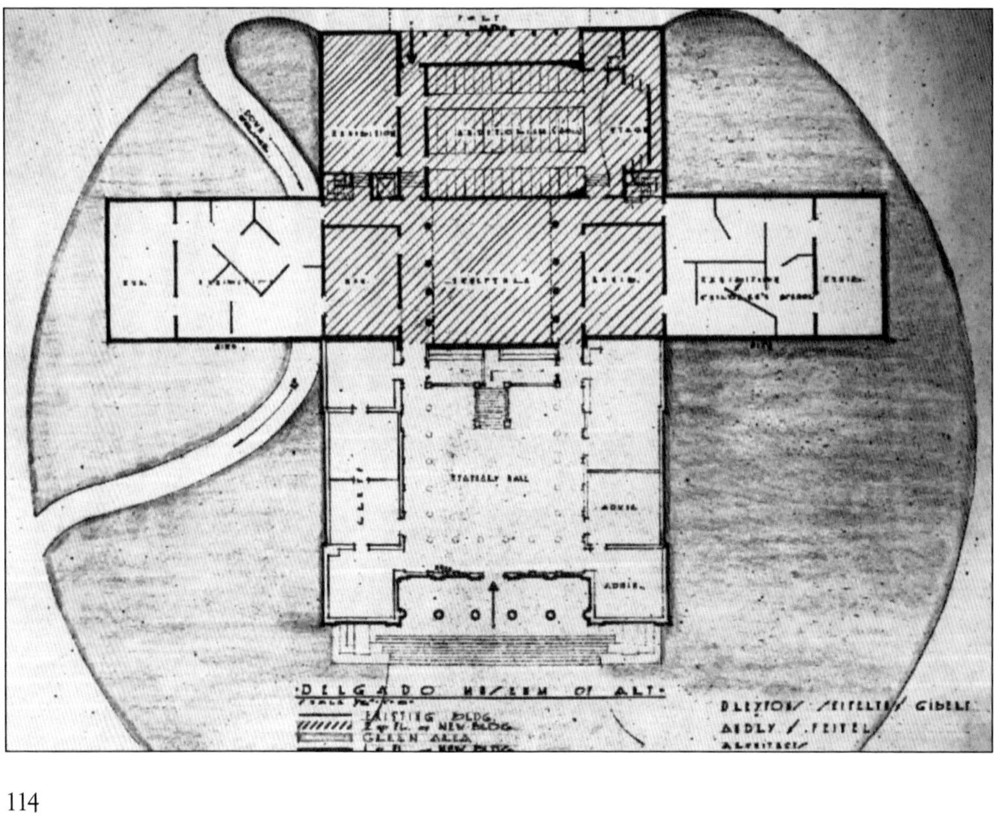

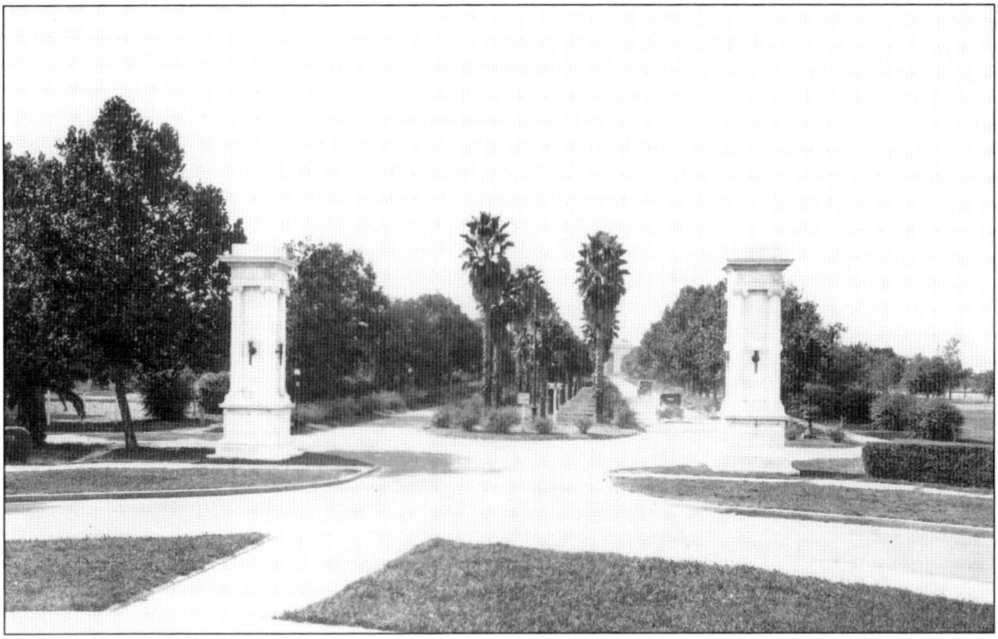

Lelong Avenue, pictured here in the 1920s, is named for French-born park commissioner and friend of Delgado, Pierre Antonin Lelong. He was a charter member of Sugar Exchange, owner of A.A. Lelong and Brothers, secretary of Planters Sugar Refining Company, and director of the Fisk and Free Library, which became the New Orleans Public Library. As chairman of the museum building committee, he selected the site and supervised its construction. (LDL.)

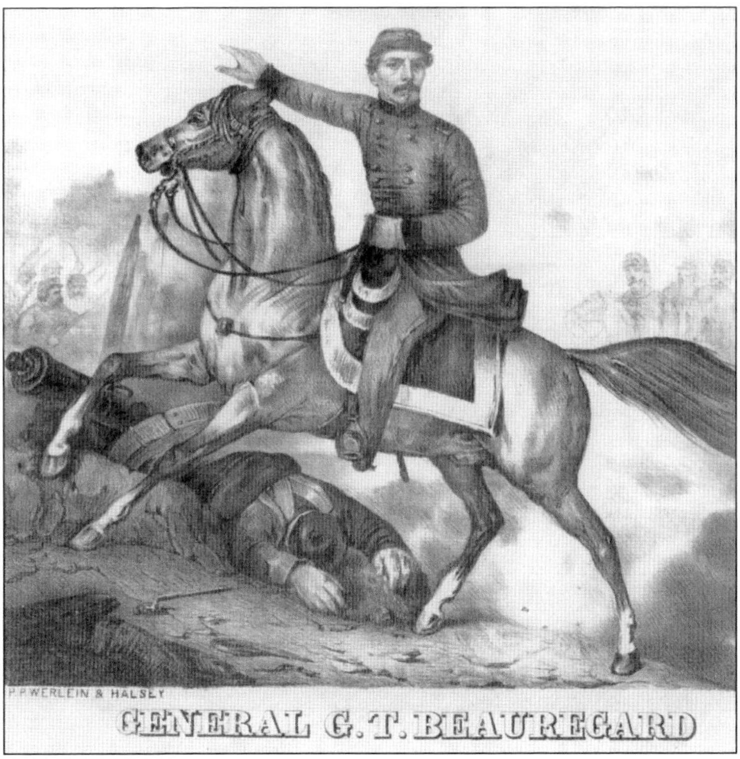

Pierre Gustave Toutant Beauregard (1818–1893), who is memorialized with the statue at the Esplanade Avenue entrance (see page 64), was a Louisiana-born politician, inventor, writer, civil servant, and general of the Confederate Army. After the Civil War, he promoted the Louisiana Lottery and advocated civil and voting rights for the recently freed slaves. Pictured is the sheet-music cover for "Beauregard Quickstep," issued by Philip Werlein at his Canal Street store. (LDL.)

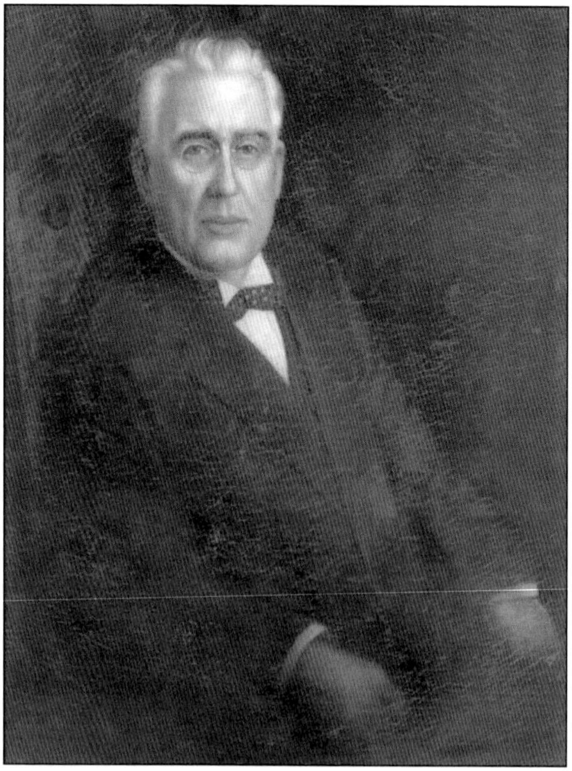

In 1924, William Ratcliff Irby donated $60,000 to build the swimming pool (see page 82) and bathhouse, which was named for him. As the owner of W.R. Irby Tobacco Company, Ltd., he employed 150 workers at his Gravier Street factory and produced La Flur de Irby, Climax, and Cotton Exchange cigar brands and sold cigar lamps, cigarettes, cutters, playing cards, and more. Irby's philanthropic endeavors included willing the Lower Pontalba Buildings, which he had bought them from Pontalba heirs in 1921 for $68,000, to the Louisiana State Museum and giving the French Opera House to Tulane University, which owned it when it was destroyed by fire in 1919. Below on the left in a white suit is Marcel Montreuil, park commissioner from 1925 to 1950 and general manager from 1934 to 1950. The bridge at De Saix Avenue was dedicated to him in 1949, as was the Camellia Garden (now the Sculpture Garden) in 1952. (Both, LDL.)

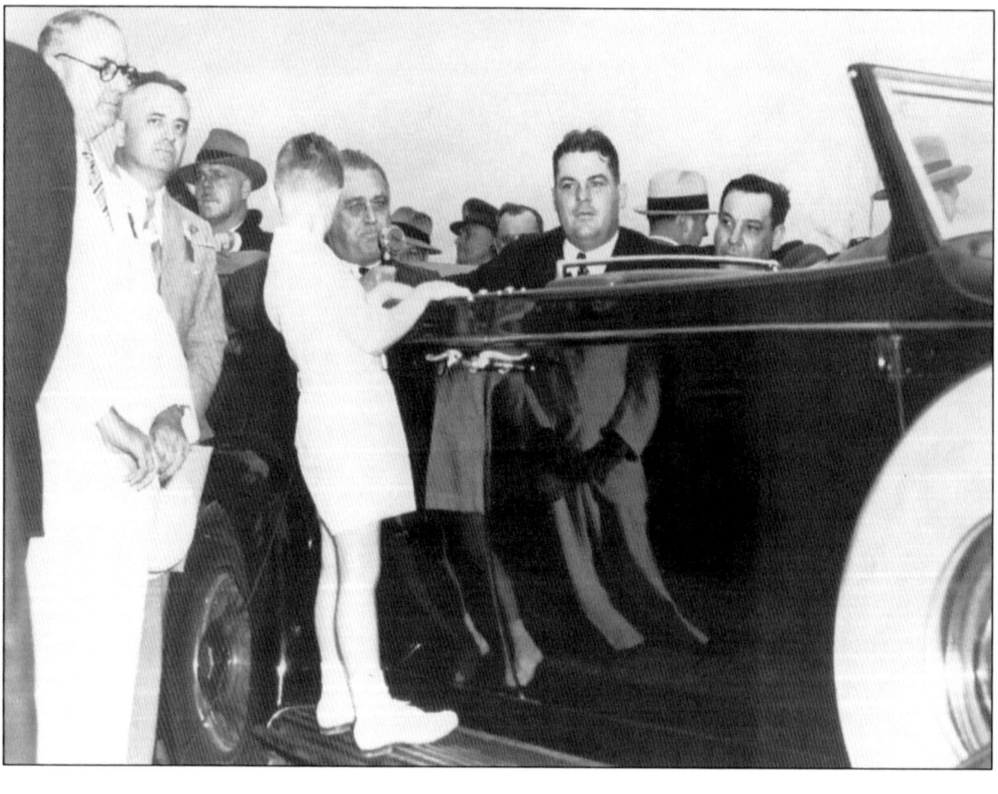

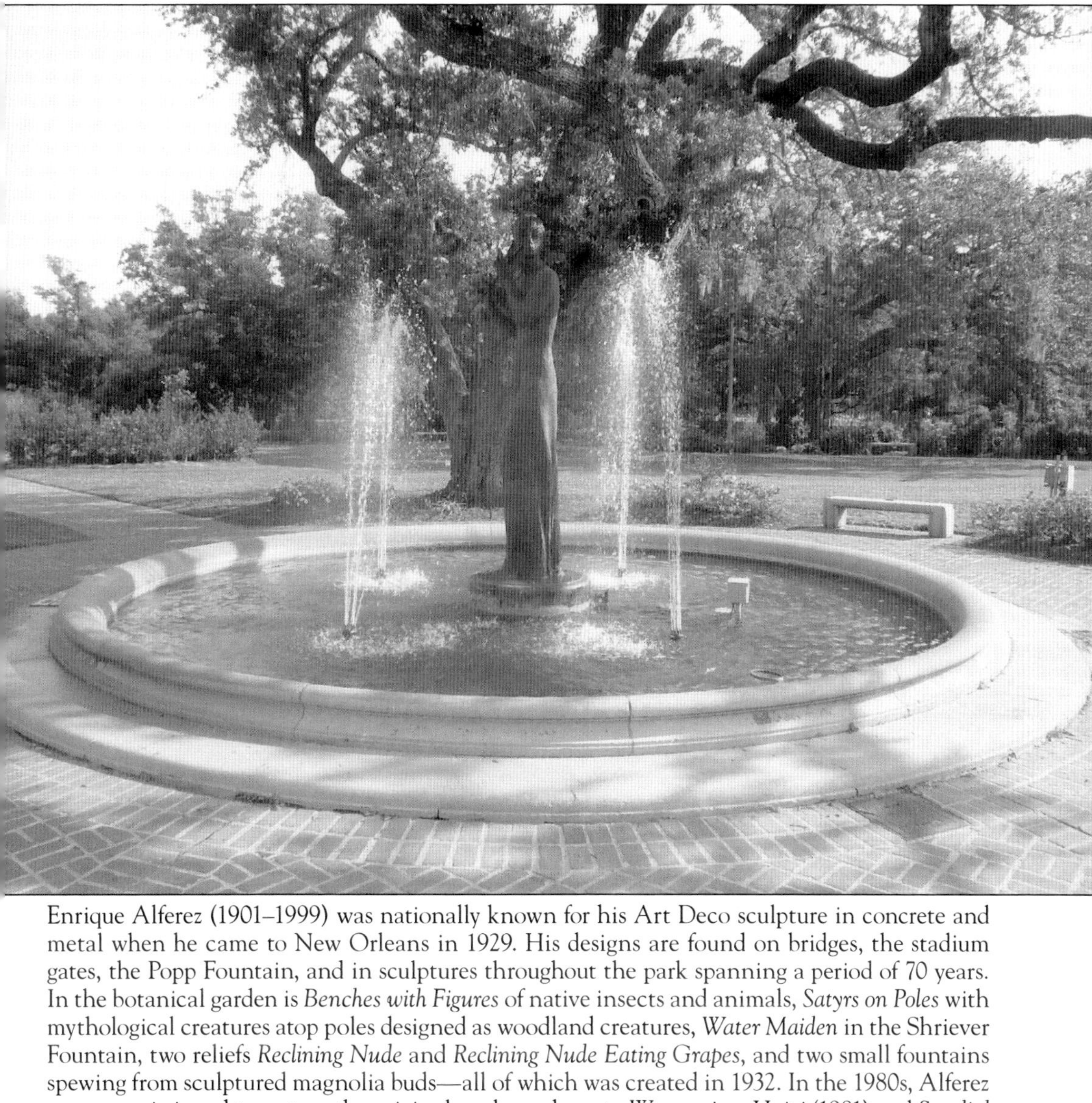

Enrique Alferez (1901–1999) was nationally known for his Art Deco sculpture in concrete and metal when he came to New Orleans in 1929. His designs are found on bridges, the stadium gates, the Popp Fountain, and in sculptures throughout the park spanning a period of 70 years. In the botanical garden is *Benches with Figures* of native insects and animals, *Satyrs on Poles* with mythological creatures atop poles designed as woodland creatures, *Water Maiden* in the Shriever Fountain, two reliefs *Reclining Nude* and *Reclining Nude Eating Grapes*, and two small fountains spewing from sculptured magnolia buds—all of which was created in 1932. In the 1980s, Alferez was commissioned to restore the original works and create *Woman in a Huipi* (1981) and *Sundial* (1983) in the center of the *Benches with Figures*. He also created *Flute Player* (1995). His final return to the park resulted in his last work, *Renascence* (1998), located west of the pavilion. His presence in the park is unmistakable, but he is also remembered by an oak named for him in 1980 as well as a street near the museum dedicated in 1983. (DCM.)

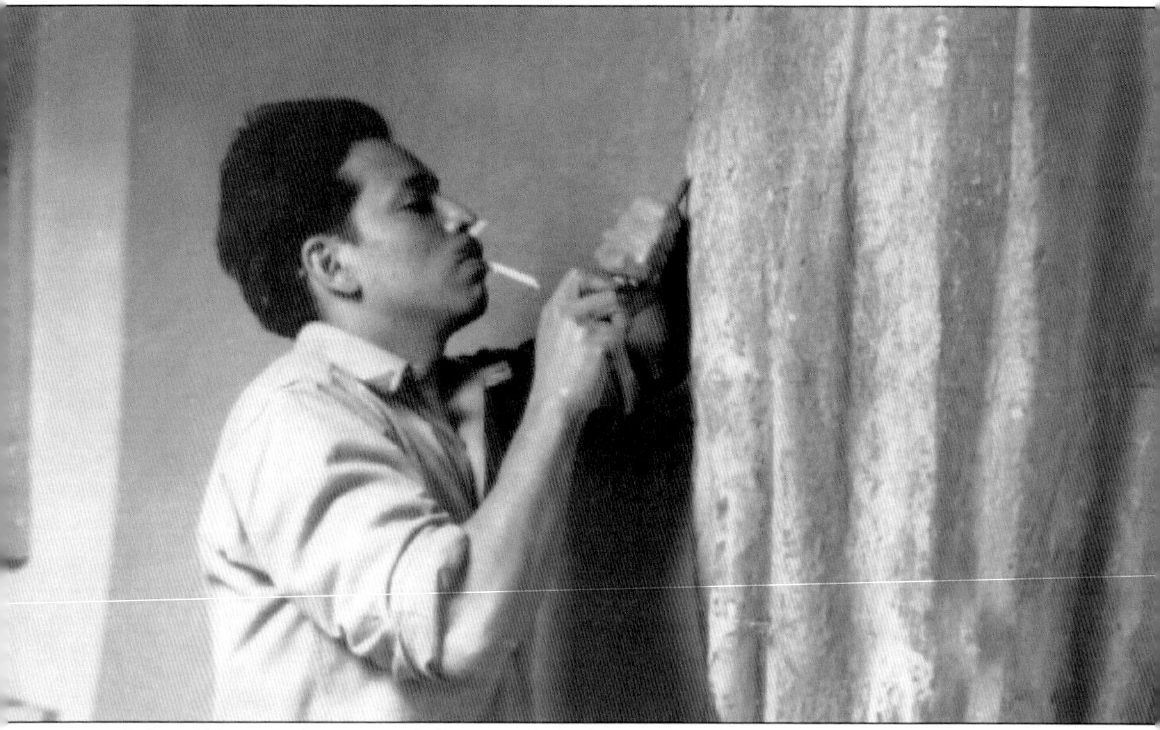

Other Alferez works in New Orleans include the metal sculpture screen at Charity Hospital over the emergency entrance, *Fountain of the Winds* at Shushan Airport, and *Molly Marine* at Elks Place and Canal Street. His birthplace is debatable—some say Mexico and others El Paso—and according to the Ogden Museum of Southern Art, tales of his life are spectacular, if not believable: "Early on he was taken into the band of infamous Mexican Revolutionary Pancho Villa. In Chicago, he earned a living climbing the Wrigley Building wearing a pair of tennis shoes to raise and lower the flag. He was mistakenly declared dead in Mexico in the late 1930s; his obituary was published in New Orleans, and he was mourned in the French Quarter. In 1930, he became a teacher at the Arts and Crafts School, and was soon known as one of the most distinctive characters living in the French Quarter." (HNOC.)

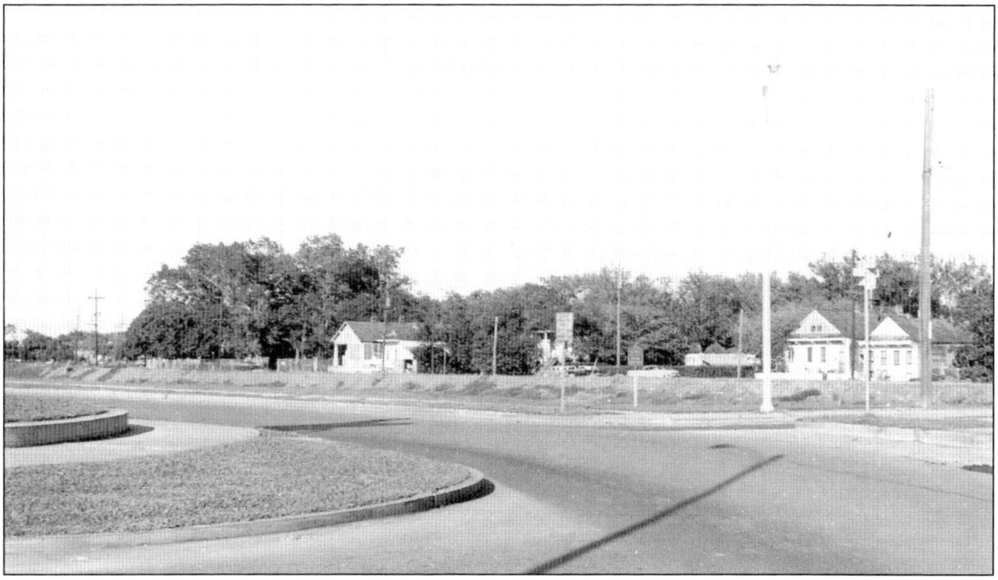

Called the "father of land reclamation," Edward Wisner bought hundreds of thousands of acres of south Louisiana swampland beginning in 1900 with plans to reclaim them for farming interests. (The boulevard named for him is seen here.) After a 1915 hurricane impeded his progress, Henry Timken took over some of the land intending to lease 600,000 acres to fur trappers. (Henry's Timken-Detroit Axle Company of Detroit, Michigan, is pictured in the early 1900s.) In 1925, oil speculator Edward Simms approached Timken with an offer to exchange some of his land for shares in Border Research Corporation, which would become Louisiana Land and Exploration Company. Meanwhile, Wisner made a fortune improving and trading land, but the Gulf of Mexico took much of it back. (Both, LDL.)

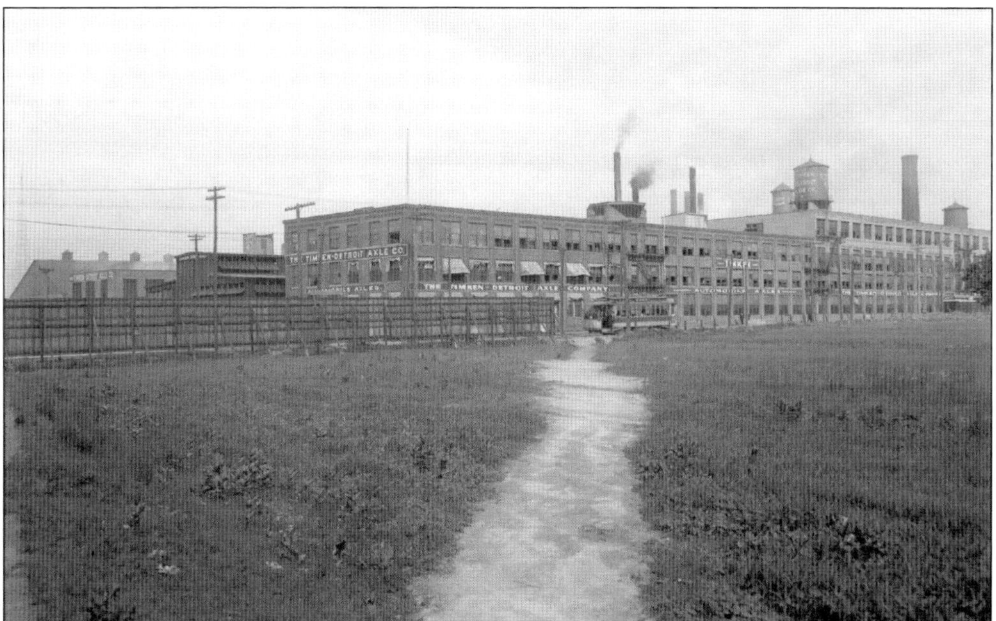

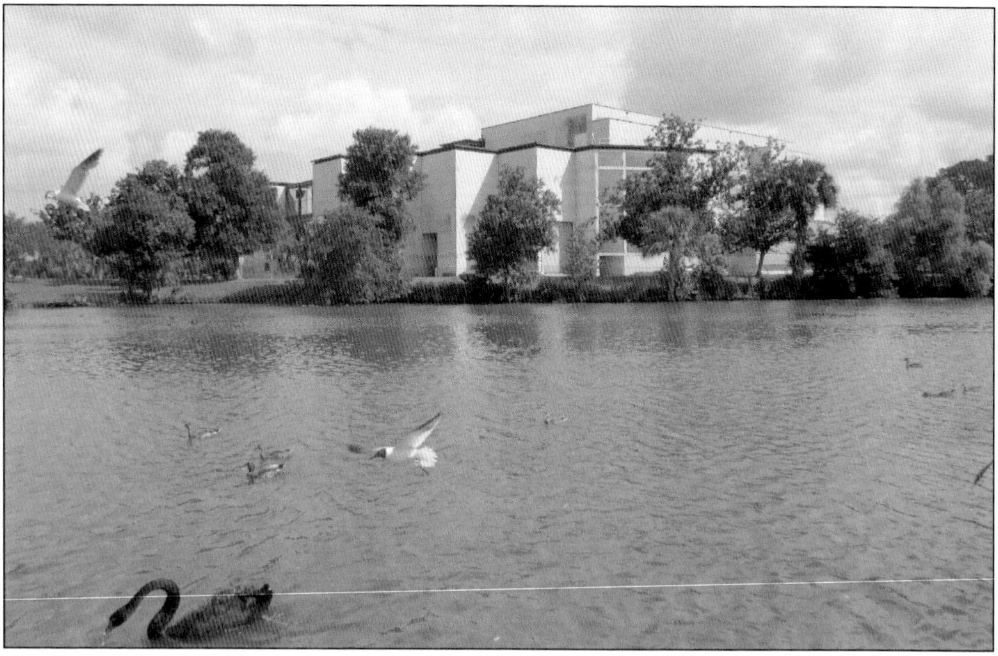

Both Wisner and Timken, who became friends, made a fortune in a prospect they had not foreseen—oil. The Wisner Tennis Center was opened in 1968, which was later demolished in 2008, and Wisner Boulevard, originally developed by City Park, was improved via revenue from oil wells willed to the park. The Wisner Wing of NOMA (above), dedicated in 1970, keeps his memory alive. The renaming of the Casino to Timken Center, shown below, in 2000 memorializes the man who donated an island in marshy land, which he acquired in 1920, to the park in 1996. (Both, DCM.)

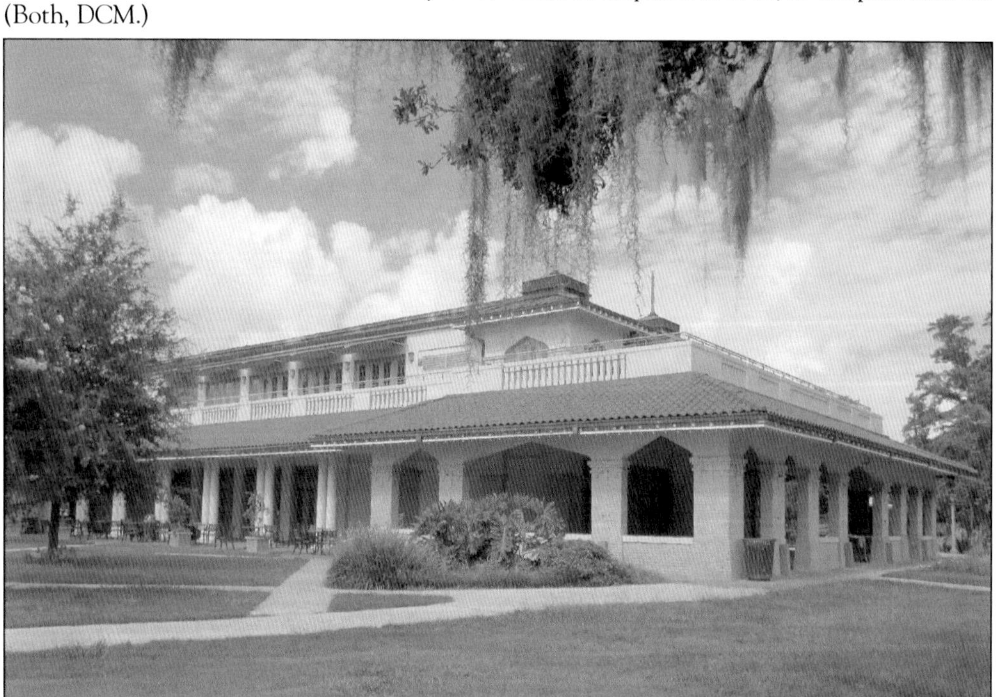

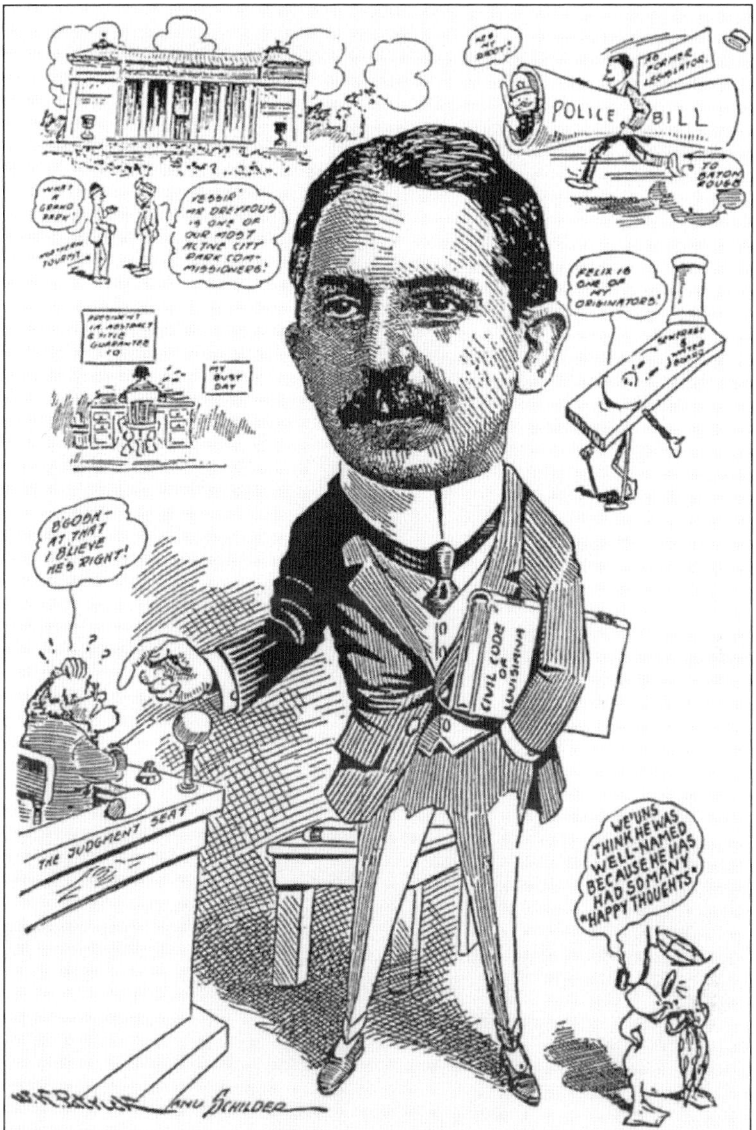

FELIX J. DREYFOUS
Attorney at Law

This 1899 editorial cartoon illustrates how involved Felix Jonathan Dreyfous (1857–1946) was in his community. Under the Delgado Museum, a tourist quips, "What a grand park," to which the response is "Yessir Mr. Dreyfous is one of our most active park commissioners." Near his left ear the Sewerage and Water Board says, "Felix is one of my originators." On the top right, Dreyfous carries the police bill to Baton Rouge, while the cop says, "He's my Daddy." At his desk, "President La. Abstract and Title Company" can be seen. His list of accomplishments are many; he was admitted to Louisiana Bar and elected State Legislator on an anti-lottery ticket in 1888, where he pushed for flood control and police protection and passed a bill to create levee boards throughout the state. He held the positions of president of the Orleans Levee Board (1890), city councilman (1895), and vice president of the Milne Boys' Asylum (1898); established the Sewerage and Water Board (1899); became a city drainage committeeman (1904); was director of La Homestead Association, which became NBC; a real estate investor, and an avid gardener. (Author's collection.)

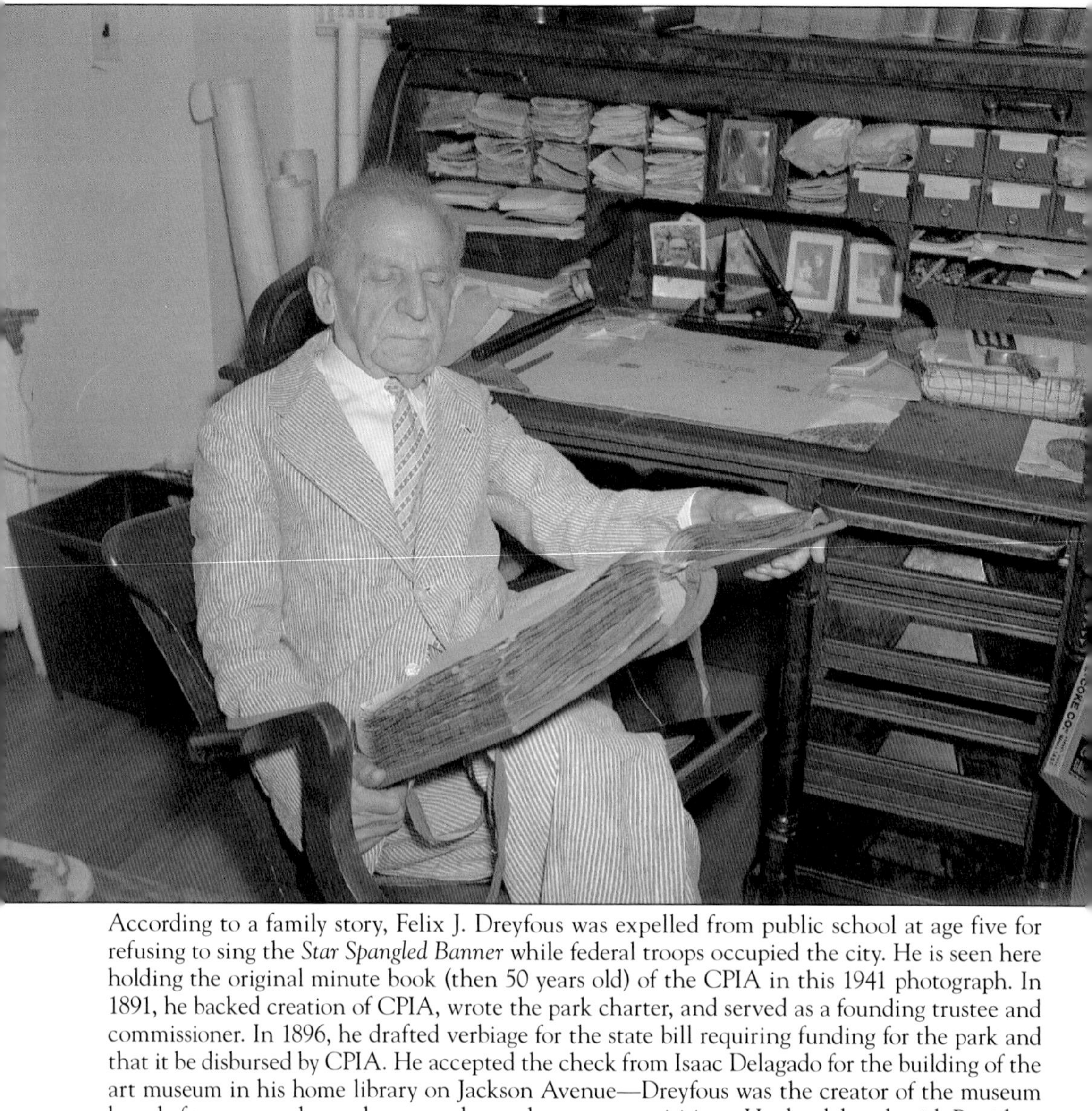

According to a family story, Felix J. Dreyfous was expelled from public school at age five for refusing to sing the *Star Spangled Banner* while federal troops occupied the city. He is seen here holding the original minute book (then 50 years old) of the CPIA in this 1941 photograph. In 1891, he backed creation of CPIA, wrote the park charter, and served as a founding trustee and commissioner. In 1896, he drafted verbiage for the state bill requiring funding for the park and that it be disbursed by CPIA. He accepted the check from Isaac Delagado for the building of the art museum in his home library on Jackson Avenue—Dreyfous was the creator of the museum board of trustees and served as a member and oversaw acquisitions. He shook hands with President Roosevelt during the 1937 WPA dedications. The Dreyfous name is memorialized on the pigeon house (see page 65), the Dreyfous Bridge (see page 86), and Dreyfous Drive (see page 26). In 1933, the *Times-Picayune* Loving Cup was given to him. Upon his death in 1946, he had served City Park for 55 years. (NOPL.)

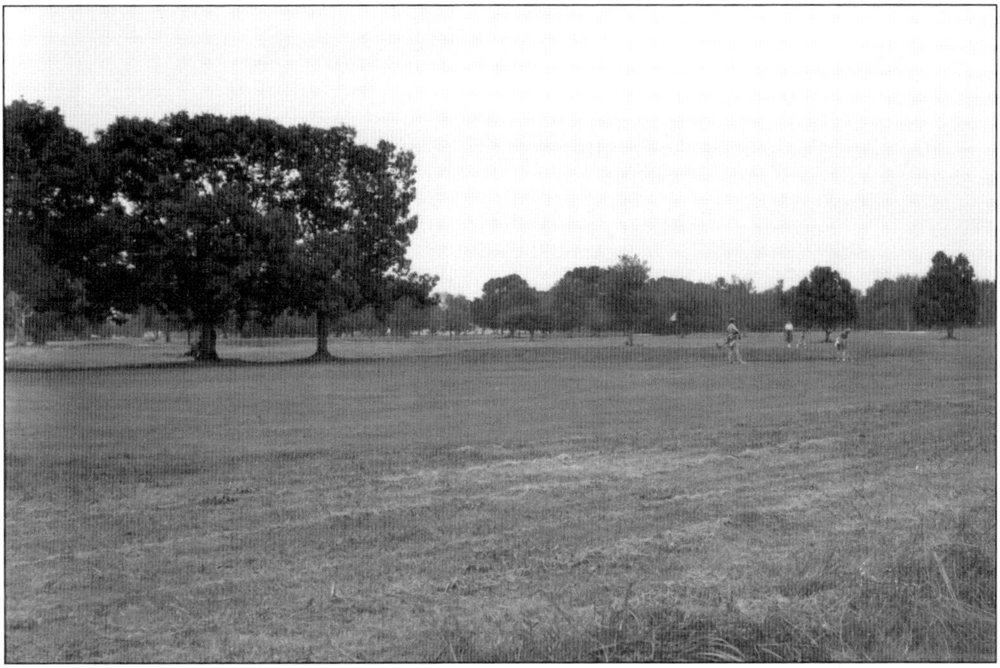

"In lieu of flowers, please make donations to rebuild City Park Golf Course," requested the *Times-Picayune* obituary for Francis Henry Thomas, who died on December 2, 2005, in Houston, just months after Katrina displaced so my New Orleanians. Thomas began working at the park course, pictured here in 1960, when he was nine years old and then moved to Colonial Country Club until 1933, when he returned to the park until 1987. During his tenure at the park, he taught golf on television in the 1940s and recorded long-playing records of his lessons. He later opened a golf shop near the park and returned to the park to teach at the driving range. After retirement, he visited the range monthly until Katrina. Henry Thomas Drive, which meanders through the course between Roosevelt Mall and Interstate 610, is named in his memory. (Both, LDL.)

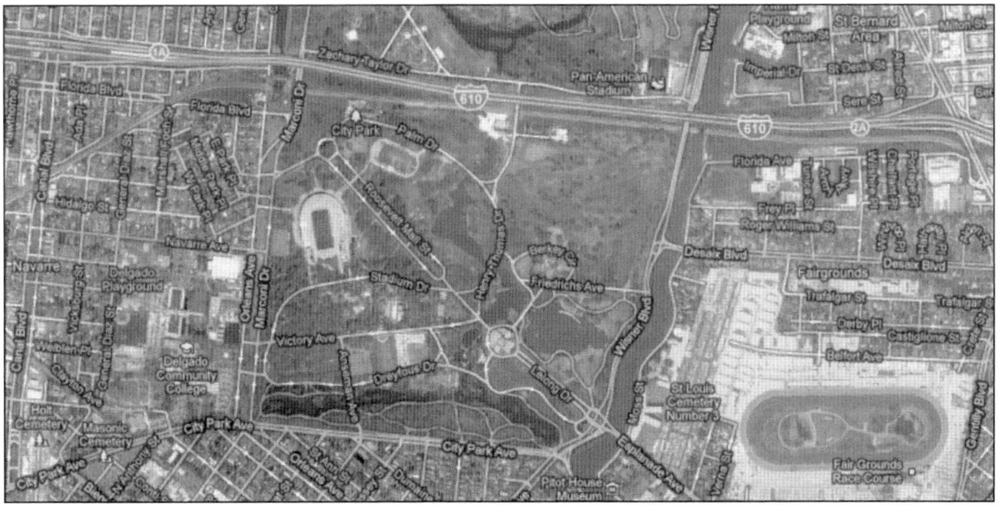

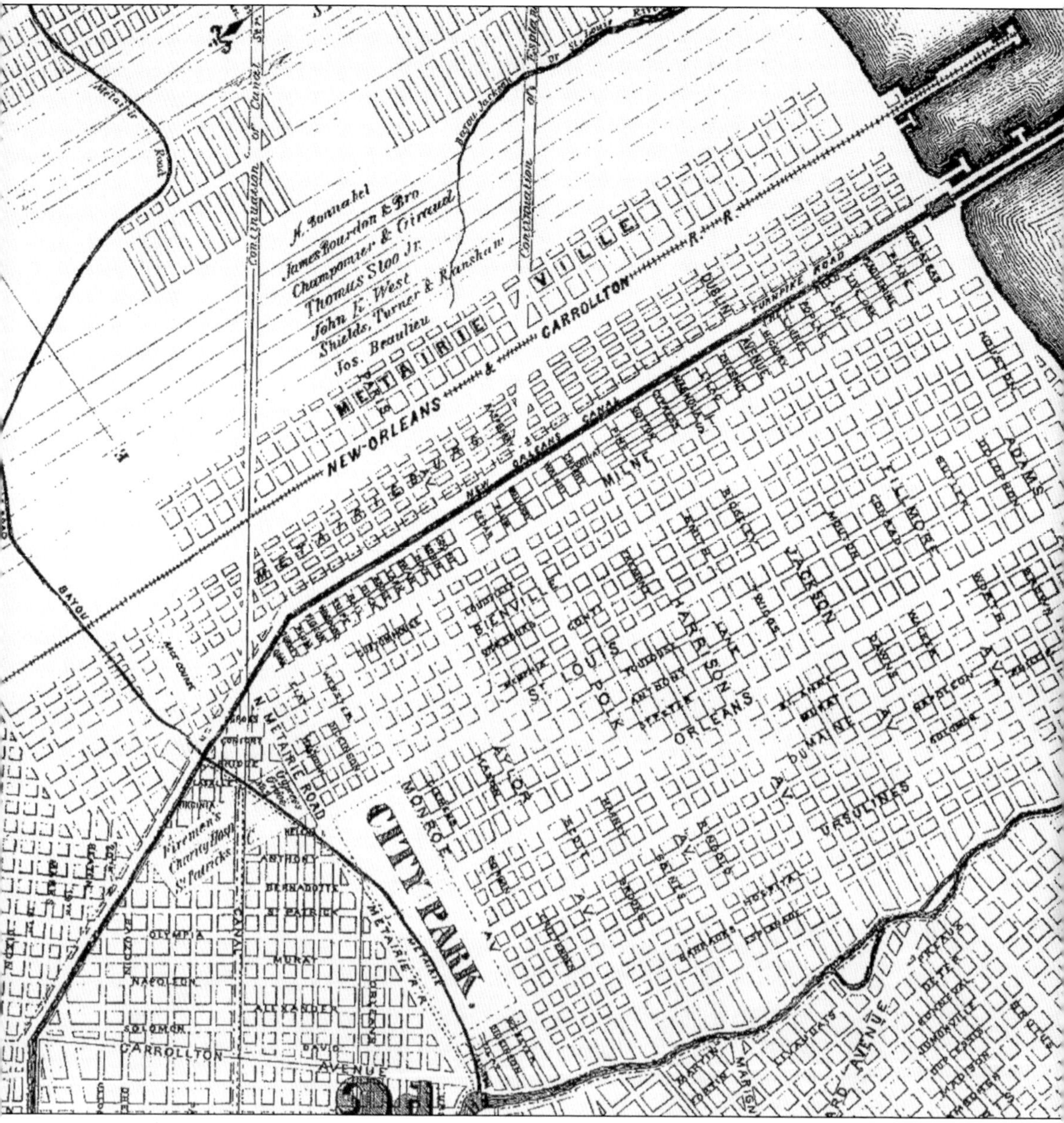

Board member George G. Friedrichs advocated renaming the park for John McDonogh (45 years after his death). The CPIA contested that 30 schools had already been named for him and that he had originally donated half of his land to Baltimore. The *Daily Picayune* reported on November 30, 1895, "If the name McDonogh Park was substituted, there would be nothing the commissioners to do but resign . . . An unfavorable report was made of the ordinance." It is possible that McDonogh's reputation as an unsociable tightwad, known to many as "McDonogh the Miser," still weighed on the commission's mind. Friedrich was a realtor who made a fortune in land—he owned Metairieburg, seen in the center of this map, north of the New Orleans & Carrollton Railroad. It is now Bucktown and beyond. A street in the park is named for Friedrichs. It runs from Wisner Boulevard to Henry Thomas Drive as it passes Christian Brothers School. (NA.)

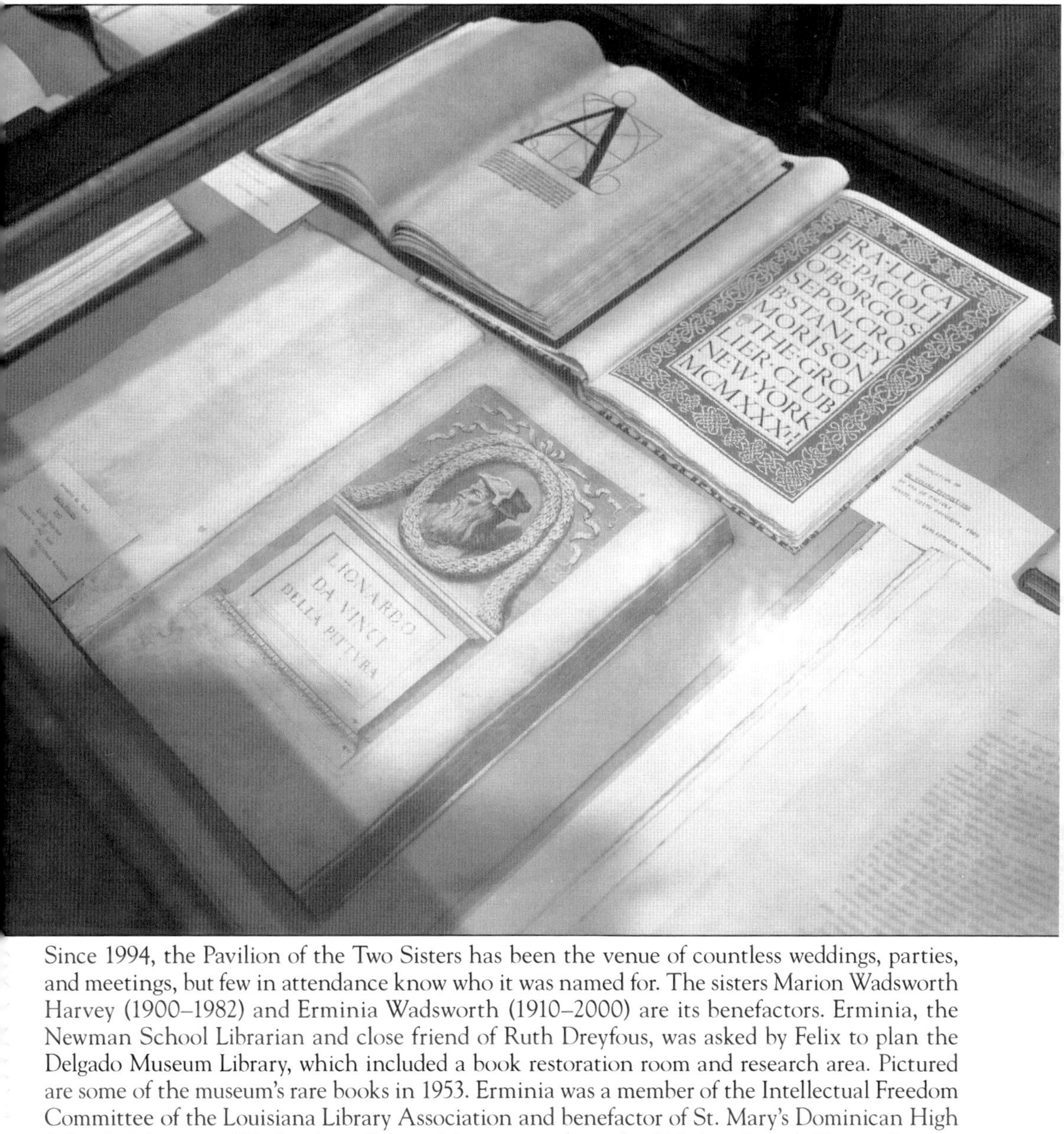

Since 1994, the Pavilion of the Two Sisters has been the venue of countless weddings, parties, and meetings, but few in attendance know who it was named for. The sisters Marion Wadsworth Harvey (1900–1982) and Erminia Wadsworth (1910–2000) are its benefactors. Erminia, the Newman School Librarian and close friend of Ruth Dreyfous, was asked by Felix to plan the Delgado Museum Library, which included a book restoration room and research area. Pictured are some of the museum's rare books in 1953. Erminia was a member of the Intellectual Freedom Committee of the Louisiana Library Association and benefactor of St. Mary's Dominican High School's Library and Technology Center. Marion was the wife of Herbert Joseph Harvey Sr.; one of his ancestors dug the Harvey Canal and another owned Destrehan Plantation. As a widow in 1969, Marion and her son Herbert Joseph Harvey Jr. established the Azby Fund with assets in real estate, timber, oil, and gas worth approximately $15 million. The fund is named for last male heir of the Destrehan family, Nicholas Azby Destrehan, who had grown up on the plantation. (LDL.)

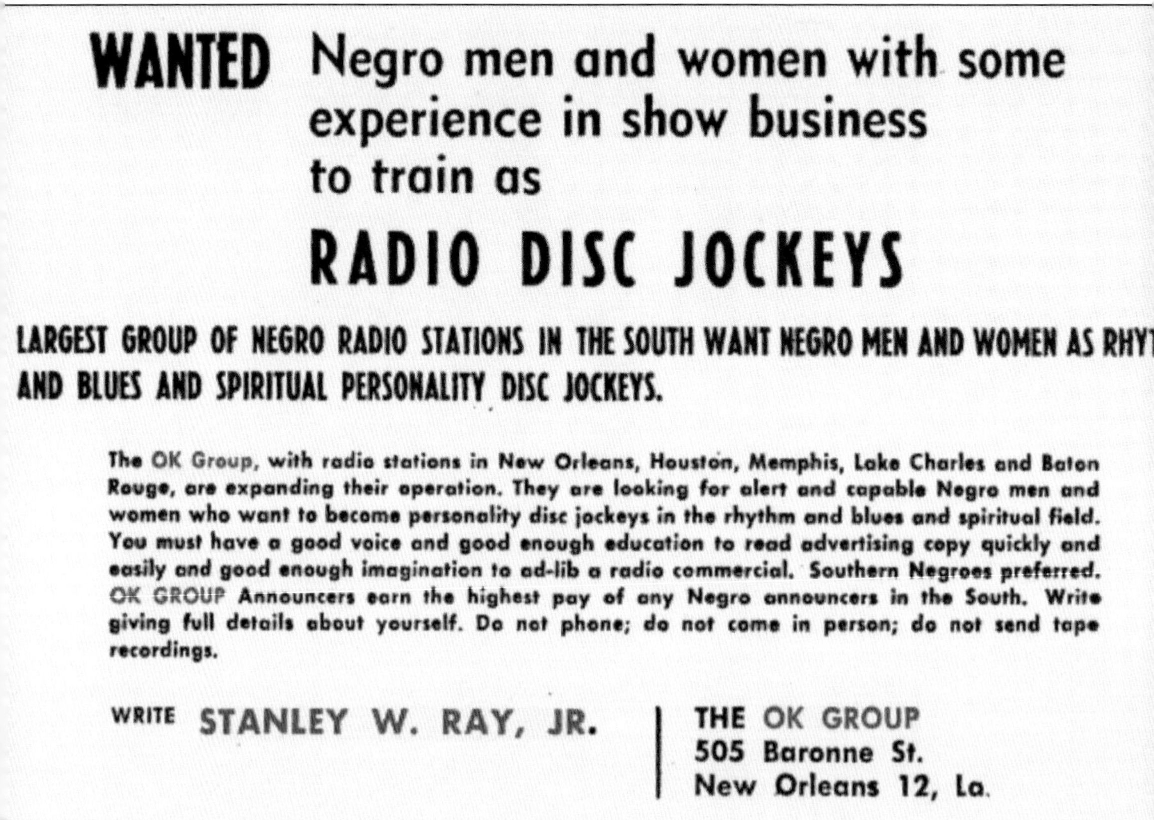

A young New Orleans native who raised his younger siblings after their parents died in a car crash went on to build a radio empire. All of Stanley W. Ray Jr.'s stations included the call letters "OK;" many New Orleanians have long listened to his station WBOK. Pictured is a 1957 *Billboard* magazine advertisement. Stanley W. Ray Jr. (1915–1970) wrote prep sports reports for the *Time-Picayune* while a student at Jesuit, lettered in basketball at Tulane while editing the campus newspaper, graduated from Tulane Law School in 1941, and served in the Army Air Corps during World War II. He established the Stanley W. Ray Jr. Philanthropic and Civic Trust to provide for unmet needs, particularly those of students who have lost one or both parents. In 2008, the trust contributed $250,000 toward the park's endowment to maintain the large playground located between the Peristyle and Popp Bandstand. An arch bearing his name marks the wheelchair-accessible, traditional playground that was designed for children between two and five years old. (*Billboard* magazine.)

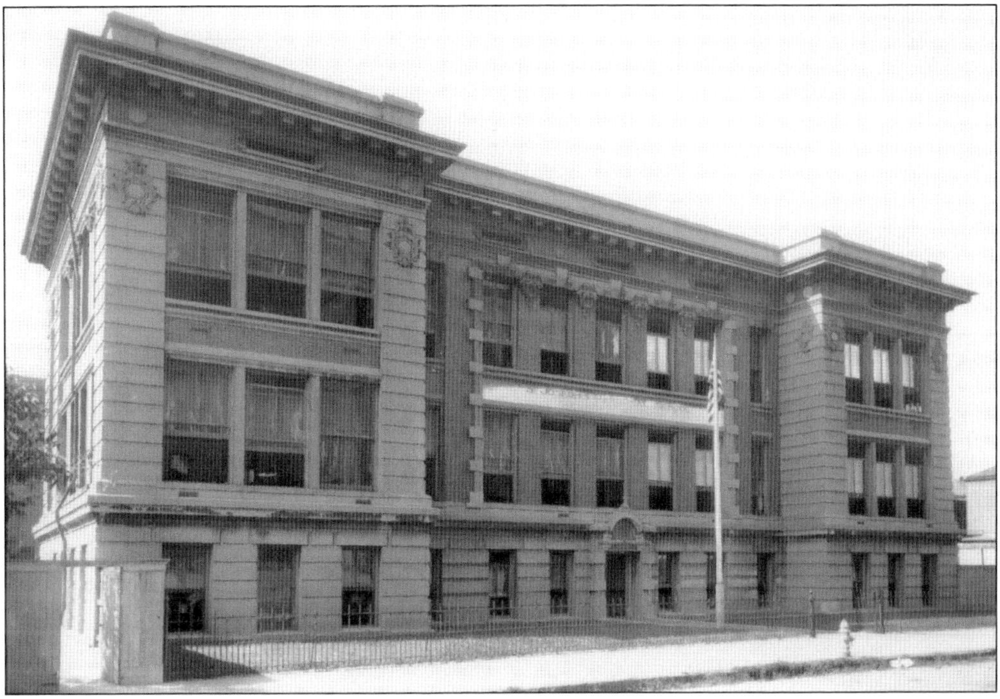

A Sicilian immigrant who made his fortune as a steamboat captain importing tropical fruit to New Orleans donated $75,000 to Mother Cabrini in 1906 to build her orphanage on Esplanade Avenue. He was also a patron of St. Joseph's Parochial School, located at 417 South Roman Street, where his name "Captain Salvatore Pizzati" was inscribed in stone above the main entrance. Captain Pizzati was also the benefactor of the beautiful 100-year-old gate on City Park Avenue. A new chapter begins, as this book ends, of the future growth and improvement of City Park. Please consider supporting those efforts by becoming a member or donating to Friends of City Park (www.friendsofcitypark.com). (Both, LDL.)

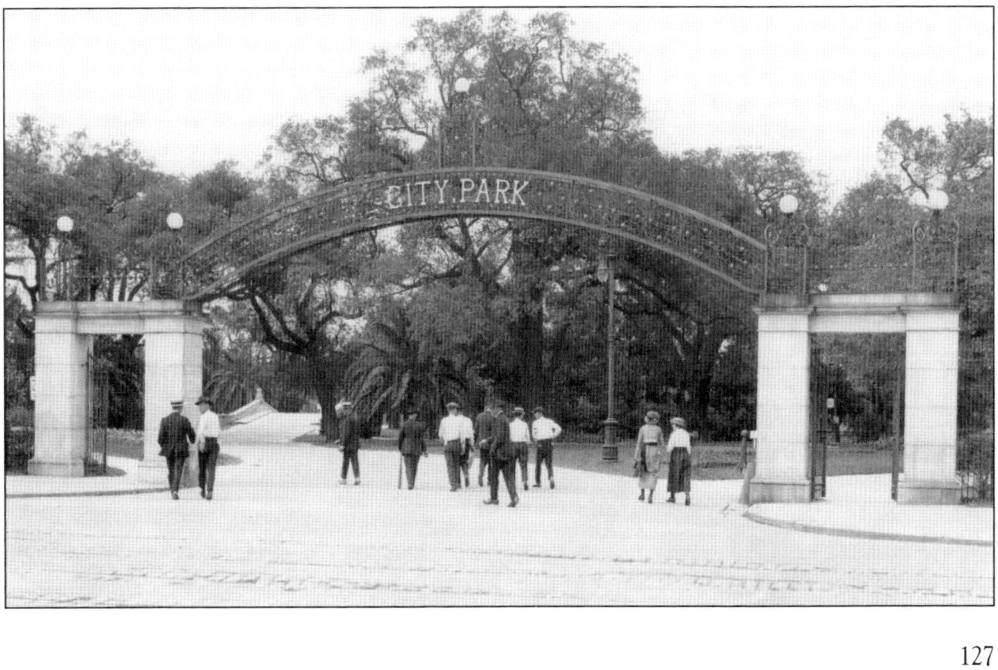